TITLE II

THE MAN IN THE NAME

So since this name was cut
When love and griefe their exaltation had,
  No doore 'gainst this names influence shut . . .

A Valediction:
of My Name, in the Window. JOHN DONNE

He was just a word for me. I did not see the man in the name
any more than you do. Do you see him? Do you see the story?
Do you see anything?

Heart of Darkness. JOSEPH CONRAD

We had the experience but missed the meaning,
And approach to the meaning restores the experience
In a different form . . .

The Dry Salvages. T. S. ELIOT

THE MAN IN THE NAME

❧ Essays on the Experience

of Poetry ❧ LEONARD UNGER

The University of Minnesota Press, Minneapolis

PRINTED AT THE NORTH CENTRAL PUBLISHING COMPANY, ST. PAUL

Library of Congress Catalog Card Number: 57-5801

PUBLISHED IN GREAT BRITAIN, INDIA, AND PAKISTAN BY THE
OXFORD UNIVERSITY PRESS, LONDON, BOMBAY, AND KARACHI

The quotations throughout the book from the following works of T. S. Eliot are reprinted by permission of Harcourt, Brace and Company, Inc.: *Selected Essays 1917–1932*, copyright, 1932, by Harcourt, Brace and Company, Inc.; *The Rock*, copyright, 1934, by Harcourt, Brace and Company, Inc.; *Murder in the Cathedral*, copyright, 1935, by Harcourt, Brace and Company, Inc.; *Collected Poems 1909–1935*, copyright, 1936, by Harcourt, Brace and Company, Inc.; *The Family Reunion*, copyright, 1939, by T. S. Eliot; *Four Quartets*, copyright, 1943, by T. S. Eliot; *The Cocktail Party*, copyright, 1950, by T. S. Eliot; *The Confidential Clerk*, copyright, 1954, by T. S. Eliot. The publisher of *The Use of Poetry and the Use of Criticism*, by T. S. Eliot, from which I also quote, is Faber and Faber, London (1933); of *The Music of Poetry*, by T. S. Eliot, Jackson, Son and Company, Glasgow (1942).

For my mother and father

For my mother and father

 Preface

IT WILL possibly be of some service to the prospective reader to describe these essays beyond what their titles indicate. "Deception and Self-Deception in Shakespeare's *Henry IV*" is an attempt to read a greater complexity and depth of meaning in the play (both parts) than has been generally allowed. This essay would have been longer if I had not discovered that several facets of my reading had already been made by D. A. Traversi (in his essay in *Scrutiny*) and by the late Harold Goddard (in *The Meaning of Shakespeare*). "Keats and the Music of Autumn" was written to express my admiration of *To Autumn* and because I felt that the poem has been peculiarly neglected in the recent comment and study that have been given to the other great odes. One of the purposes of the essay is to show how a single poem may illuminate and be illuminated by other poems of the same author — and also to show the continuity and wholeness of Keats' poetry.

"Donne's Poetry and Modern Criticism" is an argument with prevailing notions of Donne's poetry (and of metaphysical poetry) that have been fostered by Sir Herbert Grierson, T. S. Eliot, George Williamson, John Crowe Ransom, Allen Tate, and Cleanth Brooks. Much of the essay is given to analyses of the poems of Donne's *Songs and Sonets*. Emerging from the analyses is a characterization of Donne's poetry which differs basically from the characterization which has been made familiar by modern criticism. "Fusion and Experience" is a recently composed sequel to the preceding essay. It is, on a modest scale, a critical history of ideas — and especially of the ideas, as they have operated in the criticism of Eliot and others, that metaphysical poetry contains a fusion of thought and feeling and that the metaphysical poets possessed a unified sensibility. A section of the essay is devoted to a discussion of poems of Donne and Marvell, with some consideration of their relations with Renaissance Humanism. (I should like to say here that in these two essays Ransom, Brooks, and Tate — the first two my former teachers and all three my present friends — are treated "impersonally." In other words, they are subjected to the devices of my rhetoric and, I trust, of my logic for the sake of the truth as I see it and also *pour le sport* of literary criticism. If I have achieved anything of value here, then my book is but partial evidence of my grateful indebtedness to these men.)

The last three essays are on the poetry of T. S. Eliot. "Ash Wednesday" is an interpretation of the poem of that title and offers a detailed account of its sources, development, and meaning. "T. S. Eliot's Rose-Garden" traces the rose-garden and related imagery as a persistent symbolic theme throughout the whole range of Eliot's poetry and as an essential element in the continuity of his work. "Laforgue, Conrad, and T. S. Eliot" is concerned with the influences of Laforgue and Conrad on Eliot's poetry and with the relationship of these influences. While the essay offers some new assessment and documentation of Laforgue's influence, it treats more extensively Eliot's literary relations with Conrad's *Heart of Darkness*. If my observations are valid, then Conrad's story has a singular and major relevance to the style and themes of Eliot's poetry, and of his plays as well — and ultimately a relevance to our *reading* of Eliot's work. Several "after-notes" to this essay consider correspondences between Eliot's poems and passages in Conrad's other works of fiction.

At an early stage in the preparation of this book for publication, the highly reasonable suggestion was made that I write an introduction which would indicate and clarify the unity of the book. Since it was only a suggestion, and not a requirement, I have omitted such an introduction. My reasons for turning down the invitation to write another essay seem clearer to me now than they did when I first declined. For as I now contemplate the contents of the book, I discover myself wishing that it had less rather than more unity. A greater variety of subjects and ideas would have produced a more flattering image, and I dare fancy that the unity would have taken care of itself.

On the other hand, I acknowledge my gratefulness for what there is to show. Such unity as the book has was not planned until the very latest stages of production — indeed, it was not so much planned as it was actually determined by the momentum and direction of what I had already done in past years. In other words, the most recent essays — "Laforgue, Conrad, and T. S. Eliot" and "Fusion and Experience" — are further records of my response to Eliot's poetry and of my arguments with his criticism.

Anyone who is familiar with the literary discourse of the century will recognize from these essays that I am a child of the Age. I am obviously indebted to those programs and techniques which were devised by various eminent fathers of the Age. For this, too, I am grateful. But there are no programs or techniques toward which I feel any loyalty or commitment. And that is another reason why I did not choose to write an introduction. The ultimate value of literary study, as of literature itself, is for me its relevance to the quality and meaning of experience — of living. There is no other critical position that I can claim, or might like to claim, as my own. So I claim this one, for it is as much mine as anybody's. And it is from this position that I should like to claim an ultimate unity for my book. I could grant that this is not precisely a position — but then I would be satisfied to insist that it is at least, and at best, a goal.

I am aware that it is not my habit to write anything without submitting my efforts — and I mean efforts and not just the final product — to the attention of my friends. Among these, thanks are especially due to Murray Krieger, William Van O'Connor, Allen Tate, and Philip Young. They have been extremely helpful and encouraging, and also admirably patient. To this list I add separately the name of Samuel Holt Monk, for he has combined interest, understanding, and criticism in a way that has been peculiarly stimulating and persuasive. It is a pleasure to express my appreciation to Joseph Warren Beach and his wife Dagmar Beach for their unfailing friendship and for the confidence and

The Man in the Name

enthusiasm which their wise and gracious conversation has steadily inspired. Robert Humphrey and Robert Penn Warren have for too long been too far away, but their counsel in years past and my sense of their enduring friendship and understanding have been of inestimable value. My wife, Sherley Glasscock Unger, has been inescapably, but always loyally, involved in my work, and any acknowledgment of her indispensable cooperation would be an understatement.

My relations with the staff of the University of Minnesota Press have been consistently pleasant throughout all stages of the production of this book. I am grateful to Helen Clapesattle, Director of the Press, for the freedom I have enjoyed through her cordiality and generosity. The leisure necessary for the study and writing which have produced some of these essays was made possible by the generous financial assistance of the John Simon Guggenheim Memorial Foundation, and by the friendly cooperation of its Secretary, Henry Allen Moe, and the members of his staff.

Grateful acknowledgment for permission to reprint materials is due as follows: to Rinehart & Company, Inc., for passages from *Poems for Study* (prepared in collaboration with William Van O'Connor) which have been incorporated into some of these essays, and for "Ash Wednesday" and "T. S. Eliot's Rose-Garden," which appeared in my book *T. S. Eliot: A Selected Critique*; to the Henry Regnery Company for "Donne's Poetry and Modern Criticism," which was first published as a book of that title; to *The Western Review* for "Keats and the Music of Autumn."

LEONARD UNGER

Minneapolis
October 1956

 Contents

THE MAN IN THE NAME

Deception and Self-Deception in Shakespeare's *Henry IV*

I do not believe that any writer has ever exposed this bovarysme, *the human will to see things as they are not, more clearly than Shakespeare.* T. S. ELIOT

Such a far-reaching agreement as found between the means of wit-work and those of dream-work can scarcely be accidental. FREUD

IF SHAKESPEARE held the mirror up to various ideological, dramatic and literary conventions, he also held it up to nature. And like nature, the reflections have an almost endless intricacy of parts. I make these general announcements because my purpose is to show that certain things exist in the *Henry IV* plays but not to argue that other things do not exist in them. Certainly, the plays are about the development of an unconventional and unprincely Prince into an ideally regal King. This was the subject that Shakespeare borrowed from history and legend. They are also about the violence, confusion, and disorder which result when the divinely decreed social order is upset — as it had been upset when Bolingbroke forcibly took the crown from Richard II. In the play *Richard II* the Bishop of Carlisle prophesied

> The blood of English shall manure the ground
> And future ages groan for this foul act.
>
> *IV.i.137–138*

And Richard had prophesied

> The time shall not be many hours of age
> More than it is, ere foul sin gathering head
> Shall break into corruption.
>
> *V.i.57–59*

In *Henry IV* these prophecies are fulfilled. But according to Renaissance thought the social structure and the human psychol-

3]

ogy were seen as closely analogous (the macrocosm-microcosm) and the literature of the period (and of Shakespeare) abounds in metaphors relating the two. That the social disorder of Henry IV's reign and of Shakespeare's play should be reflected by the psychological disorder of the characters would be no more original than the basic plot is. But it is in the realm of the psychological that Shakespeare transcended the particulars of his sources and the generalities that he shared with his age. In holding the mirror up to doctrines about society and human psychology he also held it up to nature and thus reflected a vision of human motivation that is persuasive beyond the peculiar doctrines of any age.

This Shakespeare did in all the great plays, but he first did it with greatness in *Henry IV*. In *Richard II* he showed how social disorder resulted from Richard's egotistical theatricality and Bolingbroke's political ambitiousness. Richard's self-dramatizing, the indulgence of his ego to the neglect of his regal responsibilities, is fully represented. But the development of Bolingbroke's motivation — from his reasonable determination to have the title and estates of Gaunt, to his ambition for the crown — Shakespeare treats vaguely, almost evasively. The development merely happens — off stage, as it were. It is as if Shakespeare, at this still early stage of his career, was not yet artistically ready to involve fully, exhaustively, in a single play two such psychologically complex situations as those of Bolingbroke and Richard.

In *Henry IV* Shakespeare compensated for his earlier neglect of that character's motivation. Here it is the King who is sometimes vague and evasive. In Part II, recalling Richard's prophecy, Henry also recalls Richard's accusation that he would usurp the throne, and pleads,

> Though then, God knows, I had no such intent,
> But that necessity so bowed the state
> That I and greatness were compelled to kiss —
>
> *III.i.72-74*

thus disclaiming any personal guiltiness of ambitious thought and action. But in the next act, in the reconciliation speech to Hal, he says,

[4

Deception and Self-Deception in *Henry IV*

> God knows, my son,
> By what by-paths and indirect crooked ways
> I met this crown, and I myself know well
> How troublesome it sat upon my head.
>
> *IV.v.184–187*

These passages both account for the same problem, and the repetition of "God knows" gives a curious emphasis to their relationship. If the accounts are not quite contradictory, they do seem to represent variant attitudes — the first innocent and the second admittedly guilty. In its first use "God knows" is like the expression "as God is my witness," giving positiveness and certainty to whatever issue is involved. The second use seems to have the same meaning, but for a different verdict. But the second verdict is, after all, not a complete reversal of the first. "God knows" can also mean "only God knows" in the sense that the issue is utterly beyond any man's knowledge or understanding. This meaning is suggested by the words "and I myself know well," as if to distinguish between what only God knows and what Henry knows. The two passages, taken together, say in effect, "Everyone should know, as God knows, that I never had any wrong intentions, and if I did happen to commit some misdemeanor, God alone knows what it was — I don't." There would be less ambiguity in the second passage if the word *and* in "and I myself know well" were replaced by the word *but* — for *and* has here something of the force of *but*, as it does occasionally in the language.

The reconciliation speech continues with confessions of guilt that are ambiguously and therefore defensively qualified.

> For all the soil of the achievement goes
> With me into the earth. It seemed in me
> But as an honor snatched with boisterous hand.
>
> *IV.v.190–192*

The qualifying value of *seemed* is familiar enough in problems of appearance and reality. But "the soil of the achievement" demands more attention. In its narrowest context here *soil* means *stain*, but when a few words later we arrive at *earth* we see that there is a pun. In relation to the character and questions considered, it is not a trifling pun, but an opening wedge through which we may pursue relevant meanings. With the help of *earth*, we may go on to *ground* and *grounds*, and from there to *basis* and *justification*. And if the justification goes with Henry into the earth, then it becomes, like other matters, exclusively God's knowledge. The speech ends with a forthright plea that God forgive his sins.

> How I came by the crown, O God, forgive,
> And grant it may with thee in true peace live!
>
> *IV.v.219–220*

This *How* may be spoken with the inflection of uncertainty. It was a question that Henry was impelled to raise but never to answer with any finality or clarity.

Throughout the plays we see Henry cherishing his crown and at the same time facing the guilt for the way in which he took it. And, still at the same time — so complex and confused are his motivations — his gestures for expiating his guilt are also intended as a practical means of retaining the crown. The pious resolve spoken at the end of *Richard II* —

> I'll make a voyage to the Holy Land
> To wash this blood off from my guilty hand —
>
> *V.vi.49–50*

is repeated in the opening speech of *I Henry IV*:

> To chase these pagans in those holy fields
> Over whose acres walked the blessed feet
> Which fourteen hundred years ago were nailed
> For our advantage on the bitter cross.
>
> *I.i.24–27*

But as we learn later from the dying King's counsel to the Prince, this religious purpose was also a trick, a shrewd plan

> To lead out many to the Holy Land
> Lest rest and lying still might make them look
> Too near unto my state. Therefore, my Harry,
> Be it thy course to busy giddy minds
> With foreign quarrels, that action, hence
>   borne out,
> May waste the memory of the former days.
>
> *Part II, IV.v.211–216*

[6

Deception and Self-Deception in *Henry IV*

Henry would have killed two birds, of quite different feather, with a single stone, and one bird would have been a penitential sacrifice for the slaughter of the other. It was a good trick, not only for "giddy minds," but good enough for Henry himself — and, as it turned out, never applied beyond himself, for his former supporters never did rest and lie still long enough to permit such a venture.

This theme of deception and self-deception, of motive obscuring motive, of confusion and rationalization, is not only developed in the character of the King but is given full orchestration throughout the plays. At the opening of Part I we find the King and his helpers to the crown mutually suspicious. He suspects them of feeling that he is inordinately indebted to them for their help. They suspect him of having this suspicion. And thus each party is justified in its own extravagant and unyielding selfishness. The King had at least two good reasons for not wanting to ransom Mortimer from the Welsh, and the one which he does not reveal is that the dying Richard had proclaimed Mortimer his heir. Hotspur, even before he has learned this fact, dares comment to the King on Mortimer's wounds:

> Never did base and rotten policy
> Color her working with such deadly wounds.
>
> *I.iii.108–109*

And when he does learn it shortly, he uses it to color his own policy, to bait his hunger for heroics and "bright honor."

One could follow the theme of egotistical motivation, of suspicion, deception and self-deception in such characters as Northumberland, Worcester, and Glendower. But it is with the protagonists, Falstaff and Prince Hal, that Shakespeare gives the theme its central operation and its structural significance in the plays, thus emphasizing the essential unity of the two parts of *Henry IV*. In addition to being the central characters of the dramatic surface, these two are centrally placed in psychological perspective on the gallery of the other characters. They see through all the others, and as well, through each other. It is they who concentrate and intensify the vision of human motives that Shakespeare has

7]

otherwise elaborated in the plays. Hal encompasses the pattern of the manipulating of motives in his whole career as prince, and Falstaff embodies it in almost every moment, we may say in the very fact, of his existence. Their relationship with each other, their common and individual adventures, are a ritualistic parody of the larger plot in which they are involved, and a symbol of that aspect of humanity which Shakespeare has dramatized.

One of the most obvious characteristics of Falstaff is his ironical parallelism to, his debunking of, the noble characters. The "honor" which is their common code and which is epitomized in Hotspur, is for Falstaff "a mere scutcheon" and it belongs to "he that died o' Wednesday." That Prince Hal, to his father's grief, shares this critical detachment from the code is shown by his whole Falstaffian career, and particularly by his comment on Hotspur:

> I am not yet of Percy's mind, the Hotspur of the North, he that kills me some six or seven dozen Scots at a breakfast, washes his hands, and says to his wife, "Fie upon this quiet life! I want work." "O my sweet Harry," says she, "how many hast thou killed today?" "Give my roan horse a drench," says he, and answers "Some fourteen" an hour after — "a trifle, a trifle."
>
> *Part I, II.iv*

Hal's similar contempt for the solemnity of court and crown is shown in the same scene. Although he ends the speech above with the plan that he and Falstaff mockingly "play" at being Hotspur and his wife, he decides later that they "play" at being the King while he is scolding and advising the Prince.

This critical perspective on honor and solemnity is but incidental as compared to that on the question of motivation. First consider Falstaff. "Sir John, Sir John, I am well acquainted with your manner of wrenching the true cause the false way," said the Chief Justice (Part II, II.i), and this manner is profusely illustrated throughout the plays. "Was it for me to kill the heir apparent" explains his cowardice at Gadshill. "I dispraised him before the wicked, that the wicked might not fall in love with him" explains his slandering the Prince. As the Chief Justice's words so aptly put it, Falstaff never tells a mere lie. He twists the truth into falsehood — and vice versa. In these examples, his lies are but pretenses of falsity, deliberately and delightfully transparent. Caught in an awkward situation, he would rather be forgiven than believed. Caught in an unintended human awkwardness, he will cover it up with an intended, absorbing one into the other, thus at once pleading, asserting, and sharing his humanity. Other examples are less specifically purposeful. They represent his unsuppressible relishing of the truth, not only the truth of incidental facts, but the general and timeless truth of human nature, and it is with the transparency of the lie that he relishes the latter. Such examples are "A plague of sighing and grief! It blows a man up like a bladder," and "They hate us youth . . . Young men must live." Still other examples are purposeful beyond their occasion. When the Prince observes that the men whom Falstaff has impressed for military service are "pitiful rascals," Falstaff does not deny it but shifts the issue with his famous *non sequitur*: "Tut, tut, good enough to toss, food for powder, food for powder. They'll fill a pit as well as better. Tush, man, mortal men, mortal men" (Part I, IV.ii). Falstaff has a ready answer, but it is not relevant to the Prince's meaning, although it is full of other meanings. The statement is a cynical comment on the selfish ambitions of the noble characters, whose quarrels result in a waste of human life. Falstaff has such poor soldiers because he has been interested in lining his own pocket, and he will send them to a death that is wasted except that he will pocket their wages. If he is indifferent to this waste, at least he acknowledges that it is a waste. "Mortal men" signifies not only that these men are capable of dying, but that all men are basically the same, in their dying and in their living.

While Falstaff's humorousness is primarily related to the question of motivation, it does not always follow the pattern of indirection. Often his humor results from his confession of clear and simple truths, from his shocking frankness and actual negligence of pretense. He means himself when he says

> To the latter end of a fray and the beginning of a feast
> Fits a dull fighter and a keen guest.
>
> *Part I, IV.ii*

The Man in the Name

Just before the battle he remarks, "I would 'twere bed-time, Hal, and all well." In judging Master Shallow he does not fail to include himself: "Lord, Lord, how subject we old men are to this vice of lying." When Hal charges him with his sins, he admits them, but not without including the rest of mankind: "Thou knowest in the state of innocency Adam fell, and what should poor Jack Falstaff do in the days of villainy? Thou seest I have more flesh than another man, and therefore more frailty" (Part I, III.iii). Although Falstaff's character and behavior provide an indirect illumination of the other characters' motives, on a few occasions he is made to comment directly. When the King is examining Worcester on the reasons for his rebellion, Falstaff brazenly intrudes with the words "Rebellion lay in his way, and he found it." This explanation, combining a false innocence of tone with downright truth to fact, implies all the complexities of deceptive motivation of the nobles characters. Falstaff presumes the role of the allowed fool in uttering this insight, but the noble characters dare not recognize what he so clearly sees.

While Prince Hal shares in some measure Falstaff's critical perspective on the other characters, it is he who is drawn most fully in ironical parallelism with the fat knight. It is these two who carry the theme of deception and self-deception as a continuous strand throughout the plays. Prince Hal's great deception is, of course, announced in his first soliloquy:

> I know you all, and will a while uphold
> The unyoked humor of your idleness.
> Yet herein will I imitate the sun,
> Who doth permit the base contagious clouds
> To smother up his beauty from the world,
> That, when he please again to be himself,
> Being wanted, he may be more wondered at
> By breaking through the foul and ugly mists
> Of vapors that did seem to strangle him.
> If all the year were playing holidays,
> To sport would be as tedious as to work.
> But when they seldom come, they wished-for come,
> And nothing pleaseth but rare accidents.
> So, when this loose behavior I throw off

And pay the debt I never promised,
By how much better than my word I am,
By so much shall I falsify men's hopes.
And like bright metal on a sullen ground,
My reformation, glittering o'er my fault,
Shall show more goodly and attract more eyes
Than that which hath no foil to set it off.
I'll so offend, to make offense a skill,
Redeeming time when men think least I will.

Part I, I.ii.218-240

The dramatic significance of this passage, like the rejection of Falstaff at the end of Part II, has been much disputed. Our inter-pretation of the play is here in accord with Dr. Johnson's admi-rable comment: "The speech is very artfully introduced to keep the Prince from appearing vile in the opinion of the audience; it prepares them for his future reformation, and *what is yet more valuable, exhibits a natural picture of a great mind offering ex-cuses to itself, and palliating those follies which it can neither justify nor forsake.*" The italics are mine, but the emphasis is Dr. Johnson's — "what is yet more valuable." Dr. Johnson recognized the complex purposes to which Shakespeare had adjusted his material and saw the self-deception that was being practiced behind the announced deception. Prince Hal says that his riotous living is just a technique for appearing all the more regal when he has made a sudden reversal at the appropriate time, but he has other reasons. He was already given to this way of life at the time he became Prince, frequenting the London taverns "with unre-strained loose companions," as Bolingbroke laments toward the end of *Richard II* (V.iii.1-22). In an extremely interesting scene in II *Henry IV* (II.ii) — to which I will return — he admits to Poins a desire for "small beer." And as we have already noted, he shares with Falstaff a contempt for the court and the noble code. Hal is an egotist like Falstaff, Henry IV, and the other characters, but with his own special differences. His egotism is profounder, more isolated, and more efficient. The speech we discuss shows an obvious egotism and implies an even greater egotism. To get to the point quickly: Hal is too egotistical to be satisfied with being

a half-king, a merely good prince. As a good prince he would still
have been in the shadow of the King and the brightness of his
princely virtues would have been mere appendages to the inherent
glory of the King. So he chose to be with Falstaff and the tavern
crowd, a prince among small beer, a big fish in a little pond until
he could be the biggest fish in the ocean. But the little pond is of
course only incidental, or instrumental, to the satisfaction he
sought in being a bad prince and not just a prince. Until he could
have the ultimate distinction of kingship, he chose the distinctness
of being a bad prince: "I'll so offend, to make offense a skill." He
could thus be a prince to the tavern and an offender to the court,
something out of the ordinary in either case and hence something
whole and independent to himself.

Another significance of Hal's soliloquy appears when the King
takes the Prince to task for his offenses, as Hal and Falstaff had
mockingly anticipated he would. In a lecture-like speech of the
King's there are two elements which call to mind the soliloquy.
These are the rarity *versus* commonness theme and the sun imagery. The King charges that Hal is comparable to Richard II, who
was too lavish of his presence to vulgar company, and for the same
reason in contrast with Henry himself.

> By being seldom seen, I could not stir
> But like a comet I was wondered at,
>
> . . . .
>
> He was but as the cuckoo is in June,
> Heard, not regarded; seen, but with such eyes
> As, sick and blunted with community,
> Afford no extraordinary gaze,
> Such as is bent on sunlike majesty
> When it shines seldom in admiring eyes;
> But rather drowsed and hung their eyelids down,
> Slept in his face and rendered such aspect
> As cloudy men use to their adversaries,
> Being with his presence glutted, gorged and full.
> And in that very line, Harry, standest thou.
>
> *Part I, III.ii.46–85*

An effective dramatic irony is produced by this recurrence of theme and imagery. The King fails to see that there is a skill in Hal's offense and that father and son have essentially the same policy and even express it in the same terms. Henry, less subtle than his son, fails to see this correspondence of means and ends because Hal's different circumstances call for a superficially different means, and because at the present time the King's motives and the Prince's motives are, after all, not identical.

The ironical parallelism between Hal and Falstaff appears most vividly in the scene where Hal is caught in a desperately awkward situation. Caught holding the crown of the still-living King whom he took for dead, he can at first only weakly explain, "I never thought to hear you speak again." But before looking at this scene more closely we shall consider a pattern of actions to which it belongs and which is relevant to an aspect of Hal's character. Hal has a knack of reaping where another man has sown. He is inclined to remain detached and uninvolved until just the right moment — that is one meaning of the "I know you all" soliloquy. The first action serving this motif is the Gadshill robbery, where he robs Falstaff of the thousand pounds Falstaff has robbed from the travelers. Tillyard has observed a kind of tit for tat between the Gadshill robbery and the slaying of Hotspur, where Falstaff takes credit for Hal's deed. But the slaying of Hotspur also carries the theme of Hal's taking the short cut to rewards. Hal had promised his father that

> the time will come
> That I shall make this Northern youth exchange
> His glorious deeds for my indignities.
> Percy is but my factor, good my lord,
> To engross up glorious deeds on my behalf.
>
> *Part I, III.ii.144–148*

Shakespeare leaves it rather vague whether or not Hal let Falstaff have the credit, but we can see that Falstaff's claim provided Hal with attractive alternatives. Either he had reaped Hotspur's glories or that irksome warrior — "he that kills me some six or seven Scots at a breakfast" — had fallen ignobly at the hands of Falstaff. The Prince's father had a habit of comparing him unfavorably with

Hotspur, and the latter account of Hotspur's death would certainly put a stop to that in a satisfying way. The climax in this pattern of actions is Hal's return to the court and to the bedside of the dying King. Although he makes few appearances in Part II, it is clear that he has continued his tavern life and kept away from the court and its troublesome affairs. After last seeing him in Act II with Poins and Falstaff, we do not see him again until the close of Act IV, when he comes to the deathbed of the King. It is here that Hal's reform is first actually revealed, for we see him showing remorse and expressing virtuous and noble feelings.

But I shall attend more closely to what are perhaps less obvious meanings. For one thing, the reform has come at the last moment, when Hal knows that his father is dying and then when he mistakenly thinks he is dead. What Falstaff had said of himself —

> To the latter end of a fray and the beginning of a feast
> Fits a dull fighter and a keen guest —

is, in its essential meaning, also applicable to Hal. As far as Hal knows, his reform is just in the knick of time, too late even to be known by his father, for the King says, when he awakes, "Thy life did manifest thou lovedst me not." Hal's mistaking his father's sleep for death and his taking the crown from the room show his keenness for the noble role he has at last assumed. The Falstaffian aspect of Hal's character and behavior is epitomized in his being discovered with the crown and in his weak and brief excuse, "I never thought to hear you speak again" — a situation bordering closely on the comic. He remains holding the embarrassing crown, while his father opens a bitter tirade against him with the accusation, "Thy wish was father, Harry, to that thought." That Hal has had time during his father's speech to collect his wits and prepare a more forceful justification is pointed up by the opening words of his own speech.

> Oh, pardon me, my liege! But for my tears,
> The moist impediments unto my speech,
> I had forestalled this dear and deep rebuke
> Ere you with grief had spoke and I had heard
> The course of it so far.   *IV.v.139–143*

To make this observation is not to say that this statement, or the rest of Hal's humble and noble speech, is not sincere. The point is that Shakespeare is persuasively consistent in representing the complexity of what men call sincerity in such a way as to indicate its coexistence with unexpressed or unrealized motives. Hal had certainly not planned being caught with the crown, but he can, like Falstaff, turn a huge *faux pas* to his advantage, "Pleading so wisely in excuse of it!" as the quickly forgiving King exclaims. Hal can explain his action in such a way as to gain his father's blessing. Indeed, he can so reform as to make reform a skill. In his exoneration of himself from the appearance of overeagerness for the crown, one can see again the theme of motive concealing motive. If there is something Falstaffian about the awkwardness of Hal's situation, there is also about his successful escape from it. Even the King recognizes that the *faux pas* was a lucky occasion, leading to a fuller and more impressive reconciliation than might otherwise have occurred.

> O my son,
> God put it in thy mind to take it hence,
> That thou mightst win the more thy father's love
> Pleading so wisely in excuse of it.
> *IV.v.178–181*

In his wise pleading Hal even dares admit that he tried the crown on for size — but he doesn't put it that way, of course.

> I put it on my head,
> To try with it, as with an enemy
> That had before my face murdered my father,
> The quarrel of a true inheritor.
> *IV.v.166–169*

We may find that Hal's self-exoneration sets up echoes of such declarations as "Was it for me to kill the heir apparent," "They hate us youth," and so on. But Hal's expressed motives, unlike those of Falstaff, are not supposed to be transparent, even to himself.

The final scene of Part II, in which Hal turns away Falstaff, has been much discussed and debated. I wish to emphasize here a few lines in the speech with which Hal rejects Falstaff and publicly announces his reformation:

> I have long dreamed of such a kind of man,
> So surfeit-swelled, so old and so profane,
> But, being awaked, I do despise my dream.

V.v.53–55

We remember, of course, that Hal's reformation was planned, calculated to make him the more conspicuously glorious when he finally became King. Now that the reformation has taken place, we may ask, Is it really felt or is it just a skill? I submit that while it is a skill, it is also really felt and that we are meant to take it as such. The whole speech, and especially the lines quoted here, have a quality that is peculiarly subjective and not just that of the public statement. Falstaff assures Master Shallow that this is just an act, that "he must seem thus to the world." But Hal has the capacity for not detaching himself from the more flattering parts of his shrewd political strategy. He is the sort of person who must seem thus to himself. While his father was King, it was a fine and clever joke for the Prince and Heir to consort with thieves and drunkards. Now that Hal is King, that chapter is ended! Jokes and dreams have much in common — absurdity, for example. But while one is responsible for a clever joke, an absurd dream may be disowned. The joke has served its purpose and become a dream. Falstaff has ceased to exist, for he is banished from the new King's presence.

It has been observed that Brutus is a precursor of Hamlet in the development of Shakespeare's pageant of characters. And Hal is a still earlier precursor. All are characters peculiarly isolated, struggling with confused motives, extremely self-preoccupied but showing attractive personal features. All show a capacity, seemingly without plan or effort, of reproducing in others the love they bear toward themselves. The "small beer" scene, mentioned earlier, is most Hamlet-like. Hal appears quite sympathetically here, letting his hair down ever so slightly and with dignity, at once melancholy, witty, and superior. Poins has chided him with the trifling life he leads while his father is sick. His reply is that his "heart bleeds inwardly" and that everyone would think him a hypocrite were he to weep openly. His sentiments here are convincing, but not his logic. He would rather be thought a waster and a heartless son than a hypocrite. He is more concerned with what men like Poins think than with what his father thinks. It would be hypocritical to weep now, it would be out of character. He will weep when he is ready to step out of that character into another, when he performs the somersault of reformation, when he and the time are ready for him to put his heart into the act and the crown on his head. Then *he* will not think himself a hypocrite, and that is what matters.

The somersault of reformation has turned Hal's joke into a dream and his revels now are ended. But there is a sense in which the dream continues and in which the joke and the dream have existed side by side. The period of Hal's "loose behavior" was a joke to the extent that it was a conscious deception, but it was like a dream to the extent that it was a self-deception. And the self-deception continues, of course, in the transformation of the joke into the dream. Hal, like his father, is impelled to recreate reality according to his own egotistical needs. Indeed, once he has properly assumed the crown, he becomes visibly much like his father. We have earlier observed an implicit parallelism between father and son, but now, when Hal is also King Henry, this likeness comes to the foreground.

At the end of Act IV of Part II, in the scene of the huge *faux pas*, Hal seems much like Falstaff, when the King is on his way out, about to die. And at the end of the play Hal seems much like his father, when Falstaff is on his way out, about to be banished. In other words, as each character is eliminated, Hal appears in the semblance of the other. The two characters, the father and Falstaff (a father-figure), blend and emerge in Hal, and in so emerging each cancels the other from the external scene. Falstaff, Hal, and Henry are all in a complicated ironical parallelism. They are strongly individualized, but beneath the sharply differing appearances, they are much the same. All have a manner of wrenching the true cause the false way. "Tush, man, mortal men, mortal men."

Keats and the Music of Autumn

WITH the possible exception of Coleridge, who has loomed large as a critic, the reputation of no romantic poet has in our century maintained so steady a course as that of John Keats. While Wordsworth, Byron, and Shelley were being attacked or neglected, Keats was spared, mentioned with a special deference, and even given admiring critical analysis and scholarly study. In recent years especially has his better work, so often designated "the great odes," received serious critical attention. F. R. Leavis, Kenneth Burke, Cleanth Brooks, and Allen Tate have all made appraisals and interpretations of one or more of these poems. *Ode to a Nightingale* and *Ode on a Grecian Urn* have been of central interest and received the fullest examination, and this is in no way surprising. It is my impression, however, that *To Autumn* has been peculiarly neglected, that it merits greater attention, both in its own right and for its significance in the interrelatedness of all the odes, than it has received. For example, there is not a single reference to it in James R. Caldwell's excellent book *John Keats' Fancy*. Tate, in an essay primarily concerned with the Nightingale ode, writes of *To Autumn* that it "is a very nearly perfect piece of style but it has little to say." This is true enough in a sense, yet I propose that it is not true in the sense in which Tate must surely be using the word *say* about a poem. Leavis, in an essay on Keats' later work, quotes Middleton Murry on *To Autumn*: "It is a perfect and unforced utterance of the truth contained in the magic words: 'Ripeness is all.'" And then Leavis makes this comment: "Such talk is extravagant, and does not further the appreciation of Keats. No one could have found that order of significance in the Ode merely by inspecting the Ode itself. The ripeness with which Keats is concerned is the physical ripeness of autumn, and his genius manifests itself in the sensuous richness with which he renders this in poetry, without

[18

the least touch of artistic over-ripeness." Leavis, too, is of the opinion that the poet *says* little. But I believe that Murry's comment on the poem shows a valid and demonstrable insight into a part of its meaning.

Leavis' seeming dictum that we should read a poem merely by itself is both surprising and confusing. I am not prepared to say where the legitimate context of a poem begins and ends, but I would argue that a poem need not and sometimes cannot be read in such isolation. It is common enough for a reader to return to the same poem several times over the years, and to find new orders of significance. He might expand, or somehow qualify, the meaning he first found by simply using a dictionary during the second reading. After we have some familiarity with Homer, can we read the *Odyssey* as if we had never heard of the *Iliad*? Perhaps Leavis has arrived at this fallacy because Keats is close to us in time, so that his individual poems, on one order of significance, are wholly available. But surely no amount of footnoting or scholarly introduction can provide the kind of illumination for the individual poem, whether Petrarch's or Yeats', which it receives from the other works of its author, and even from the works of other authors — and finally from the stage of literacy, the general fund of knowledge, which a particular reader brings to a poem. The scholar can, of course, provide some relevant signposts and reminders. Modern critics, Leavis among them, have done a truly good deed in rescuing poetry from the morgue of scholarship *pour* scholarship, but when the poem is isolated for close analysis it may remain something less than restored if too much emphasis is put on the isolation. Although there are no "authorities" on this question, it is interesting to recall that two critics who have led the way toward the analytical interpretation of poetry also insisted on the reverse of isolation. In that early and long famous essay on tradition, Eliot announced that "no poet . . . has his complete meaning alone," and his arguments are applicable to the individual poem. Ransom, evaluating and interpreting *Lycidas* in two of his earlier essays, looks backward and forward in Milton's work and suggests that the poem is "nearly anonymous." That the whole is greater than the sum of its parts is true not only of a poem but of a poet's whole work — or rather, this is true of better poems, and of poets whose achievement is most formidable. Fortunately, Leavis' own practice as a critic is not limited by the principle of reading a poem "merely by itself." As I read *To Autumn* in the light of Keats' other poems, I shall also be working in an illumination kindled by all the writers mentioned above.

It seems generally agreed that *To Autumn* is a rich and vivid description of nature, expertly achieved within a fairly intricate stanzaic pattern. The words are successfully descriptive (or evocative) in their phonetic qualities and rhythmical arrangement, as well as in their imagistic references. If we are familiar with Keats' other work, however, we can discover that the poem is not only rich in pictorial and sensuous details, but that it has a depth of meaning and a characteristic complexity of structure. *To Autumn* is allied especially to the odes on Melancholy, on a Grecian Urn, and to a Nightingale. The four poems are various treatments presenting differing aspects of a single theme.

In so far as the theme is "stated" in any of the poems, it is most clearly stated in the *Ode on Melancholy*. In fact, if we want a general formulation of the theme, we need only quote the last stanza — especially these lines:

> Ay, in the very temple of Delight
> Veil'd Melancholy has her sovran shrine,
> Though seen of none save him whose strenuous
>   tongue
> Can burst Joy's grape against his palate fine.

Keats was obviously preoccupied with the consideration that beauty and melancholy are closely related: true melancholy is to be found only in the fullness of living, in beauty, joy and delight, for these experiences make most poignant the passage of time, through which such experiences and then life itself must come to an end.

All this is clear enough in the *Ode on Melancholy*. There is, however, the implication that the relationship between beauty and melancholy works both ways. That is, either joy or sadness is most intensely felt when it is attended by a consciousness of the experience which is opposite and yet so closely related to it. The theme, then, is more complex and subtle than the aspect of it which appears on the surface in *Ode on Melancholy*. Other implications of the theme may be found throughout the four poems, which illuminate and clarify each other. This is not to say that the poems are merely repetitions of the same theme, which Keats had in mind before he wrote any of them. When we understand the poems we might find it more accurate to say that each is the exploration of a certain theme.

With so much of its context in mind, let us examine closely *To Autumn*. The poem opens with an apostrophe to the season, and with a description of natural objects at their richest and ripest stage.

> Season of mists and mellow fruitfulness,
>   Close bosom-friend of the maturing sun;
> Conspiring with him how to load and bless
>   With fruit the vines that round the thatch-eaves run;
> To bend with apples the moss'd cottage-trees,
>   And fill all fruit with ripeness to the core;
>   To swell the gourd, and plump the hazel shells
>   With a sweet kernel; to set budding more,
> And still more, later flowers for the bees,
> Until they think warm days will never cease,
>   For Summer has o'er-brimm'd their clammy cells.

The details about the fruit, the flowers and the bees constitute a lush and colorful picture of autumn and the effects of the "maturing sun." In the final lines of the first stanza, however, slight implications about the passage of time begin to operate. The flowers are called "later," the bees are assumed to think that "warm days will never cease," and there is a reference to the summer which has already past.

In the second stanza, an imaginative element enters the description, and we get a personification of the season in several appropriate postures and settings.

> Who hath not seen thee oft amid thy store?
>   Sometimes whoever seeks abroad may find

The Man in the Name

Thee sitting careless on a granary floor,
   Thy hair soft-lifted by the winnowing wind;
Or on a half-reap'd furrow sound asleep,
   Drows'd with the fume of poppies, while thy hook
     Spares the next swath and all its twined flowers:
And sometimes like a gleaner thou dost keep
   Steady thy laden head across a brook;
   Or by a cyder-press, with patient look,
     Thou watchest the last oozings hours by hours.

As this stanza proceeds, the implications of the descriptive details become increasingly strong. For example, autumn is now seen, not as setting the flowers to budding, but as already bringing some of them to an end, although it "Spares the next swath." Autumn has become a "gleaner." The whole stanza presents the paradoxical qualities of autumn, its aspects both of lingering and passing. This is especially true of the final image. Autumn is the season of dying as well as of fulfilling. Hence it is with "*patient look*" that she (or he?) watches "the last oozings hours by hours." Oozing, or a steady dripping, is, of course, not unfamiliar as a symbol of the passage of time.

It is in the last stanza that the theme emerges most conspicuously.

     Where are the songs of Spring? Ay, where are they?
       Think not of them, thou hast thy music too, —
     While barred clouds bloom the soft-dying day,
       And touch the stubble-plains with rosy hue;
     Then in a wailful choir the small gnats mourn
       Among the river sallows, borne aloft
        Or sinking as the light wind lives or dies;
     And full-grown lambs loud bleat from hilly bourn;
       Hedge-crickets sing; and now with treble soft
       The red-breast whistles from a garden-croft;
        And gathering swallows twitter in the skies.

The opening question implies that the season of youth and rebirth, with its beauties of sight and sound, has passed, and that the season of autumn is passing. But autumn, too, *while* it lasts — "While barred clouds bloom the soft-dying day" — has its beauties, its music, as Keats' poem demonstrates. The imagery of the last stanza contrasts significantly with that of the first, and the final development of the poem adds meaning to its earlier portions. The slight implications are confirmed. We may recall that "maturing" means aging and ending as well as ripening. The earlier imagery is, of course, that of ripeness. But the final imagery is more truly autumnal. The first words used to describe the music of autumn are "wailful" and "mourn." The opening stanza suggests the height of day, when the sun is strong and the bees are gathering honey from the open flowers. But in the last stanza, after the passing of "hours and hours," we have "the soft-dying day," the imagery of sunset and deepening twilight, when the clouds impart their glow to the day and the plains. The transitive, somewhat rare use of the verb *bloom*, with its springlike associations, is perhaps surprising, and certainly appropriate and effective in suggesting the tensions of the theme, in picturing a beauty that is lingering, but *only* lingering. The conjunction of "rosy hue" and "stubble-plains" has the same significant incongruity, although the image is wholly convincing and actual in its reference. While the poem is more descriptive and suggestive than dramatic, its latent theme of transitoriness and mortality is symbolically dramatized by the passing course of the day. All these characteristics of the poem are to be found in its final image: "And gathering swallows twitter in the skies." Here we have the music of autumn. And our attention is directed toward the darkening skies. Birds habitually gather in flocks toward nightfall, particularly when they are preparing to fly south at the approach of winter. But they are still gathering. The day, the season, are "soft-dying" and are both the reality and the symbol of life as most intensely and poignantly beautiful when viewed from this melancholy perspective.

This reading of *To Autumn* is obviously slanted in the direction of a theme which is also found in the other odes. The theme is, of course, only a part of the poem, a kind of dimension, or extension, which is almost concealed by other features of the poem, particularly by the wealth of concrete descriptive detail. Whereas in *Ode on Melancholy* the theme, in one of its aspects, is the immediate subject, in *To Autumn* the season is the subject and the details which describe and thus present the subject are also the medium by which the theme is explored. It may be of interest, at this point, to distinguish between exploration and illustration. For example, Herrick's *To Daffodils* has a theme which is at least superficially similar to Keats'. But in Herrick's poem the theme is openly stated, and it is, in fact, the subject, which is illustrated by logical analogy with the daffodils. In *To Autumn*, however, the relationship between subject and theme is not one of analogy. The theme inheres in the subject, and is at no point stated in other terms. That is why we could say, in our reading of the poem, that the subject "is both the reality and the symbol," and to say now that the development of the subject is, in a respect, the exploration of a theme.

The poem has an obvious structure in so far as it is a coherent description. Its structure, however, is not simple in the sense of being merely continuous. For example, the course of the day parallels the development of the poem. And an awareness of the theme gives even greater significance to the structure, for the theme merges with increasing clarity and fullness throughout the poem until the very last line. Because the theme is always in the process of emerging without ever shaking off the medium in which it is developed, the several parts of the poem have a relationship to each other beyond their progression in a single direction. The gathering swallows return some borrowed meaning to the soft-dying day with substantial interest, and the whole last stanza negotiates with the first in a similar relationship. (If we had a special word for this kind of structure in poetry, we should be less inclined to discuss it figuratively. The words *organic* and *dynamic* have been used, as well as the word *dramatic*. Particularly in regard to Keats' poetry has *spatial* been used as a critical term [by Tate]. For example, we might say that the structure of *To Autumn* is *spatial*, not only because of the quality of the imagery, but because the structural elements exist, or coexist, in a relationship with each other which is different from the temporal progression that constitutes, on one level, all descriptive, narrative, and discursive writing. This *spatial* metaphor is applicable in more or less degree to any piece of writing in so far as it fulfills the formal conditions of art. It is by such considerations that we move in an ever widening circle away from the particular poem or experience, and the expressions which were initially metaphors thus tend to become abstract critical terms. *To Autumn* itself, as we have seen, has implications about space and time, but because it scarcely takes the first step into metaphor, which is also a step toward statement, it is of all the odes at the farthest extreme from abstraction.)

We have observed the descriptive, temporal (course of day), and thematic aspects of the structure. Another aspect of structure appears when, once more, we consider the poem within the context of Keats' work. *To Autumn* shares a feature of development with the odes on the Nightingale and the Grecian Urn. Each of these poems begins with presentation of realistic circumstances, then moves into an imagined realm, and ends with a return to the realistic. In *Ode to a Nightingale*, the most clearly dramatic of the poems, the speaker, hearing the song of the nightingale, wishes to fade with it "into the forest dim" and to forget the painful realities of life. This wish is fulfilled in the fourth stanza — the speaker exclaims, "Already with thee!" As the poem proceeds and while the imagined realm is maintained, the unpleasant realities come back into view. From the transition that begins with the desire for "easeful Death" and through the references to "hungry generations" and "the sad heart of Ruth," the imagined and the real, the beautiful and the melancholy, are held balanced against each other. Then, on the word "forlorn," the speaker turns away from the imagined, back to the real and his "sole self."

Ode on a Grecian Urn opens with an apostrophe to the actual urn. In the second stanza the imagined realm, the "ditties of no tone," is invoked, and the "leaf-fringed legend" comes to life. And here, too, the imagined life and real life are set in contrast against each other — the imagined is the negation of the real. It is in the fourth stanza that the imagined life is most fully developed and at the same time collapses into the real. The urn is left behind and the people are considered as not only in the scenes de-

picted on the urn, but as having left some little town. With the
image of the town, desolate and silent, the imagination has completed its course. The people can never return to the town. In
the final stanza they are again "marble men and maidens" and the
urn is a "Cold Pastoral." The statement about truth and beauty
with which the poem ends is famous and much debated. It is conceivable that Keats is saying here what he has said elsewhere and
in another way — in the *Ode* that begins

> Bards of Passion and of Mirth,
> Ye have left your souls on earth!
> Have ye souls in heaven too,
> Double-lived in regions new?

Toward the end of the poem there are these lines:

> Here, your earth-born souls still speak
> To mortals, of their little week;
> Of their sorrows and delights;
> Of their passions and their spites;
> Of their glory and their shame;
> What doth strengthen and what maim.
> Thus ye teach us, every day
> Wisdom, though fled far away.

Keats is not didactic here, nor does he claim didacticism for the
bards. Their earth-born souls, their works, teach wisdom in speaking of the lives of men, and in bringing to men, generation after
generation, an intensified awareness and thrill of being alive. It
is the same wisdom which the urn will continue to teach "in midst
of other woe." Keats believed that man's life, though rounded
by a little sleep, is the stuff of which "a thing of beauty" is made.
Art takes its truth from life, and then returns it to life as beauty.
The paradox that "teases us out of thought" is that in a work of
art there is a kind of life which is both dead and immortal. But,
a melancholy truth, *only* the dead are immortal. If there is a
heaven, Keats wanted it to be very much like earth, with a Mer-
maid Tavern where poets could bowse "with contented smack."
Delight is inseparable from melancholy because it is not conceivable apart from the mortal predicament. The answer to the question at the end of *Ode to a Nightingale* — "Do I wake or sleep?" —

is, Both. In the structural imaginative arc of the poem, the speaker is returned to the "drowsy numbness" wherein he is awake to his own mortal lot and no longer awake to the vision of beauty. Yet he knows that it is the same human melancholy which is in the beauty of the bird's "plaintive anthem" and in the truth of his renewed depression. His way of stating this knowledge is to ask the question. Such considerations may clarify the truth-beauty passage. Whether they justify artistically Keats' use of these clichés of Platonic speculation is another matter. Keats was no Platonist, and if he had avoided those terms or if he had indicated more obviously, within the poem, that he was using the word *truth* in a sense close to the materialism of his own times, *Ode on a Grecian Urn* would have had a different career in the history of literary criticism. It is unlikely that any amount of exegesis can rescue those last lines of the poem from associations with Platonic pietism, for Keats was not enough of a witty and conscious ironist to exploit successfully the philosophical ambiguities of *truth*. His romanticism was neither reactionary nor modernist in that way, and he may not even have been clearly aware of the ambiguity involved. If it could be proved that he was innocent of the ambiguity, and wanted only the philosophical prestige of the Platonic associations, then from his point of view the poem would not suffer from the difficulties which the merest sophistication can ascribe to it. Whether such ignorance of the law would be too outrageous to merit critical exoneration is a nice problem for critical theory.

In considering the arc of imagination as an aspect of structure, we have noticed that *Ode to a Nightingale* approaches general statement and that *Ode on Grecian Urn* arrives at it. *To Autumn* is obviously less explicit, although it shows the same structural aspect. The lush and realistic description of the first stanza is followed by the imagined picture of autumn as a person who, while a lovely part of a lively scene, is also intent upon destroying it. The personification is dropped in the final stanza, and there is again a realistic description, still beautiful but no longer lush, and suggesting an approaching bleakness.

The imaginative aspect of structure which the three odes

have in common illustrates opinions which are in accord with the thought of Keats' times and which he occasionally expressed in his poetry. The romantic poets' preoccupation with nature is proverbial, and there are a number of studies (e.g., Caldwell's on Keats) relating their work and thought to the associationist psychology which was current in their times. According to this psychology, all complex ideas and all products of the imagination were, by the association of remembered sensations, evolved from sensory experiences. Keats found this doctrine interesting and important not because it led back to the mechanical functioning of the brain and the nervous system, but because sensations led to the imagination and finally to myth and poetry, and because the beauty of nature was thus allied with the beauty of art. In the early poem which begins, "I stood tip-toe upon a little hill," Keats suggests that the legends of classical mythology were created by poets responding to the beauties of nature:

> For what has made the sage or poet write
> But the fair paradise of Nature's light?
> In the calm grandeur of a sober line,
> We see the waving of the mountain pine;
> And when a tale is beautifully staid,
> We feel the safety of a hawthorn glade:
> . . . .
> While at our feet, the voice of crystal bubbles
> Charms us at once away from all our troubles:
> So that we feel uplifted from the world,
> Walking upon the white clouds wreathed and curled.
> So felt he, who first told, how Psyche went
> On the smooth wind to realms of wonderment.
> . . . .
> What first inspired a bard of old to sing
> Narcissus pining o'er the untainted spring?
> In some delicious ramble, he had found
> A little space with boughs all woven round;
> And in the midst of all, a clearer pool . . .

In the *Ode to Psyche*, which was written during the same year as the other odes (1819),* Keats claims a similar experience for

* The Psyche, Melancholy, Nightingale, and Grecian Urn odes were written in May, and *To Autumn* in September.

himself and contrasts it with those of the "bards of old." He has come upon Cupid and Psyche while he "wandered in a forest thoughtlessly." Although the times are "too late for antique vows" and the "fond believing lyre," he is still by his "own eyes inspired." If he cannot celebrate this symbolic deity with rites and shrine, then he proposes to do so with the service of the imagination, with "the wreath'd trellis of a working brain, . . . all the gardener Fancy e'er could feign" and with all that "shadowy thought can win." Conspicuous throughout Keats' work, blended and adjusted according to his own temperament and for his own purposes, are these *données* of his time: a theory of the imagination, the Romantic preoccupation with nature, and the refreshed literary tradition of classical mythology. These are reflected by the structure of his most successful poems, and are an element in their interrelatedness.

To Autumn is shorter than the other odes, and simpler on the surface in several respects. The nightingale sings of summer "in full-throated ease," and the boughs in the flowery tale on the urn cannot shed their leaves "nor ever bid the Spring adieu." The world in which the longer odes have their setting is either young or in its prime, spring or summer. Consequently, in these poems some directness of statement and a greater complexity are necessary in order to develop the paradoxical theme, in order to penetrate deeply enough the temple of Delight and arrive at the sovran shrine of Melancholy. The urn's "happy melodist" plays a song of spring, and the "self-same song" of the nightingale is of summer. One of these songs has "no tone," and the other is in either "a vision or a waking dream," for the voice of the "immortal Bird" is finally symbolized beyond the "sensual ear." But the music of autumn, the twittering of the swallows, remains realistic and literal, because the tensions of Keats' theme are implicit in the actual conditions of autumn, when beauty and melancholy are merging on the very surface of reality. Keats' genius was away from statement and toward description, and in autumn he had the natural symbol for his meanings. If *To Autumn* is shorter than the other odes and less complex in its materials, it has the peculiar distinction of great compression achieved in simple terms.

Donne's Poetry and
Modern Criticism

THE CRITICS

IT IS my impression that in modern criticism of poetry the word *metaphysical* has been used more frequently than any other comparable term — if there is one comparable. The term has become, moreover, categorical in a way for a body of modern critical theory and the contemporary poetic practice associated with that theory. Yet, if this word suggests a category, it is a very loose one. My intention is to examine some of the criticism employing the word and some of the literature embraced by it, to make the category tighter and clearer, or else to discover that it is unfit for categorial pretension — at least beyond its historical origin.

As a result of Dryden's reference to Donne as "affecting the metaphysic" and more particularly of Dr. Johnson's naming as "metaphysical" Donne and the seventeenth-century poets showing his influence, historians of English literature have persistently used the term for grouping together certain poets of the seventeenth century. Modern critics, passing favorable judgment upon the work of these poets, often use the term to imply — and even make explicit — an aesthetic formula by which a kind of poetry may have been written before or since the time of Donne and his immediate followers. One finds critics writing the word *metaphysical* with a capital letter, in italics, or within quotation marks. This suggests that they do not always mean simply what the philosophers have meant by it. And a survey of their writings finds the term used with no consistent significance throughout, at times with a lack of clarity, and often in questionable propositions.

A review of comment upon metaphysical poetry may well begin with Sir Herbert Grierson, the foremost editor of Donne and one

[30

of the earliest in this century to write admiringly upon the subject. Introducing his edition of *Metaphysical Lyrics and Poems of the Seventeenth Century*, Grierson uses *metaphysical* in its customary philosophic meaning: he says that metaphysical poetry was written by Lucretius, Dante, and Goethe; that it is poetry that "has been inspired by a philosophical conception of the universe and the role assigned to the human spirit in the great drama of existence." * This definition could certainly be applied to poetry (e.g., Shelley's *Prometheus Unbound*) with which that of the seventeenth century is often contrasted. Donne and his followers wrote poems of no such proportions, were metaphysical in not so large a way, yet Grierson finds it especially adequate to call them metaphysical. His characterization of the poetry, to show the justness of the title given it, deserves quotation, for we find echoes of it and statements of a similar nature in the discussions of later writers. The term *metaphysical*

"lays stress on all the right things — the survival, one might say the reaccentuation, of the metaphysical strain, the *concetti metafisici ed ideali* as Testi calls them in contrast to the simpler imagery of classical poetry, of mediaeval Italian poetry; the more intellectual, less verbal, character of their wit compared with the conceits of the Elizabethans; the finer psychology of which their conceits are often the expression; their learned imagery; the argumentative, subtle evolution of their lyrics; above all the peculiar blend of passion and thought, feeling and ratiocination which is their greatest achievement. Passionate thinking is always apt to become metaphysical, probing and investigating the experience from which it takes its rise. All these qualities are in the poetry of Donne, and Donne is the greatest master of English poetry in the seventeenth century" (pp. xv–xvi).

Grierson's remarks are certainly instructive, and one has faith in the soundness of his historical references; yet one could wish that his statements were developed from analyses of particular poems, or that his own propositions were always such that they could be analyzed with reference to particular poems. Expressions like "blend of passion and thought" and "passionate thinking"

* H. J. C. Grierson, *Metaphysical Lyrics and Poems of the Seventeenth Century* (Oxford, 1921), p. xiii.

may well suggest the quality of one's experience upon reading the poetry, and they might reasonably be used in making good guesses about the minds of the authors, but they can hardly be used for discussing the structure of a poem or a poetic method. What Grierson says may seem, for readers of Donne, to follow from the poetry, and he has been repeated in one way and another by several writers since his essay appeared. But if this poetry is to be distinguished from other kinds, it would be well to follow impressionistic statements with analysis of the poetry in terms that refer to the poetry, not the poet's hypothetical personality or a reader's private articulate response. The phrase "passionate thinking" can convey but little knowledge to us when even the psychologists are not satisfied with their understanding of passion and thinking; how such thinking becomes metaphysical cannot be less mysterious than the thinking itself. Grierson's mention of "wit" and "conceits" is the beginning of the kind of definition that is desirable, if possible (i.e., a "public" or structural account), and we shall attend more fully to these matters in discussing later commentators.

T. S. Eliot, whose essay "The Metaphysical Poets" was written as a review of the book edited by Grierson, is generally acknowledged to be largely responsible for the growth of popular and critical interest in metaphysical poetry. He, too, discusses the reader's experience and the psychological constitution of the poets. This he does with many quotations and remarks that suggest a genuine appreciation, an appreciation and delicacy of feeling which many readers have found contagious, which have stimulated many practicing poets. And one suspects that Eliot is quite aware of what he is doing. He does not argue that the term *metaphysical* in its philosophical sense is an apt description of the poetry nor does he cut the term loose from its historical moorings, as Grierson partly does, and as some later critics emphatically do. When he turns to a characteristic structural problem he makes an observation which may be the only structural generalization a close study of the poetry can yield:

"It is difficult to find any precise use of metaphor, simile, or other conceit, which is common to all the poets and at the same time important enough to isolate these poets as a group. Donne, and often Cowley, employ a device which is sometimes considered characteristically 'metaphysical'; the elaboration (contrasted with the condensation) of a figure of speech to the farthest stage to which ingenuity can carry it." *

It should be noticed that Eliot does not raise the question of value in mentioning the characteristic elements of the poetry; in this he is more cautious than other critics. He gives a definition of the conceit which agrees with the *discordia concors* that Dr. Johnson saw in it; and he does not, as other critics have done, place the conceit topmost upon a hierarchical scale of poetic devices: "The conceit itself is primarily an eccentricity of imagery, the far-fetched association of the dissimilar, or the overelaboration of one metaphor or simile." † Nevertheless, there are many statements in Eliot's essays similar to the expression about the combination of thought and feeling; and later critics have borrowed his phrases and used them as if they were propositions having reference to the structural aspects of a poem: "In Chapman especially there is a direct sensuous apprehension of thought, or a re-creation of thought into feeling, which is exactly what we find in Donne. . . . Tennyson and Browning are poets, and they think; but they do not feel their thought as immediately as the odour of a rose" (*Selected Essays*, pp. 246, 247). One may be curious to know how the seventeenth-century poets used language that these things can be said of them with more justice than of Milton, Wordsworth, Shelley, and Browning — if someone wanted to argue that these later poets were unrivaled "passionate thinkers," and so on. Since it reappears in the writings of others, it should be pointed out that the expression "a tough reasonableness beneath the slight lyric grace" (p. 252), which Eliot puts in apposition with Marvell's wit, tells us nothing about the wit or the poetry, although it may intimate the quality of one's feelings (Eliot's, originally) about these. At any rate, with *wit* and what is meant by a *conceit*, we are moving

* *Selected Essays 1917–1932* (New York: Harcourt Brace and Company, 1932), p. 242.
† "Donne in Our Time," in *A Garland for John Donne* (Cambridge, 1931), p. 16.

closer to the poetry and are being provided with propositions that can be tested by poems.

The Donne Tradition * by George Williamson springs, as the author acknowledges, from the suggestions and statements of T. S. Eliot. Williamson discusses the seventeenth-century group of poets called metaphysical, with special attention to John Donne as the founder and supreme example of a certain way of writing poetry. There is much in the book concerning what Eliot had called the unified sensibility of the seventeenth century, with considerable imaginative ramification by Williamson on the nature of this sensibility. And there are extended and frequent discussions of wit and the conceit, and comments on particular passages of poetry, mostly in phrases that are variations of the *combination of thought and feeling.* "It is in such combination (of the ingenious and the imaginative) that the conceit attains to high poetic value; the idea and the figure become one, and we have Donne's *Valediction*, King's *Exequy*, Herbert's *Pulley*, or Marvell's *Coy Mistress* . . . for these poems are moving and sincere" (p. 29). Eliot's phraseology on the minds of the poets echoes and re-echoes through the book. Williamson's habit is to use, as counters for recording his feelings about the poetry, expressions invented by Eliot; his remarks are indeed witness to the suggestibility of the poetry. We are, however, left curious to know what a conceit is doing in and to a poem, in addition to wondering what its effect is upon the reader:

"The expanded conceit is successful when the idea and the figure become one, and the condensed conceit when the image is the very body of the thought. Thus we see the close relation of the conceit to the sensuous thinking of Donne which I have already described. The conceit, playing like the shuttle between his mind and the world, wove the fabric of the thought, and gave the pattern in which he united his most disparate knowledge and experience into an image witty or imaginative, novel or compelling, but always rising from a tough reasonableness and often attaining startling insight, with moments of breathtaking beauty. In short, the conceit, with its wit and surprise and bias of reason, suited his mind, his many-sided interests and his poetic nature" (pp. 31–32).

* Cambridge, 1930.

Donne's Poetry and Modern Criticism

The wit and the conceits are generously illustrated, but there is no venture beyond them by way of further analysis of poems. There is, however, frequent reference to the subject matter and recurrent themes of the poetry; this indicates that an examination may be made for determining to what extent the quality of a poem depends upon these, to what extent upon the technique, and upon the relationship between technique and subject matter. But these considerations are not kept distinct in Williamson's book. When he would appear to be talking about the technique of composition or the structure of a poem, he reiterates approvingly statements made by a poem. Upon Donne's *Extasie*, a poem about the relationship of the bodies and souls of lovers, he offers this comment: "Here a Dionysian ecstasy is supported by the coolest reason, and neither feeling nor thought can be separated from its sensuous embodiment. This is no poetizing of thought, but thought in the flesh of sensuous and emotional perception, or mind expressing itself in the book of the body" (pp. 22–23). An observation is made upon the conceit in somewhat the same manner: "We shall not be wrong if we conclude that the conceit is one of the principal means by which Donne chained analysis to ecstasy; never, we remember, more characteristically than in a poem called *The Extasie*" (p. 34).

Williamson's book has a section especially devoted to a discussion of the conceit. Here he quotes definitions that have been made by others, and he agrees with the stress that is put upon certain aspects. These are the *discordia concors*, the intellectuality and the sincerity that obtain — in the words of T. E. Hulme — "when the whole of the analogy is necessary to get out the exact curve of the feeling or thing you want to express" (p. 84). Here again, except for the *discordia concors*, which is another name for the conceit, general qualities are attributed and references are made to the author's mind: "sincerity" is particularly such a reference. Though he applies in detail the suggestions made by Eliot, Williamson makes no further advance in analysis of the poetry.

In the writings of John Crowe Ransom we find a conception of metaphysical poetry which is categorial, beyond being historical.

The Man in the Name

The term, as Ransom uses it, is evaluative, referring to a superior kind of poetry of which the seventeenth-century poets are the most successful practitioners. Although it is never explicitly stated, the theory that the poetry is characterized by an actually metaphysical content seems at first to be implied by some of Ransom's remarks. What, for instance, does he mean by miraculism?

" 'Metaphysics,' or miraculism, informs a poetry which is the most original and exciting, and intellectually perhaps the most seasoned, that we know in our literature, and very probably it has few equivalents in other literatures. But it is evident that the metaphysical effects may be large-scale or they may be small-scale. (I believe that generically, or ontologically, no distinction is to be made between them.) If Donne and Cowley illustrate the small-scale effects, Milton will illustrate the large-scale ones, probably as a consequence of the fact that he wrote major poems." *

Unfortunately, though he does attend to specific poems for other purposes, Ransom never shows clearly how this *miraculism* is allied with a single poem. Such a demonstration would be most desirable, since he is clear enough about the technique of figurative language that results in the poetry he esteems most highly, and uses it as a measure for making critical judgments upon all poetry. In Ransom's opinion, there is a kind of knowledge — of the metaphysical aspects of human experience, as he might call it — which poetry alone can articulate. This opinion and his sweeping generic use of *metaphysical* are evident in the following quotation:

"The intention of Metaphysical Poetry is to complement science, and improve discourse. Naturalistic discourse is incomplete for either of two reasons. It has the minimum of physical content and starves the sensibility, or it has the maximum, as if to avoid the appearance of evil, but is laborious and pointless. Platonic Poetry is too idealistic, but Physical Poetry is too realistic, and realism is tedious and does not maintain interest. The poets therefore introduce the psychological device of the miracle. The predication which it permits is clean and quick but it is not a scientific predication. For scientific predication concludes an act of attention but miraculism initiates one" (*World's Body*, pp. 141–142).

* *The World's Body* (New York, 1938), p. 135.

Donne's Poetry and Modern Criticism

One wishes that Ransom, so respectful to particulars, would point to a particular miracle. In poetry, before there can be a psychological device there must be a linguistic device. With such a device he does not fail to provide us, though when we would have him attend analytically to the device his utterance becomes psychological, and the transition from the device to the psychological seems yet to be explained. Ransom, like others, regards the conceit as this device: "For the critical mind Metaphysical Poetry refers perhaps almost entirely to the so-called 'conceits' that constitute its staple. To define the conceit is to define small-scale Metaphysical Poetry." And in his definition of the conceit he again turns psychological (i.e., the terms of his statement make reference to impression, or feeling), although a certain use of the conceit is intimated: "A conceit originates in a metaphor; and in fact the conceit is but a metaphor if the metaphor is meant; that is, if it is developed so literally that it must be meant, or predicated so baldly that nothing else can be meant. Perhaps this will do for a definition" (*World's Body*, pp. 136, 137).

Meant is again one of those words that refer to a reader's final attitude toward a poem, but we cannot arrive at it by limiting discussion to terms that are an immediate reference to the poem. What Ransom is saying, obviously, is that the conceit is an extended comparison, a procession of statements that do not depart in figurativeness from a single metaphor. He says as much elsewhere: "The impulse to metaphysical poetry, I shall assume, consists in committing the feelings in the case — those of unrequited love for example — to their determination within the elected figure" (*World's Body*, p. 286). It is easily understood that such adherence to a figure may suggest that the figure is intended seriously or "meant." Yet Ransom surely would not contend "that nothing else can be meant." The figure is, after all, the mechanical device that represents or conveys what is meant — if one would bring up the difficult problem of meaning and the individual consciousness. What Ransom probably does intend is that the figure is not merely a mechanical intermediary, but an object with a peculiar individuality, and is to be contemplated as such. And one may add, as such to be studied and explained, for certain purposes. A distinction may be made between the structure of an object, and the quality of an object when related to human attention. There are times when one might wish that references to these in comment on poetry were less mixed, for the terminology of quality is always more variable — as distinguished from constant — than the terminology of structure. We find such a mixture when Ransom speaks of poetry that has "a single extended image to bear the whole weight of the conceptual structure, as is the way of that precision method of poetical composition which flourishes in the 'metaphysical' style." * The *extended image* is a detail of structure; *precision*, as Ransom uses it, is a quality attributed to the poetry. Extension of image is a method, but what it brings precision to, and why it does so, are left unexplained. That it does so pre-eminently for a concept is arguable, though it may suggest that a concept, with its qualitative accompaniments, is meant, is seriously intended.

A single extended metaphor constituting the whole poem is the primary definition in Ransom's conception of metaphysical poetry. This definition may be tested by looking for examples of it in the seventeenth century and by studying that poetry to determine whether its "success" — the dominant and most frequent structure of the poems — is in the direction of the definition. At present it is interesting to note the consistency of the highly restrictive definition with Ransom's pronouncements on other, extraliterary subjects. He has been much concerned, especially in his earlier writings,† with religious myth, orthodoxy and ritual, uttering a philosophy that held these things valuable and found them wanting in modern society; our misfortune, he argued, is that we have no single consistent myth which is acceptably representative of life beyond its mere economic and biological aspects and which provides adequately for articulation of this life. When no single myth is meant, ritual, which is a kind of articulation, becomes meaningless or impossible. Ransom was not calling simply for a

* "Honey and Gall," *Southern Review*, VI (1940), 10.
† *God without Thunder*, New York, 1930.

religious creed: "Manners, rites, and arts are so close to each other that often their occasions must be confused, and it does not matter much if they are" (*World's Body*, p. 42). The "occasion" for ritual generically includes the occasion for writing a poem, and Ransom would have the poet *mean* a single metaphor just as society should *mean* a single myth, which is a kind of cosmic metaphor that can be extended to every peculiar detail of human experience. Perhaps the critic should hesitate before Ransom's analogies. Possibly on linguistic-aesthetic-psychological grounds he is right, but only possibly, by no means certainly. His social philosophy, with its dicta and evaluations, merges so continuously into his literary criticism that one wonders whether an unprejudiced — a "scientific" — analysis of poetry would fall neatly into the same locus or not.

The poem-ritual occasion is also connected with the term *metaphysical* and Ransom's definition of it. It seems that he uses *metaphysical* as if it were other than an accidental term. Yet its meaning — e.g., miraculism — derives more from his own psychologizing than from customary philosophical usage; it refers to the sentiments and sensibilities of the individual: "The poet perpetuates in his poem an order of existence which in actual life is constantly crumbling beneath his touch" (*World's Body*, p. 348). The result of Ransom's habit of bringing into synthesis his several opinions may be briefly indicated: metaphysical (seventeenth-century poetry → extended metaphor → order of existence); the terms in parentheses may be put in any order. Whether these references hang together by their own nature remains to be learned, although here we have taken note of such expressions as "order of existence" for learning the sources and implications of Ransom's definitions and need not retain them in a fresh analysis of poems.

We may expect that the criticism of Allen Tate * will contain much of the same import to be found in that of Ransom, for each has announced his indebtedness to the other, and they have held similar attitudes on matters other than metaphysical poetry. We find indeed that this is true. Both critics hold metaphysical poetry in high esteem and see in it the same characteristics. One

* *On the Limits of Poetry*, New York, 1948.

noticeable difference, however, is that Tate is less rigorous and positive in the technical lineaments that he attributes to the poetry. For him, as for Ransom, characterization of metaphysical poetry entails definition of the conceit. In this definition he concurs with Ransom, but he does not insist that the conceit of a metaphysical poem is necessarily or typically a metaphor so extended that it is coterminous with the whole structure of the poem (though he suggests that it may be so at times): "Therein lies the nature of the 'conceit.' It is an idea not inherent in the subject, but exactly parallel to it, elaborated beyond the usual stretch of metaphor into a supporting structure for a long passage or even an entire poem" (p. 331).

When Tate treats of the matter at greater length his slight divergence from Ransom becomes clearer. Instead of committing himself to terminology such as *meantness* and such strict definition as a *single extended metaphor*, he gives his statements the qualifications of approximateness, thus making for a looser category than that offered by Ransom. Tate sees in metaphysical poetry not "meantness," but an explicit logical order; not "a single extended image," but the characteristic development of imagery by logical extension. These correlatives to Ransom's terms are found in Tate's statement:

". . . in metaphysical poetry the logical order is explicit; it must be coherent; the imagery by which it is sensuously embodied must have at least the look of logical determinism: I say the look of logic because the varieties of ambiguity and contradiction possible beneath the logical surface are endless . . . Here it is enough to say that the development of imagery by logical extension, the reasonable framework being an Ariadne's thread that the poet will not permit us to lose, is the hallmark of the poetry called metaphysical" (p. 80).

We may restate this in other words: in metaphysical poetry there is conceptual development in imagistic terms, and the images can be recognized as connected with and following each other by their own nature, or else their relationship and sequence is explained within the poem. Such an account is fully applicable to poems, whether or not it would be found valid as a description when applied to Donne's. In testing this proposition one would not look for adherence to a single metaphor throughout a poem, but simply for a series of images that follow each other according to an intellective basis, this basis itself being suggested by the images.

Tate further characterizes metaphysical poetry by distinguishing it from poetry constituted by a series of images having no discernible intellective basis: "Strategy [metaphysical] would here indicate the point on the intensive-extensive scale at which the poet deploys his resources of meaning. The metaphysical poet as a rationalist begins at or near the extensive or denoting end of the line; the romantic or Symbolist poet at the other, intensive end; and each by a straining feat of the imagination tries to push his meanings as far as he can toward the opposite end, so as to occupy the entire scale" (p. 86). Tate's own language is not so near the denoting end of the line as one would have it. By "meanings" does he refer to distinguishable terms in poems that have been written, or does the word include the most ineffable intentions of a poet? Even if we could settle upon a definite reference for "meanings," we would still want a clear mechanical description of the process and product intimated by "a straining feat of the imagination." Whether or not it is reducible to actually descriptive definition, and whatever the terms of such definition might be, Tate does supply a general hypothesis: metaphysical and symbolist poetry are of similar linguistic materials (i.e., images), but these materials are organized in respective patterns that are technically the obverse of each other. Like the pronouncements of other critics, this hypothesis and Tate's definition of metaphysical poetry as "the development of imagery by logical extension" must be shown to rest upon analyses of particular poems.

In his *Modern Poetry and the Tradition,** Cleanth Brooks treats at considerable length several problems concerning metaphysical poetry. He states in the Preface that his book is in some measure the extension, application, and synthesis of ideas borrowed from other critics, including Eliot, Ransom, and Tate. Consequently, in discussing Brooks some repetition will be likely.

* Chapel Hill: University of North Carolina Press, 1939.

The Man in the Name

It should first be noted that, to put it as simply as possible, Brooks regards metaphysical poetry as the best kind of poetry — as, indeed, of the condition toward which any poem tends in so far as it is successful. Consequently, in characterizing the poetry, he is evaluative as well as descriptive. In his most elementary definition he is closer to Tate than to Ransom, for like Tate he refrains from insisting upon the single extended metaphor as normally the framework of a metaphysical poem, although he does of course identify metaphorical device with the body of the poem: "Most clearly of all, the metaphysical poets reveal the essentially functional character of all metaphor. We cannot remove the comparisons from their poems, as we might remove ornaments and illustrations attached to a statement, without demolishing the poem. The comparison *is* the poem in a structural sense" (p. 15). This, like similar statements previously observed, suggests the question: Is a typical poem by Donne and his fellow poets based on a conceit or unbroken chain of conceits, or can we say only that it is a poem in which the conceit appears frequently?

In further development of the subject Brooks suggests that he considers *metaphysical* as an arbitrary name, that it designates a poetry the definition of which is partially fulfilled by other poetry in more or less measure. Moreover, with the definition he has already given, he identifies the term *wit*: "One might, indeed, let the matter rest on the definition of wit: viz., metaphysical poetry (whatever the term metaphysical may mean or may have meant) is witty poetry. . . . Our definition of metaphysical poetry, then, will have to treat the difference between metaphysical poetry, and other poetry as a difference of degree, not of kind" (p. 39). Brooks has singled out what he considers to be the essential feature of metaphysical poetry and applied it to other poetry; and obviously this process gives hierarchical advantage to the metaphysical. Whether this is demonstrable and just, remains problematical. What is to prevent the advocate of another poetry from laying down as the rule what he considers essentially poetical, even if Brooks is altogether accurate in his description of metaphysical poetry?

Donne's Poetry and Modern Criticism

With the identification of the definitions of metaphysical poetry and wit Brooks goes beyond what is primarily structural description. This would not be the case if he meant simply that statement made by metaphor and imagery is fundamentally the device of wit, as he uses that term. But he makes clear that by wit he means not structure alone: "Wit is not merely an acute perception of analogies; it is a lively awareness of the fact that the obvious attitude toward a given situation is not the only possible attitude" (p. 37). This awareness must be ascribed to the poet; though it is deduced from the poetry, it does not inhere in the poetic technique and consequently is not pertinent to technical distinctions, which are those first insisted upon by Brooks and other critics. If we are to accept the first definition as distinguishing the poetry we must see how the generalizations departing from the terminology of structure are consequent upon this definition.

Brooks' contribution in emphasizing the wittiness of metaphysical poetry is to suggest that this poetry is characterized not only by the manner of its statement but also by the import of its statement (i.e., the thought ultimately represented by the words of a passage or poem). He denominates the metaphysical poet as witty because of the poet's use of metaphor and because "he converges his lines from the farthest possible distances" (p. 43) — the *discordia concors* again; and the same wit he credits for the irony and complexity of attitudes to be observed in the statement of the poem. The connection between the structure and the kind of statement is left in question. Does the nature of the statement follow causally from the structure, or are such statement and structure in combination merely coincidental in the poetry of the seventeenth century? This question may in some measure be settled by attending to the poetry; we may determine whether the wit of a passage is felt because of the technique used or because of the thought contained; and if the force of the passage is found to arise from the thought, then we should want to know what is contributed by the technique and what is the relationship between technique and thought in so far as the force or effect of wit is concerned.

The Man in the Name

Brooks presents another problem, one we have already met in the comment of Tate. He suggests that metaphysical poetry and symbolist poetry share essentially characteristic features. In doing so he indicates further the qualified emphasis he gives to the structural aspect of metaphysical poetry. Instead of placing symbolist poetry in positive structural relation to metaphysical, he seems to belittle the importance of structure with regard to all poetry: "Lack of dependence on logical structure distinguishes symbolist poetry from simple expository prose; but this is also true of poetry in general" (p. 60). The strategy, or technique, of metaphysical poetry, which he and other critics have considered so seriously, diminishes in importance when he relates this poetry to another kind: "There are various strategies which the poet may employ, but we shall only confuse matters if we try to make more than a distinction of strategy between the characteristic methods of the metaphysical poet and the symbolist poet" (p. 66). A more rigid formulator of structural pattern for metaphysical poetry, Ransom has not failed to take issue with Brooks on this score: "But I think that the matter of the logic might have engaged him a little more deeply. In view of the logical showing of the seventeenth century he might have argued that the old poets were wasting some of their labors, for the logical nicety is much the most visible of their superficial techniques, and goes far beyond what Mr. Brooks cares to require." *

However this issue may eventually be settled, it is apparent that Brooks presents a new point of view on metaphysical poetry. For him, definition of its structure in technical terms is insufficient characterization of the poetry. He eventually forsakes explanation that is objectively determinable in the structure of the poetry, and he arrives at a description of the poetry by laying stress rather upon its pervasive features and communicative service to the poet than upon its pattern of organization: "With the acquisition of these qualities — irony, realistic diction, wit — symbolist poetry coalesces with metaphysical" (p. 61). "There was in Donne's

* John Crowe Ransom, "Apologia for Modernism," *Kenyon Review*, II (1940), 249.

poetry an ambiguity which went far deeper than the mere use of obscure and difficult references. There was — as there is in the case of tragedy — an ambiguity as to the poet's ultimate attitude" (p. 209). The account of the subject which Brooks presents is not wholly consistent; he fails to indicate the development from the structure of a poetry to the "poet's ultimate attitude." But it is likely that his complicating of problems and difficulties does a kind of justice to the subject.

We may now bring together those remarks, singled out from comment on metaphysical poetry, which actually can be referred to the poetry itself. Our critics agree in the generalization that the poetry is characterized by the conceit and by wit. The conceit is regarded as a comparison of the dissimilar, frequently an extended comparison. As to the exact relationship of the conceit to metaphysical poetry, there is no final and common explanation among the critics. The several statements on the subject are, in effect, as follows:

The conceit is simply a frequent, a habitual device in the poetry.

The conceit, as it is distinctive of an exemplary metaphysical poem, is a single extended metaphor comprising the whole poem.

The metaphysical poem, not necessarily based on a single metaphor, at no point departs from the manner of the conceit, the poem showing a development of imagery by logical extension.

Whatever thought may be extracted or restated from a typical passage of metaphysical poetry is, in the passage, expressed by a trope.

As a characterization, wit, of course, remains more general than conceit. If the poetry is to be distinguished by structural device alone, one may mean simply that the conceit is a device of wit. One can also mean that there are in metaphysical poetry the conceit and other wit devices comparable to it, though such devices have not been specified by any critic. One critic, regarding metaphysical poetry as witty, departs from a rigidly structural aspect and sees wit as a pervasive quality of the poetry. A more specific observation from this point of view is to the effect that metaphysical poetry is witty by its expression of irony and complexity of attitude.

THE POEMS

John Donne is considered the most prominent of the group of seventeenth-century poets called metaphysical, and statements on metaphysical poetry most often refer to the poems of his *Songs and Sonets*. It is, therefore, natural that further study of the subject should attend to these.*

The opening lines and title of *The Good Morrow*, as well as other parts of the poem, indicate that it is addressed by a lover to his loved one after a night of love. Speculation on what the lovers did until they loved is in the form of a conceit; the lovers are equated with suckling children:

> . . . were we not wean'd till then?
> But suck'd on countrey pleasures, childishly?

The poem does not develop by an extension of this conceit nor are references to infancy or the stages of human growth made again as statements upon the condition of the lovers, past or present. Instead, the conceit is followed by an alternative conceit; previous to this love the lovers were as infants, or their unawareness was a condition of sleeping in the legendary den of the seven sleepers. So the speculation runs. But there is hardly a development of thought in the sequence of these two conceits, and there is no linkage between them in figurative terms. And since the two conceits are independent of each other and yet reiterative in statement, their possibilities of precision and significance of detail become less likely when it is affirmed concerning both of them that "T'was so." First the conceits are on a par with each other and then they are lumped together, so that what issues from them is a general implication, not a conceptual argument developed by a single figure or even a series of figures. In the closing lines of the stanza the speaker turns from the pre-love condition to the present: except for his love, he says, all pleasures are fancies, and

* The text consistently used here is *The Poems of John Donne*, ed. H. J. C. Grierson, London: Oxford, 1933.

[46

all his former experience of beauty was but a dream of the loved one. These statements, although suggestive of conceits, are hardly more than the idioms of hyperbole. They do not continue previous references in the poem, nor are they recalled in later references.

As the lover's speech continues in the second stanza, there is no continuation of either argument or terminology from the first stanza. It is not until the fourth line that the figurative language of a conceit occurs. Following the generalization,

> For love, all love of other sights controules,

there comes the particular example,

> And makes one little roome, an every where.

The conceit is constituted by the identification of a room with the world. Other geographical references follow this conceit, but the conceit itself is not in any way extended. The lines that follow,

> Let sea-discoverers to new worlds have gone,
> Let Maps to other, worlds on worlds have showne,

are rhetorical imperatives exclaimed by the lover in expression of his indifference to and independence of affairs other than his own. There is nothing figurative in these statements. Their terminology, however, serves as a referential background for the conceit used in the final line of the stanza:

> Let us possesse one world, each hath one, and is one.

This time each of the lovers is identified with a world. To call this trope a conceit is perhaps questionable, unless one means by a conceit any metaphor or other figure that is not utterly conventional.

The third stanza opens with literal description: the lovers' faces are reflected in each other's eyes. The second line, "And true plain hearts doe in the faces rest," is hardly less literal, since the word *heart* is considered synonymous with *affections* rather than figuratively representative of *affections*. In the next two lines we do have a conceit:

> Where can we finde two better hemispheares
> Without sharpe North, without declining West?

The Man in the Name

This is not the first use of geographical terms. Previously it was said that each lover was a world, that each possessed a world. However calculated and noticeable the use of two "geographical" conceits may be, one is in no way the logical extension or justification of the other. The conceits stand independently side by side; one does not continue from the other. A connection between them is suggested by the fact that each makes reference to the same material, but the connection is general, even vague. Moreover, the second conceit, though it develops its own meaning, does not add meaning to the first. The second conceit says that the faces in which hearts rest are hemispheres, but of a kind that presents no perils to mariners. The implication is that the lovers have nothing to fear from each other and may be confident about the course of their love. The poem ends with a new conceit:

> What ever dyes, was not mixt equally;
> If our two loves be one, or, thou and I
> Love so alike, that none doe slacken, none can die.

Here the conceit is constituted by the application of a proposition from physical science to the relationship of the lovers. If their love is a single unity or is made of equal parts, then, like similar mixtures, the relationship will hold fast and neither party will cease loving the other. The idea of equal parts may refer to the hemispheres of the earlier conceit, but the connection between the two conceits is so slight it can hardly be considered that one is the extension of the other. If one attempts to include the hemispheres in the conceit of the mixtures, it becomes apparent that no meaningful resolution is possible, although the final conceit is otherwise a development in the meaning of the poem.

This examination of *The Good Morrow* is not an attempt at evaluating the poem. Our concern is to discover which statements about the structure of metaphysical poetry are borne out by it. The only statement that is found to be wholly valid with regard to *The Good Morrow* is that the conceit often occurs. It can also be said that the ideological burden of the poem is to a considerable extent conveyed by the use of tropes, though not consistently. An obvious, or superficial, wit inheres in the conceits and such devices

as the hyperbole of the first stanza and the rhetorical imperatives
of the second. Another kind of wit, less local and rhetorical, may
be considered as present in the poem. This wit consists in the
contrast between the two *worlds*: the world of the lovers, and the
geographical world. It is, moreover, not merely a verbal wit, for
each world represents an attitude — the worldly attitude and the
lover's attitude. There is, then, a complexity of attitudes in the
poem. But the lover, who speaks the poem, gives no hint of being
involved in an ironical situation, of entertaining any complexity
of attitudes. He dismisses the geographical world and affirms the
world of love.

The first stanza of *The Canonization* constitutes an apostrophe
to anyone who might try to distract or persuade the lover from his
loving. The lover, implying that he is determined upon loving,
suggests that his critic admonish him upon other grounds, or that
the critic attend to his own advancement, but at any rate leave the
lover undisturbed. Aside from the apostrophe, there is no figurativeness in this stanza, and there is no development or addition
of statement after the first line. A wittiness results from grouping
together the several specific actions, each of which might be performed as alternatives to criticizing the lover; from the critic's
point of view it is irrelevant and absurd to consider such alternatives. Though the stanza is from one point of view repetitious,
though it contains no trope or material that is to be figuratively
elaborated, its wit does characterize the speaker and establish a
tone.

This tone is maintained with little change throughout the
second stanza, which is similar to the first in its construction and
scarcely different in its statement. The speaker continues the
argument for his love, this time in the manner of rhetorical inter-
rogations. He asks what injuries may be charged against his loving,
and then, in the form of questions, lists specific possibilities: have
his sighs drowned ships? have his tears flooded grounds? have his
lover's-chills affected the weather? have his lover's-fevers affected
the health of society? These possibilities, by the extent of their
exaggeration, border upon metaphor, but the obvious function of

the exaggeration is the absurdity which makes for wit. An additional element in the wit is the fact that the issues raised by the lover are irrelevant to — are a digression from — sensible arguments which might be brought against him. The same kind of wit is produced by the literal statement of the lines concluding the stanza:

> Soldiers finde warres, and Lawyers finde out still
> Litigious men, which quarrels move,
> Though she and I do love.

This observation, though it may be witty by its absurdity in the apparent argument, is on another level of reading not absurd at all, though still witty.

With these final lines of the second stanza it becomes obvious that the lover is doing more than making a witty appeal for permission to continue his loving undisturbed. He is saying that his loving has no effect upon soldiers, lawyers, and litigious men; and he is implying, here and throughout the preceding part of the poem, that the values of the lover and those of the world are wholly different and unconnected. In the first two stanzas the speaker has illustrated the thesis that it is absurd to make worldly values bear upon the lover. His absurd defiance of the world is, indirectly, the suggestion of a serious defiance, and this practice of indirection is witty. It should be noticed that this wit does not depend upon the particular devices used for overt absurdity. Like the wit of *The Good Morrow*, it proceeds from the contrast of the two attitudes: that of the world, and that of the lover. Here, however, the lover does not easily dismiss the world. He is cognizant of the contrasting attitudes as being in conflict, and he is opposing one to the other. He is insisting upon a complexity of attitudes, arguing that one attitude should not be confused with or subordinated to the other. Throughout the rest of the poem he continues to argue for the merit and self-sufficiency of the lover's world, the lover's attitude.

The third stanza begins with the lover's statement of his indifference to what others think of or call the lovers. And the stanza continues with the lover's own suggestions as to how they may be characterized: they are tapers, dying at their own cost; in them may be found the Eagle and the Dove; finally, they are comparable to the riddle of the Phoenix:

> The Phoenix ridle hath more wit
> By us, we two being one, are it.
> So to one neutrall thing both sexes fit,
> Wee dye and rise the same, and prove
> Mysterious by this love.

These comparisons, particularly the latter, may be regarded as conceits. There is, however, no connection between the conceits in so far as their terms are concerned; but each one does make the witty point of the paradoxical — the mysterious — nature of the lovers' relationship.

None of the earlier conceits is drawn upon in the fourth stanza, which begins with the statement that the lovers can die by love, a possibility suggested in the preceding stanza. The statement is without metaphor and says in effect that when the lovers have died, their legend may not be fit for tombs and hearse, but it will be fit for verse. In the lines that follow, the subject is further developed, this time with an abundant use of metaphor:

> And if no peece of Chronicle wee prove,
> We'll build in sonnets pretty roomes;
> As well a well wrought urne becomes
> The greatest ashes, as halfe-acre tombes,
> And by these hymnes, all shall approve
> Us *Canoniz'd* for Love.

Though there are several metaphors here, the passage is not constituted by a single conceit; we do not have logical extension in the terms of an initial image or other metaphorical situation. There is, however, no lapse of metaphorical statement. The conceits follow immediately upon each other and are joined to each other by obvious association. One example of such association is the shift from *verse* to *sonnets* to *hymns*. Another example: the sonnets containing the story of the lovers are like pretty rooms in which the lovers themselves are contained; the sonnets — or pretty rooms — are like a well-wrought urn, as distinguished from some monument of greater proportions. And finally, having shifted from sonnets to hymns, the passage ends with the statement that the lovers are canonized. This conclusion is reached by no argument, it is not contained within a metaphorical development: as we have already observed, it proceeds simply by an obvious association.

The conceit of canonization continues throughout the final stanza of the poem. This continuation of the conceit may be regarded as a single segment of extension, for the extension is effected by a statement, comprising the whole stanza, which invokes the lovers as canonized — as saints:

> And thus invoke us; You whom reverend love
>   Made one anothers hermitage;
> You, to whom love was peace, that now is rage;
>   Who did the whole worlds soule contract, and drove
>   Into the glasses of your eyes
>   So made such mirrors, and such spies,
>   That they did all to you epitomize,
>   Countries, Townes, Courts: Beg from above
>   A patterne of your love!

The elements contained in this stanza are themselves tropes proper to the religious invocation which is the embracing conceit: the lovers had a hermitage — one another — in which they found peace and performed the miracle of contracting the world. The stanza ends with a request to the lovers that they "beg from above" a pattern of their love, which is their special function as saints.

We may turn now to observation of the general structure of the poem in its entirety. It may be said of the last three stanzas of *The Canonization* that the conceit is frequent. A negative argument could be made, however, on the basis that there are no conceits in the first two stanzas. At any rate, even if the issue of frequency could be settled in the affirmative, this affirmation would contribute little of importance to the more complicated and systematic definitions of metaphysical poetry which several critics have ventured.

Our analysis has shown that *The Canonization* is not built on a single extended metaphor that is coterminous with the poem.

Donne's Poetry and Modern Criticism

One could argue that the embracing metaphor is constituted by the situation out of which the poem is supposedly uttered — the lover in defense of his loving — and that the poem has implications beyond its obvious verbal reference; but then such argument must make allowance for dramatic monologues and poems with other kinds of unity to be included under *metaphysical,* and as a result the term and its definition become meaningless and unprofitable. It is true that the conceit that gives the poem its title has considerable extension, but it is unanticipated and unpredictable until reached in the poem; the extent of the conceit is too slight in relation to the rest of the poem to justify its being regarded as characterizing the general structure of the entire poem.

According to our analysis of the first two stanzas, one cannot say of *The Canonization* that it departs at no point from the manner of the conceit, or that a prose restatement of the poem's meaning is within the poem always expressed by a trope. There are, however, passages in the poem made up wholly of conceit following upon conceit, and often it is a conceit or sequence of conceits which expresses whatever thought may be inferred or restated from the poetry. Our analysis confirms that *The Canonization* is witty in that it contains the devices of wit: the absurd apostrophes of the first stanza, the exaggerations and rhetorical questions of the second, and the associations and conceits in the remaining stanzas. We observed, moreover, that there is in the poem wit which results from a complexity of attitudes, which is conceptual originally, and which does not follow from local rhetorical device.

Donne's *Twicknam Garden* is, in its title and structure, unlike many of his other poems. For instance, poems having some figurative use of titles within the poetry are *The Sunne Rising, The Flea, The Will,* and other poems, and even *A Nocturnall upon Saint Lucies Day,* which is peculiarly similar to *Twicknam Garden* in several respects. Unless we seek in the biography of the poet for additional meanings, the title of this poem is to be taken simply and literally: the speaker of the poem is present in the garden and makes references to its details.

The garden, then, may be regarded as an immediate material

of the poem. Another immediate material would be the speaker's feelings, his emotional condition. These two materials are introduced and developed side by side: the poem begins

> Blasted with sighs, and surrounded with teares,
> Hither I come to seeke the spring . . .

And not until the end of the poem does the speaker pursue any argument or set up any extended metaphor as a seeming fulfillment to the direction of the whole poem. He continues speaking in the terms with which the poem begins, and the terms are actually what the poem is about — the garden and his emotion. The speaker actually discusses the relationship between these; he refers to the garden as it is seen in the light of the emotion and, thus seen, as it reflects the emotion. We have, consequently, an essentially dramatic poem: a speaker in a specific situation making utterances about the situation:

> Blasted with sighs, and surrounded with teares,
> Hither I come to seeke the spring,
> And at mine eyes, and at mine eares,
> Receive such balmes, as else cure every thing;
> But O, selfe traytor, I do bring
> The spider love, which transubstantiates all,
> And can convert Manna to gall,
> And that this place may thoroughly be thought
> True Paradise, I have the serpent brought.

Although the dramatic situation of the speaker is to be taken literally, his utterance does none the less contain figurative expressions. The speaker, given over to sighs and tears, comes to the garden at the spring season, seeking some relief. The garden, with its pleasant aspects of sight and sound, would work a healing effect upon him but for the fact that he has brought the "spider love." Here we have the first conceit of the poem. This conceit — love as a spider — is extended, but with the extension the metaphor changes its terms. The emotion of love, like the spider, corrupts the pleasures of the garden. And, like religious love, it "transubstantiates" these, only with an ironical difference; for instead of providing healthy spiritual nourishment, this love changes a provident remedy — manna — into unpalatable bitterness. The speaker leaves this complex figure and continues his irony, saying that he has brought along the serpent in order that this garden may be considered a true paradise, for the traditional paradise — the Garden of Eden — had a serpent in it. This statement is far more complicated dramatically than it is rhetorically. It is in sheer irony that the speaker says he has brought the serpent purposefully. Though with the addition of the serpent the garden is made comparable to the traditional paradise, no paradisiacal benefits are implied: one garden is like the other because both are invaded by evil. We see, thus, that the *serpent* is related to the general logic of its context: it is conveyed by the speaker to the garden, and this is said as part of a consistent comment upon the garden.

But how, in the first place, is the presence of the serpent to be explained? Certainly it is not to be pictured as part of a physical setting suggested by the poem. (Of course, it is there in the garden, but not in a physical sense, not as an image.) Obviously, the serpent represents that emotion of the speaker which makes it impossible for him to appreciate the pleasures of the garden, which turns these to displeasures. (One may be reminded of "a serpent in the breast.") This equation between serpent and emotion is, however, not stated. We have, consequently, an implied metaphor: a symbol is used in the place of the thing symbolized while there is no grammatical connection between the two — the thing symbolized, in fact, being omitted. An effect of the poetry is this suggestion of the nature of the emotion: we may have here something comparable to the technique of symbolist poetry. The emotion is the *subject* of the poem, and the speaker, in order to specify its character, must go beyond the statement that all is not well with him; to characterize the emotion he must discuss it in terms other than itself. And such terms are the peculiar aspect of the garden, the spider, and the serpent. All these are meaningful in that they suggest characterizations of the emotion. It is, I believe, terms such as these that would be important in a consideration of poetic effect. A symbolist poem of comparable terms would be "difficult" in so far as one could not determine the *subject* of which the terms are characterizations, the theme by which they cohere.

The Man in the Name

In the second stanza of the poem the speaker continues referring to his emotion by elaborating upon the fact that he is unable to appreciate the pleasant garden; a dismal garden would be more tolerable to his mood:

> 'Twere wholsomer for mee, that winter did
>   Benight the glory of this place,
>   And that a grave frost did forbid
> These trees to laugh, and mocke mee to my face;
>   But that I may not this disgrace
> Indure, nor yet leave loving, Love let mee
>   Some senslesse peece of this place bee;
> Make me a mandrake, so I may groane here,
> Or a stone fountaine weeping out my yeare.

Here again it is apparent that the passage is not constituted by conceit — one or more. There is, of course, some figurativeness, but the meaning or effect of the passage depends upon its dramatic significance, figurative or not. Everything the speaker says, like the mention of the serpent in the first stanza, serves to intimate the quality of his emotion. The stanza begins with a conditional statement: a winter garden would be more tolerable and fitting to his feelings than a spring garden; in such a garden the trees would not laugh and mock him to his face, as they do now. The laughing, mocking trees are a metaphor (or personification), but this metaphor does not determine or extend the structure of the poem. And it is no criticism of the passage to say this. The trees become terms in a figurative expression because they are part of a situation that the speaker observes to be ironical. Here the figurativeness is dramatic rather than structural, as we have been using that word. It is dramatically significant that the speaker should make the figure, and the intimation already noted continues. It does, indeed, continue through the entire stanza. The spring garden remains unchanged, of course, so the speaker requests of "Love" (obviously the deity) that, in order not to endure "this disgrace" of mockery and yet to cease not from loving, he be made a "senslesse peece" of the garden — a groaning mandrake (of folklore) or a weeping stone fountain. There is no logic and certainly no feasibility to the request. How, as a senseless object, though "groaning" or "weeping," would he continue to love? The question is a confusing one if we try to follow it literally and rationally. But this is beside the point. Because it is thus confusing, the more obviously is the question, again like other parts of the poem, connotatively an intimation of the speaker's emotion. And here, too, we may notice, there is some figurativeness, but it is incidental in the passage and subordinate to it. This is not to say that it is a detachable ornament; it is an element of the intimating rhetorical question that we have discussed.

In this second stanza there is some development of the subject of the poem, and this advance is contained in the phrase "nor yet leave loving." Such characterization of the emotion, which has been called "spider" and "serpent," suggests its tension and complexity. It should be noticed, however, that in the poem as we have read it thus far there has been no development of idea through argument or extended metaphors (cf. *A Valediction: Forbidding Mourning, The Extasie, A Lecture upon the Shadow*) but rather a developmental reference to the emotion which is the subject of the poem.

The opening of the third and final stanza is, in a way, comparable to extended metaphor, and the whole stanza differs, by its argumentative nature, from the first two.

> Hither with christall vyals, lovers come,
>   And take my teares, which are loves wine,
>   And try your mistresse Teares at home,
> For all are false, that tast not just like mine;
>   Alas, hearts do not in eyes shine,
> Nor can you more judge womans thoughts by teares,
>   Then by her shadow, what she weares.
> O perverse sexe, where none is true but shee,
>   Who's therefore true, because her truth kills mee.

The metaphor extended is that of the speaker as a weeping stone fountain, this having been suggested at the end of the preceding stanza. Extension of this metaphor, however, does not consist in elaboration but rather in maintained reference to the initial metaphorical situation. The speaker bids lovers to come with vials and take the tears which he, as fountain, is weeping. He calls the tears "loves wine," thus implying that they are a liquid accompaniment to the occasion of love and that they belong to a class within which distinctions may be made, as the connoisseur distinguishes among wines. The lovers are to compare these tears with those of their mistresses in order to discover the genuineness of the latter: "For all are false, that tast not just like mine." Thus the speaker exclaims upon the genuineness and seriousness of his own emotion; and at the same time suggests the source and experiential context of the emotion. That he has been personally affected by the nature of woman is emphasized by the "Alas" which introduces his dictum: woman's heart and thought are no more to be learned from her eyes and tears than is what she wears from her shadow. In other words, women are dissemblers, making for inconsistency, illogicality, and disorder. They are a "perverse sexe," for, in the experience of the speaker, one of them by being true causes him to suffer. Her trueness consists in that she does not love him and gives him this plainly to understand. Hence in a perverse and ironical sense of true, she is true in her attitude of not being his true love.

If we look back now over the stanza we find in it several metaphors: the speaker as fountain, tears as wine, the taste of tears as an indication of sincerity, and eyes as reflecting the heart. No one of these metaphors, however, includes all the others or provides the terms which are used in an expression of the central thought or subject of the poem. And though the metaphors are close upon each other, there is no logical extension of imagery. For example, the lovers' tasting the tears of their mistresses is not important as an image. If we want to make a comparable description for the development of the stanza, we might call it an associational procession of ideas. The concluding passage of the stanza ("O perverse sexe . . .") contains no metaphor ("her truth kills me" is hardly considerable for its figurativeness); nor can the passage be figuratively connected with any preceding metaphor.

It was observed above that the final stanza differs somewhat from the others. These stanzas, we noticed, made no argument, developed no idea, but as a dramatic utterance made reference to the garden and the emotion of the speaker, thus apparently characterizing the emotion. But in the final stanza there is argument and development of idea: women are generally false, and one woman's "truth" is peculiar in that it affects the speaker painfully. These ideas offer themselves for consideration as ideas, and because of this the stanza is not so apparently a characterization of the speaker's emotion, which in the earlier stanzas is unmistakably the subject. Such observation may be in the nature of a criticism. There is a possible reading of the last stanza, and I believe it to be not unjust, which would make this criticism less strictly applicable. This reading would take the stanza as a dramatic utterance comparable to the others, despite the obtrusiveness of its ideas. That is, it would be found significant beyond its specific structure and immediate references, significant primarily in its reference to and characterization of the speaker's emotion.

We have found that no single characterization of metaphysical poetry is wholly borne out by any of the three poems we have examined. It is true that there are some conceits in each of these, and it may therefore be said that the conceit often occurs; but, as we have observed before, this is unpretentious beside the other definitions and would probably be found acceptable by proponents of these definitions. Consequently, it will not alter our problem or our approach to the problem if these three poems are, in their content of conceits, a fair sample of the rest of Donne's *Songs and Sonets.* These other poems we shall not examine in full detail, since the three analyses already made will provide a basis of reference and allow of some economy.

It will be convenient to continue the discussion of Donne's poems by allying them with the conclusions drawn from those already analyzed; it should be noted, however, that the three poems are not offered as representing a possible grouping of Donne's poems. To begin with *The Good Morrow*: it was found that none of the definitions wholly fits. To some extent the ideological burden of the poem is conveyed by the use of tropes (metaphor-conceits and other tropes) but not in sufficient measure to justify this practice as characterizing the whole structure of the poem. Like *The Good Morrow*, the poem beginning "Goe, and catche a falling starre" is conspicuously not an example of any of the definitions. We may say that it contains no conceits at all, unless it would be argued that any metaphor is a conceit. There are three, and only three, metaphors in the poem: these are

> Or to keep off envies stinging . . .
> Till age snow white haires on thee . . .
> Such a Pilgrimage were sweet . . .

And these metaphors are obviously idiomatic (except for "Pilgrimage," perhaps) rather than of figurative force. Most of the images of the poem are contained in fanciful imperatives like the opening line. These imperatives are clearly impossible and hence are techniques of wit. The "prose meaning" of the poem is that there are no women both true and fair, under any circumstances, not anywhere in the world. This is said ironically — by devices of wit — in the first two stanzas, and it is said simply, without irony, in the last stanza. The poem, however, will not serve to illustrate the nonstructural definition; it contains ironical technique but is not itself the expression of an irony, or complexity of attitude, its attitude (no true, fair women) being uncomplicated and steadily maintained.

Though there are differences among them, neither *The Sunne Rising, The Indifferent,* nor *Confined Love* provides a basis for the definitions. *The Sunne Rising* is the most richly figurative of the three poems. Like *The Good Morrow*, it is the utterance of a lover after a night of love. (A picture of the lovers in a bedroom is suggested.) The whole poem is an apostrophe to the sun, giving it a surprising and somewhat funny personification. In addressing the sun, questioning and commanding it, the speaker says in effect that love is indifferent to all the influences that the sun has upon the world. He is thus in a position like that of the speaker of *The Good Morrow*. He does not maintain or arrive at a complexity of attitudes, but he chooses one attitude from a complexity — that of love, and dismisses the other — the attitude of the world. This is said finally, at the end of the first stanza, with directness:

> Love, all alike, no season knowes, nor clyme,
> Nor houres, dayes, moneths, which are the rags of time.

Donne's Poetry and Modern Criticism

The speaker continues to the effect that his love is complete in itself, as if it included everything in the world, everything under the sun. This is said in a conceit, the conceit being established at the end of the second stanza and extended through the third stanza, which is the final one. These lines, occurring within the conceit, will indicate the use of the metaphor:

> Thine age askes ease, and since thy duties bee
> To warme the world, that's done in warming us.

Though the conceit makes up a fairly long passage, there is no ideological development in it; it says throughout that the lovers are in themselves as complete as the world, thus, by implication, contrasting two "worlds" of value.

The Indifferent is much simpler rhetorically than *The Sunne Rising*. It has no large measure of figurativeness, few conceits — and these of brief extent. Like almost every poem of Donne's, it is the statement of a speaker. Here the speaker expresses an unconventional and unromantic attitude toward love. He is inconstant, unfaithful, indiscriminate, promiscuous, and he says that all men and women should be so. There are local ironies in the poem, such as

> Or doth a feare, that men are true, torment you?

but the speaker's attitude, the attitude of the poem, remains single and unchanged. These same conclusions will serve for *Confined Love*. Its thesis is that a woman should not be bound in love only to one man. This is expressed by implied analogies, such as: "Who e'r rigg'd faire ship to lie in harbors"; and it is stated literally and generally at the end of the poem:

> Good is not good, unlesse
> A thousand it possesse,
> But doth wast with greedinesse.

Poems having a similar relation to the definitions we have in mind are *Breake of Day, The Message, The Curse,* and others.

The Prohibition is characteristic of Donne in its argument and paradox, but none of the definitions according to conceit is applicable to it. The poem is one of counsel addressed by a lover to a woman. It is composed of three stanzas, each with its own thesis: (1) Take heed of loving me; (2) Take heed of hating me; (3) Love and hate me, too. There are no conceits in the first stanza. Here the lover cautions heed in loving him, and he explains the need of caution, thus implying the nature of the former relation between himself and the woman. There is no danger that he, when loved, will be as she was when he loved her:

> By being to thee then what to me thou wast . . .

The danger is that the joy of being loved may kill him, thus leaving her love frustrated:

> Then, least thy love, by my death, frustrate bee,
> If thou love mee, take heed of loving mee.

In the second stanza he warns her against hating him or taking "too much triumph in the Victorie." Her fear should be, not that he will retaliate, but that, destroying him by her hate, she will be deprived of her conquest. All this is expressed in military terms as a conceit, though the conceit does not extend beyond this stanza. In the final stanza the lover's argument develops into paradox: he would be both loved and hated:

> Love mee, that I may die the gentler way;
> Hate mee, because thy love'is too great for mee.

When both attitudes are maintained, they counterbalance each other and he survives, escaping the sudden and violent death which love or hate singly would effect. (In Donne's time "die the gentler way" must certainly have been a pun, since *die* was also a verb for the sexual act.) His survival is stated as profitable for the woman, for thus he remains her field of activity and she may continue to love and hate:

> So shall I, live, thy Stage, not triumph bee.

"Stage" and "triumph" are the only conceits — if they can be so called — in the stanza. The conceit of the second stanza is of slight figurative force, for most of the figurative terms there are what they would be ordinarily; if it were not for the presence of *officer* such terms as *triumph, victorie, retaliate, conquest,* and *perish* would not necessarily have metaphorical status. We find, then, that the structure and effect of *The Prohibition* would not be wholly lost in a prose paraphrase that eliminated all figurativeness. In other words, the structure is not dependent upon tropes, but upon the sequence of ideas and combination of ideas. A complexity of attitude is here the explicit, rather than implicit, subject of the poem. Not only is the speaker's attitude complex, but so is that of the one spoken to, and therefore the situation involving them is a pattern of complex attitudes. All this is immediately in the poem.

Another argumentative poem of Donne's is *Communitie*. The poem is about *good* and *bad*, the nature of women, and men's use of them. Its first three stanzas are speculative generalization meager in imagery and figurativeness. The first stanza is most general of all, wholly in terms of abstractions:

> Good wee must love, and must hate ill,
> For ill is ill, and good good still,
>   But there are things indifferent,
> Which wee may neither hate, nor love,
> But one, and then another prove,
>   As wee shall finde our fancy bent.

The rest of the poem is an application of this thesis. It is assumed in the second stanza that women are "things indifferent," and consequently are subject to the usage such things receive. In the second stanza this character of women — that they are neither good nor bad — is "proved" by false, question-begging statements, such as "Good is as visible as greene." And again the thesis is applied: "they deserve nor blame, nor praise." That is, they are not subject to moral judgment. And the argument is repeated and particularized, in violation of logic, with the development of a conceit that makes up the fourth and final stanza. Women are like fruit in the respect that they are not subject to moral judgment. It then follows, illogically as if logically, that they are like fruit in other respects: they may be used, as a mere commodity, without the raising of moral issue; the poem ends —

> And when hee hath the kernell eate,
> Who doth not fling away the shell?

The Man in the Name

There is in *Communitie* witty argument, not achieved through paradox (which is overtly an apparent contradiction of logic), but through discourse that moves with the assurance of logic and yet is obviously fallacious. The wit consists in ingenuity, in the semblance of logical support upon which an attitude is rested. As we have observed, the poem develops by proceeding from the general to the particular, ending finally with the only conceit of the poem and thus arriving at the attitude which is the destination of the argument. The attitude is not witty in itself, unless one happens to find it surprising, but the manner of stating it is witty.

Aire and Angels is perhaps the most complex of all Donne's poems, because of its manner of development, because of its subject, and because of the numerous distinctions of ideas made within a poem of moderate length. Our purpose will be best served by first attempting to make a paraphrase of the poem. It is spoken by a man to a woman. He says that he has loved her before he ever met her, as people worship angels whom they have never seen. It is thus implied that his love was directed toward an idea of a woman, for people have only ideas of angels, never having seen them. When first he met this particular woman, she was a "lovely glorious nothing." That is, she was not yet recognized as the direction or object of his love, or she was not the loved object until he made her so, this being done by his identification of her with his idea of the loved object. The process of identification is thus explained: Love is the child of his soul, and since his soul has taken a body, Love, like the parent, must do so. This it does when it is urged to discover the identity of the woman: it assumes the body of the woman, and in this way the woman becomes the physical referent of what was previously the idea of the loved object. Here the first stanza ends.

The second stanza begins with a conceit by which love is equated with a ship. The speaker of the poem says that in having love assume the body of the woman he thought to have given it stability and fixation — as one ballasts a ship with weight — but he discovers that he has overweighted it. This is explained, after the conceit has been dropped, by the statement that the woman, in all her detail, "for love to worke upon / Is much too much." In other words, it turns out that the woman, as she appears to him, as she represents the ideal object of love, is more than his love can manage to attach itself to. For as his love could not formerly come to rest, when there was no basis on which it might rest, so now it is not able to partake of an extreme and ultimate fulfillment. Consequently, it must abandon this fulfillment of the ideal and adjust itself to the love that the woman offers, not to the woman herself. This adjustment is possible because woman's love is less than man's, and hence can be the "spheare" of man's love, just as an angel's body, though pure, is less pure than the angel's soul contained therein:

> Just such disparitie
> As is twixt Aire and Angells puritie,
> 'Twixt womens love, and mens will ever bee.

So the poem ends.

In approaching a consideration of its structural aspects perhaps it will be well to summarize the paraphrase of the poem: Man has a conception of the woman whom he would love before having found the woman, but when finally an individual woman is accepted as representing this conception, man discovers that his love does not fully measure up to the woman he sees as the loved object, so an adjustment is made according to the measure, not of the woman, but of the woman's love, which is always less than man's.

It is obvious that the poem is not structurally coterminous with a single extended conceit. There is no conceit until the middle of the first stanza, where we have the conceit, extended to the end of the stanza, of love as the child of an embodied soul. Then there is a conceit extended from the beginning of the second stanza through the first four lines, this time of love as a ship that is ballasted. These two conceits are adjacent, but one does not follow the other by logical extension of imagery or even by obvious association; there is a complete break in figurativeness. Their sequence is dependent upon the fact that both are metaphors about love, which is the subject of a discourse that begins before and

extends through and beyond both conceits. At the conclusion of
the poem there is, not a conceit, but an analogy between the psychological anatomy of angels and the loves of men and of women.

And now let us examine a structural aspect of the poem other
than that which would be determined by tropes. According to the
paraphrase that was made, the lover addresses the woman he loves
in terms of praise, exalting her above himself, until almost the end
of the poem. And then it develops that this discussion leads to a
statement that the woman is in a respect lower than the lover. With
this surprising reversal, seemingly unprepared for, the poem ends.
The reversal is surprising, and a calculated surprise is witty. Moreover, the reversal makes for irony: one attitude is apparently
prepared for, and then its opposite is given. Hence the poem is not
a straightforward development of a single attitude, but provides
a complexity of attitudes.

Womans Constancy and *A Valediction: of My Name, in the
Window* are poems with a development of structure similar to that
of *Aire and Angels*. There are still others which contain opposite,
and therefore a complexity of, attitudes, but in which the complexity is not established by a sharp reversal at the end of the
poem. We find instead, in varying degrees, a complexity of attitudes developed earlier in the poem and with more obvious preparation. And the extent to which such complexity determines the
development varies from poem to poem. Sometimes, indeed, a
poem begins with the statement of a paradox, and in that case
the poem may in no way develop according to the principle we are
at present discussing. But the paradox would none the less be a
complexity, though this need not be a determining element in the
development or structure of the poem.

A feature of *Aire and Angels* making for additional irony and
complexity of attitudes is the subject matter. The several aspects
of a unit, or individual, are considered as existing independently
(somewhat in the manner of faculty psychology); then differing or
opposing attitudes are taken toward these aspects, thus making
for complexity of attitudes and possibly irony. In *Aire and Angels*
there are the lover, his soul, his love, his conception of the woman,

the woman, her love. The reversal at the end of this poem is peculiarly dependent upon this division of the individual: it turns from the attitude toward the woman to the attitude toward her love. Complexity of attitude results in other poems having the same use of subject matter: division of the individual into parts and then a separate attitude toward each part. Such poems are *The Undertaking, Lovers Infinitenesse, The Broken Heart, The Extasie, Loves Diet,* and *The Blossome.* This complexity is not in a relation to the development or structure of a poem, and irony is not always its concomitant.

In the analysis of *Twicknam Garden* it was remarked that *A Nocturnall upon Saint Lucies Day, Being the Shortest Day* is similar to that poem in some distinctive respects. We observed of *Twicknam Garden* that it is peculiarly a dramatic poem, the utterance of a speaker upon a specific situation involving the speaker, and that, in accordance with its dramatic nature, the subject of the poem is the emotion of the speaker. Our method of arriving at this observation was to regard the terms and statements of the poem as references to or reflections of the speaker's emotion, or, in other words, as a characterization of this emotion. And the problem of explicating the *Nocturnall* may lend itself to a similar handling.

The poem opens with the speaker describing an aspect of the situation. The night following the shortest day of the year (St. Lucy's Day, December 22) is coming on, and the speaker sees this longest night as comparable to himself. Winter and profound darkness are upon the world. This condition is described figuratively in negative terms, by what is absent — sap, balm, life — rather than by what is present:

> The worlds whole sap is sunke:
> The generall balme th'hydroptique earth hath drunk,
> Whither, as to the beds-feet, life is shrunke,
> Dead and enterr'd; yet all these seeme to laugh,
> Compar'd with mee, who am their Epitaph.

Thus the speaker comments upon himself. The things that are dead and interred are less mournful than he, less negative, for he is

the "epitaph" of these, the very meaning and token of negativity.
And such a view of himself implies, of course, the emotion from
which the view articulated arises.

In the second and third stanzas the emotion is more fully and
more specifically characterized. In addition to the continued stress
upon the speaker's feeling of negativity or nothingness, the source
and history of this feeling are provided. The speaker addresses
himself to those who will be lovers in "the next world, that is, at
the next Spring." By this it becomes evident that the emotion has
followed from the experience of love. And the speaker goes on to
explain what the experience was and how it worked upon him.
He advises the lovers to study him, and this advice is apparently
a warning to them. In the form of a conceit — the speaker as subject to love's alchemy — he tells of the ultranothingness into which
he has been made, for he was a kind of nothingness originally:

> For I am every dead thing,
> In whom love wrought new Alchimie,
>   For his art did expresse
> A quintessence even from nothingnesse,
> From dull privations, and leane emptinesse:
> He ruin'd mee, and I am re-begot
> Of absence, darknesse, death; things which are not.

The conceit continues into the third stanza, in which it is again
said that he is the distillation of nothingness ("by loves lim-
becke"). And then this original nothingness and the experience of
love are further explained, the background, and hence characterization, of the emotion being thus increasingly abundant as the
poem develops. Often the speaker and the woman he loved brought
themselves to a state of nothingness; they were drowned, or they
were chaoses, or carcasses:

> . . . Oft a flood
>   Have wee two wept, and so
> Drownd the whole world, us two; oft did we grow
> To be two Chaosses, when we did show
> Care to ought else; and often absences
> Withdrew our soules, and made us carcasses.

In the fourth stanza the speaker states precisely what brought him to the condition, or emotion, of which he speaks. This is the death of the woman, by which he is

> Of the first nothing, the Elixer grown.

And he proceeds to describe, negatively, what it is to be this second, more extreme, nothing. Unlike even the most limited objects, he is, since the death of the woman, without the properties of a substance, in no context at all:

> If I an ordinary nothing were,
> As shadow, a light, and body must be here.

The implication of this is that when the woman lived, he was an ordinary nothing, her shadow.

In the fifth and final stanza the speaker reasserts his nothingness and makes a witty contrast between himself and the lovers whom he is addressing. His sun, the woman, will not return, but the other sun will, bringing for the lovers the season of love:

> But I am None; nor will my Sunne renew.
> You lovers, for whose sake, the lesser Sunne
>   At this time to the Goat is runne
>   To fetch new lust, and give it you,
>   Enjoy your summer all;
> Since shee enjoyes her long nights festivall,
> Let mee prepare towards her, and let mee call
> This houre her Vigill, and her Eve, since this
> Both the yeares, and the dayes deep midnight is.

Here, at the end of the poem, the speaker turns from the consideration of his nothingness and the things with which it is contrasted, to the state of the woman and the attitude he will take toward her. Now, instead of construing her death as the event which made him the elixir of nothingness, he will regard it as the event which removed her to bliss, and he will look forward toward his death, by which he will join her in this bliss. Hence the long night is interpreted, not as partially representing his nothingness, but as representing the bliss of her who is dead, the bliss which he anticipates. The hour, symbolic for the death and interment of which he is the epitaph, is also her vigil and eve; it is hallowed for her and in commemoration of her, as it might be by a saint.

So the poem ends, maintaininig a complexity of attitudes — or we might here say a tension of attitudes. This complexity consists of the double interpretation put upon the "deep midnight." It is most conveniently illustrated with the expression "enjoyes her long nights festivall." For here *long night* and *enjoyed festival* are in a combination which includes the two attitudes toward the woman's death: death as it is significant in the mundane and human realm, and death as it initiates the supernatural bliss of Christianity. And as a matter of fact, this complexity, this irony, comes not alone at the end, but exists earlier in the poem: "I am by her death, (which word wrongs her) . . ." There is, moreover, an ironical complexity throughout the poem and at the basis of its most dominant theme. Upon the removal from a situation in which he was already nothing, the speaker becomes steeped in an even greater nothingness. He gives warning to lovers of the future, yet he predicts joy for them and remains himself, in a manner, still attached to the woman whom he loved. He laments his condition, would rather be otherwise in the terms of the world: "I should preferre, / If I were any beast . . ." Yet he anticipates a joy that is beyond that of the world. His prospect of death is both despairingly suicidal and hopefully optimistic.

Our reading of the *Nocturnall* has shown it to be the statement of a speaker at a dramatic moment in the speaker's experience. This experience, or plot, is filled out as the poem develops, for the speaker expresses what he feels about the experience. We may say, therefore, that the poem, the speaker's expression, has for its subject the speaker's emotion. With the development of the poem, this emotion is characterized by references to its context and to the complexity of attitudes which constitute it. We may repeat, then, the similarity between the *Nocturnall* and *Twicknam Garden*. Both poems are speeches within indicated dramatic situations, and each poem has a dramatic complication beyond its rhetorical complication. That is, all the tropes in the poem (and there are many) with their conceptual burdens, and other kinds of passages also, cohere in a meaningful pattern by dramatic reference, rather than by any figurative device or system of figurative devices. Every element (tropical, conceptual, and perhaps other kinds) is significant in terms of its whole context, while it gives significance to this context; just as every detail of a drama may depend for its meaning upon, and be also part of, the whole drama. Like many other poems of Donne, the *Nocturnall* has several conceits, other witty devices, and a witty, or ironically complex, aspect to its subject; and all of these are present as contributing to the whole organization, or structure, of the poem; none alone, however, is determinant of this organization.

Once again we may use analyses already made for an economical comment on new poems. There are other poems that are dramatic in the same way as *Twicknam Garden* and the *Nocturnall*, each being spoken in a situation clearly indicated and having for subject the emotion of the speaker. Such poems are *The Apparition*, *The Relique*, and *The Anniversarie*. Still others comply with this principle in varying degrees. For instance, in some poems the speaker supplies a discourse on a subject other than his own situation and emotion, not necessarily reflecting an emotion. Or a poem may begin with a specific situation and then develop to the exposition of a generalization, reference being made not to the situation and emotion of the speaker, but to some problem or idea suggested by these. Among such poems are *The Extasie* and *A Lecture upon the Shadow*. And there are poems even further removed from any connection with an emotion of the speaker. In these no situation or relationship of the speaker is indicated. Such a poem is written in the first person singular, as *Goe, and catche a falling starre*, *Loves Alchymie*, and *The Primrose*. An opinion is developed, but it is the kind of opinion that is held generally and arises from no particular situation or emotion. These poems are comparable to essays, public statements, as distinguished from dramatic statements that are *private* with respect to the speaker. An account of the speaker's relationship to other materials of the poem would be one way of distinguishing among, grouping, and characterizing the poems of Donne's *Songs and Sonets*; for all of them but two — *Confined Love* and *Communitie* — are *spoken*.

The complexity of attitudes, or the irony, found in the *Noc-*

turnall is, in its character, illustrative of such complexities as they exist in other poems. In the *Nocturnall* two standards of value are set against each other: death as it is significant in the world, and as it is significant beyond the world. Similarly, in *The Canonization* there are two standards of value: those of the lover and those of the world. In both *The Anniversarie* and *The Relique* the complexity is again derivative of a conflict between worldly values and supernatural values. For instance, in *The Anniversarie* the speaker laments that death must come for the two lovers, although he acknowledges that there is also a love which the souls shall enjoy after death:

> Alas, as well as other Princes, wee,
> (Who Prince enough in one another bee,)
> Must leave at last in death, these eyes, and eares,
> Oft fed with true oathes, and with sweet salt teares;
>   But soules where nothing dwells but love
> (All other thoughts being inmates) then shall prove
> This, or a love increased there above,
> When bodies to their graves, soules from their graves remove.

In *The Relique* there is a multiple complexity. The speaker contrasts the natural promiscuity of women with his own loved one, who is exceptional in faithfulness and spirituality; and at the same time he would delay the supreme spirituality that there is in heaven:

> When my grave is broke up againe
> Some second ghest to entertaine,
> (For graves have learn'd that woman-head
> To be to more then one a Bed)
>   And he that digs it, spies
> A bracelet of bright haire about the bone,
>   Will he not let'us alone,
> And thinke that there a loving couple lies,
> Who thought that this device might be some way
> To make their soules, at the last busie day,
> Meet at this grave, and make a little stay?

Though this kind of complexity may be developed in a poem through the use of conceits, it is not dependent for its presence in

Donne's Poetry and Modern Criticism

the poem upon figurative device. The complexity is, rather, inherent in the ideas, or conceptual content, of the poetry. In each of the poems we have just been discussing there are ideas which, in the tradition of European thought, involve two standards, and these standards are considered as conflicting: there is the world in contrast to the spirituality of love, or there is earthly existence in contrast to supernatural existence.

Before finally attempting any generalization drawn from an analysis of Donne's poetry, it appears logical first to take particular notice of those poems that are, or appear to be, coterminous with a single extended metaphor, or conceit, and also of those poems that are in large part so constituted. Such a list may well begin with *A Valediction: Forbidding Mourning*, the poem ending with the conceit of the lovers' souls as "twin compasses," perhaps the most famous of all Donne's conceits:

> If they be two, they are two so
>   As stiffe twin compasses are two,
> Thy soule the fixt foot, makes no show
>   To move, but doth, if the'other doe.
>
> And though it in the center sit,
>   Yet when the other far doth rome,
> It leanes, and hearkens after it,
>   And growes erect, as that comes home.
>
> Such wilt thou be to mee, who must
>   Like th' other foot, obliquely runne;
> Thy firmnes makes my circle just,
>   And makes me end, where I begunne.

We discover that, after all, this conceit runs through only the last three stanzas of a poem which is made up of nine stanzas. Though the conceit does not extend through the entire poem, there is a "conceptual burden," shared by this conceit and others, which does so extend. This burden is again, in its most general nature, the complexity of attitudes we have frequently observed elsewhere in Donne's poetry. Two standards of value, or interpretation, are contrasted in the poem: that of the ordinary world, and that of the spirituality of love. This distinction, which is the basic argument of the poem, is stated clearly in the second stanza by the speaker of the poem:

> T'were prophanation of our joyes
> To tell the layetie our love.

In this poem absence between lovers is interpreted by the two standards. According to one of these, when the lovers are absent from each other, a real division results. But according to the other, that of the spirituality of love, the lovers share a single, indivisible soul, and absence has no effect upon this unity, despite appearances. It is this principle which is illustrated in some detail by the conceit of the compasses. We may notice, however, that the principle is already stated in the stanza preceding this illustration, first literally, and then by the simile of beaten gold:

> Our two soules therefore, which are one,
> Though I must goe, endure not yet
> A breach, but an expansion,
> Like gold to ayery thinnesse beate.

Obviously the final conceit does not determine the poem's structure. This conceit, as well as others, may be "important" for a total characterization of the *Valediction: Forbidding Mourning,* but if there is any one element which may be singled out as basic to the whole organization of the poem, and as an element typical among the poems of Donne, it is this theme of complexity of attitudes.

The poem *A Feaver* is made up for the most part, though not wholly, of a single conceit. A woman's fever as the conflagration which is destroying the world: this is the metaphor that is extended through five stanzas — that is, through all but the first and last stanzas of the poem. The speaker of the poem addresses this woman, who is dying, and whom he loves. The metaphor says in effect that the woman is a world to the lover. She is, thus, set apart from the ordinary world, and a separate attitude exists for each. Hence, there is in *A Feaver* the typical complexity of attitudes found in many of Donne's poems. We may observe, however, that this complexity is not initiated by the metaphor. It is otherwise stated in the opening stanza of the poem, where the speaker distinguishes between the dying woman and all other women, thus implying that he loves her for some pecular aspect not pertaining to women in general, but which places her, in a respect, apart from the general class:

> Oh doe not die, for I shall hate
> All women so, when thou art gone,
> That thee I shall not celebrate,
> When I remember, thou wast one.

The distinction of the woman, as contrasted to the rest of the world, is reiterated beyond the terms of the conceit. Here are the last two stanzas:

> These burning fits but meteors bee,
> Whose matter in thee is soone spent.
> Thy beauty,'and all parts, which are thee,
> Are unchangeable firmament.

> Yet t'was of my minde, seising thee,
> Though it in thee cannot persever.
> For I had rather owner bee
> Of thee one houre, then all else ever.

The speaker says that the fever originated in his mind and that it issued to the woman when his mind fastened upon her. He concludes with a reference to the two standards of value, and he affirms one of these, that represented by the woman, as opposed to "all else ever."

In *Loves Diet*, a poem of five stanzas, a single conceit is sustained through all but the last stanza. The nature of the metaphor is implied by the title of the poem. The speaker personifies his experience, or emotion, of love, and he tells of the diet which he forced upon it. The opening stanza will illustrate:

> To what a combersome unwieldinesse
> And burdenous corpulence my love had growne,
>   But that I did, to make it lesse,
>   And keepe it in proportion,
> Give it a diet, made it feed upon
> That which love worst endures, *discretion*.

In the discussion *Aire and Angels* we have already referred to the complexity of attitudes which exists in this poem. Such complexity, it was observed, results from a division of the individual into several aspects. Then these aspects are considered as existing independently, and one may be opposed to another or to the individual as a whole. An example of this complexity in *Loves Diet* is the opposition of the individual's two impulses, love and discretion. One attitude is represented as being conditioned by other attitudes. This theme continues beyond the conceit of the diet into the final stanza:

> Thus I reclaim'd my buzard love, to flye
> At what, and when, and how, and where I chuse;
>   Now negligent of sport I lye,
>   And now as other Fawkners use,
> I spring a mistresse, sweare, write, sigh and weepe:
> And the game kill'd, or lost, goe talke, and sleepe.

An additional element of this complexity, ironical in character, results from the detachment with which the speaker regards an attitude, as if it were not his own.

At the opening of *A Lecture upon the Shadow* the speaker, addressing a woman, states his intention of making some comment upon the nature of love. First he calls attention to the shadows produced by the couple as they walked together, and to the effect which the course of the sun has upon these shadows. And then, in the form of a metaphor that is extended to the end of the poem, he explains how a complete love is comparable to noon, when the sun is at its highest and shadows are diminished:

> So whilst our infant loves did grow,
> Disguises did, and shadowes, flow,
> From us, and our cares; but, now 'tis not so.
>
> That love hath not attain'd the high'st degree,
> Which is still diligent lest others see.

The speaker of the poem does not maintain simultaneously a complexity of attitudes. He does indicate, however, that there is such complexity until love has reached its fullest and complete condition. While it has not reached this condition, there are "disguises" and diligence "lest others see." With the conclusion of the poem he insists that there is no complexity in the attitude of love, no intermediate stages or overlapping of attitudes between love and the absence of love:

> Love is a growing, or full constant light;
> And his first minute, after noone, is night.

The poems *Loves Usury*, *A Valediction: of the Book*, and *The Will* might each be considered as coterminous with a single conceit. Yet these conceits, if they are such, are different in kind from what is typically regarded as an extended metaphor. In the usual conceit there is, as the metaphor is extended, a development of the conceptual burden in terms of the object with which the conceptual burden is equated, and therefore a constant recurrence of figurativeness. But this figurativeness is not to be found in *Loves Usury*. The title of the poem may, indeed, suggest a conceit, or seem to have the potentialities of a conceit, but we do not find in the poem the necessary figurativeness. In fact, any argument for the poem's conceitedness would be less likely if it were not for the title. As we read the poem we find it to be the address of a speaker to Love, the deity. Love is described as "usurious," and reference is made to a "bargain," but the poem develops in terms of experience other than the practice of usury. Here, for example, is the second of the three stanzas which make up the poem:

> Let mee thinke any rivalls letter mine,
>   And at next nine
> Keepe midnights promise; mistake by the way
> The maid, and tell the Lady of that delay;
> Onely let mee love none, no, not the sport;
> From country grasse, to comfitures of Court,
> Or cities quelque choses, let report
>   My minde transport.

What may in some ways resemble a conceit is really the complication of the conventional myth, love as a god. The statement of a relationship between a man and a mythical god, even though it is a "usurious" yet not financial relationship, is not strictly a metaphorical statement. Possibly it is surprising, but one remembers Mephistopheles and Dr. Faustus.

A Valediction: of the Booke opens with the declaration, by a speaker to his loved one, that there is a way by which the lovers may "anger destiny"—that is, secure the endless fame of their love and of themselves. This way is explained in the second stanza:

> Study our manuscripts, those Myriades
> Of letters, which have past twixt thee and mee,
> Thence write our Annals, and in them will bee
> To all whom loves subliming fire invades,
> Rule and example found;
> There, the faith of any ground
> No schismatique will dare to wound,
> That sees, how Love this grace to us affords,
> To make, to keep, to use, to be these his Records.

In the following four stanzas these "annals" are spoken of as the book that will provide every kind of learning. Clergymen, lawyers, and statesmen will find that it contains information according to their special needs. In the sixth and final stanza the speaker says to the woman that she is to write this book, and that he, going abroad, will study her. And the poem ends with mathematical, astronomical, and geographical metaphors to the effect that love is tested by absence between the lovers. Though an extended metaphor may have been suggested by the title, we do not really find one in the poem. In so far as the poem is the *extension* of anything, it is the extension of the fabulous notion of the kind of book that may be produced from the lovers' letters. This fabulous notion is implicitly an affirmation of lovers' values, and a satire on other kinds of people.

Because of its title, *The Will* may also give promise of being a poem coterminous with a single conceit. And it is, indeed, closer to that condition than *Loves Usury* or *A Valediction: of the Booke.* The poem is addressed to Love by a speaker who is at the point of death. Throughout the poem the speaker reveals the details of the legacy he will leave, and explains them. Thus the poem opens:

> Before I sigh my last gaspe, let me breath,
> Great love, some Legacies; Here I bequeath
> Mine eyes to *Argus*, if mine eyes can see,
> If they be blinde, then Love, I give them thee;
> My tongue to Fame; to'Embassadours mine eares;

To women or the sea, my teares.
Thou, Love, hast taught mee heretofore
By making mee serve her who'had twenty more,
That I should give to none, but such, as had too much before.

In this manner the speaker lists for five stanzas (all but the last) his gifts and the recipients of his gifts. And in every case the nature of the bestowal consists of a witty incongruity, in illustration of the fact that the woman holds his love as an incongruity, as unacceptable. With the last stanza of the poem the speaker turns from his itemized legacy to a statement of his approaching death, some of the effects it will have, and his purpose in dying:

Therefore I'll give no more; But I'll undoe
The world by dying; because love dies too.
Then all your beauties will bee no more worth
Then gold in Mines, where none doth draw it forth;
And all your graces no more use shall have
Then a Sun dyall in a grave.
Thou Love taughtst mee, by making mee
Love her, who doth neglect both mee and thee,
To'invent, and practise this one way, to'annihilate all three.

Since the poem is from beginning to end the speech of a dying man concerning the legacy he leaves, it may appear at first to be coterminous with a single conceit. But unless one considers the statement of an incongruous and absurdly unfeasible gift to be metaphorical, there is really not a single conceit in the poem. The comparisons in the last stanza might possibly be regarded as conceits, but in this stanza there is no longer a recitation of the will.

To one who is already preoccupied with the notion of a single extended metaphor, *The Flea* may appear to be so constituted. But it is not really a conceit that is extended through the poem. There is, instead, a maintenance of, or continuous use of, the same witty device. This device is the insistence by the speaker that there is no difference between sexual intercourse and a man and woman being bitten by the same flea; in either case, argues the speaker to the woman, "our two bloods mingled bee." And so the witty, seductive argument continues through the poem. The wit results from the obvious logical fallacy: having sexual intercourse and being bitten by the same flea may be similar in one respect, but not in other respects. When in the second stanza the speaker argues —

> Though parents grudge, and you, w'are met,
> And cloystered in these living walls of Jet.

his statement is not figurative, but simply false in its implication. This is true also of the final lines of the poem, which the speaker says upon the woman's having killed the flea:

> Just so much honor, when thou yeeld'st to mee,
> Will wast, as this flea's death tooke life from thee.

Another poem among those which appear to be made up of a single extended metaphor is *A Valediction: of My Name, in the Window.* Here the object constantly referred to is, as the title indicates, the name of the speaker cut upon a window; the window is that of the woman he loves. Throughout the poem the speaker tells her to regard this name, during his absence, as representing himself. He states his hope that the name will act as a charm, keeping the woman faithful to him. There are in the poem many metaphors, some of them extended sufficiently to be regarded as conceits. There is not, however, continuous expression of the conceptual burden in the terms of a single metaphor. For instance, though there are some metaphors in the seventh and eighth stanzas, these are not extensions of a single initial metaphor; and the stanzas themselves are a direct statement, from the speaker to the woman, about the fact that his name is cut upon the window. He instructs her in how she is to regard this name:

> So since this name was cut
> When love and griefe their exaltation had,
> No doore 'gainst this names influence shut;
> As much more loving, as more sad,
> 'Twill make thee; and thou shouldst, till I returne,
> Since I die daily, daily mourne.
>
> When thy inconsiderate hand
> Flings ope this casement, with my trembling name,
> To looke on one, whose wit or land,
> New battry to thy heart may frame,
> Then thinke this name alive, and that thou thus
> In it offendst my Genius.

Donne's Poetry and Modern Criticism

At the end of the poem, in the eleventh stanza, the speaker turns from the comment upon his name and his hope for faithfulness in the woman, to an observation upon this very comment:

> But glasse, and lines must bee,
> No meanes our firme substantiall love to keepe;
> Neere death inflicts this lethargie,
> And this I murmure in my sleepe;
> Impute this idle talke, to that I goe,
> For dying men talke often so.

It is noteworthy that the final lines of the poem are without any terms that derive from the name or the window. These lines are of special significance, for with them there develops the complexity of attitudes found in many of Donne's poems. The speaker of the poem has been expressing hope because all hope is lost. This is his own conclusion.

THE PROBLEMS

We may now draw upon our analyses of poems from Donne's *Songs and Sonets* to make a more final comment on the definitions discussed in the first section, and to proceed to generalizations about the poetry which are suggested by our analyses.

The extended metaphor, or conceit, appears frequently in the poetry, and would certainly figure in a full characterization of Donne's style. But it is not, we have observed, an element by which the poetry is primarily and essentially characterized. Consequently, it must be concluded that those definitions are not accurate which are based upon the conceit as determining the structure of a metaphysical poem — if we mean that metaphysical poetry is the kind of poetry written by John Donne.

Poems that are coterminous with a single extended metaphor are exceptional rather than representative. Indeed, there is not a single poem in the *Songs and Sonets* which fits exactly the terms of the critic offering this definition. Ransom, we may recall, declared that there is in metaphysical poetry "a single extended image to bear the whole weight of the conceptual structure." If a physical image is meant, then even such poems as *The Will* and

Loves Usury could not be considered examples. We found, more-over, that few images are extended in the terms of imagery; the conceit of the compasses in *A Valediction: Forbidding Mourning* is one of these few. More frequently, however, there are various interpretations of the same image, or there is an accumulation of statements made by reference to a single image. And sometimes a conceit may not originate with a physical image at all, as the conceit of the lovers being canonized in *The Canonization*.

These observations apply also to the definition that metaphysical poetry shows a development of imagery by logical extension, as Tate suggests.* In our analyses we did not find that poems are characteristically developed by physical imagery. Though physical images are abundant in the poems of Donne, no one device of a relationship among the images can be singled out as exclusively typical. This definition will not hold even if *imagery* is not interpreted as physical references alone. We may again turn to *The Canonization*, this time for an example of the logical development of terms that are not strictly images. The fourth stanza of that poem, we noticed, has a sequence of terms that are allied with each other by obvious association: *legend, verse, sonnets, hymns, canonization*. These terms might be associated with each other even outside their present context; the association of the terms is possible because of their own nature, and not merely because they are used for a particular conceptual development. But there is no reason for regarding this stanza as characterizing or determining the structure of the whole poem. Nor are such examples frequent enough in the poetry to be regarded as the characteristic means by which the poems develop.

We have been saying, in effect, that there is no basis in the *Songs and Sonets* for the statement that a metaphysical poem departs at no point from the manner of the conceit. It will be recalled that the majority of the poems we examined do depart from this manner. And hence, we may say that the conceit is not essentially the "manner" of a metaphysical poem. As we have often observed, the conceit is frequent; and Brooks is no doubt correct in his con-

---

* *On the Limits of Poetry*, p. 106.

tention that the metaphors are not indifferently detachable from a metaphysical poem; but our analysis of the poetry compels us to remark that there is no validity to his dictum, "The comparison *is* the poem in a structural sense." A comparison is often an integral element in the entire complicated structure of a poem, but no justification has been found for generally identifying comparison with the structure of whole poems.

It also follows from our examination of the poems that the conceptual burden is not habitually conveyed by tropes. There are passages in which the conceptual burden *is* thus conveyed. But since such passages are not exclusively typical, there is no basis for saying that the conceptual structure of a metaphysical poem is generally within a figurative structure. A more accurate statement is that tropes are frequently elements in the development of conceptual structure. In other words, the thought abstracted or restated from a passage of metaphysical poetry may or may not be originally expressed by a trope. We noticed, for instance, that conceptual structure develops with slight use of figurative devices in such poems as *Goe, and catche a falling starre, The Indifferent, Confined Love* and *Communitie.* The obvious structure of *The Prohibition* is conceptual, and this structure is not lost in a prose paraphrase devoid of tropes. Even the condensed and generalized paraphrase of *Aire and Angels* is structurally a closer parallel to the whole poem than is any metaphor or group of metaphors. That is, structure is not generally related to a certain use of metaphor, as the several critics have incorrectly stated it to be. Metaphors and other tropes are often devices for the development of structure, but structure itself is, by figurative standards, looser than such devices. In so far as the structure of an entire poem is in any way determined, it is determined by the sequence of ideas in the poem and the relationship of these ideas to each other. There are, from this point of view, several poems in the *Songs and Sonets* which have a common structure, but we do not find that the poems as a whole yield any single formula of structure that is generally applicable. We do find basis, however, for other kinds of generalization; and hence we can give Donne's poetry a specific characterization, though it will not be structural.

In the first section, while reviewing the modern comment on metaphysical poetry, we observed a striking difference between the characterization given this poetry by Brooks and that of other critics. He departs from considerations of structure and figurative device. In so doing, he gives an account of the poetry by referring not to the details of technique, but to the attitudes that are expressed in a poem: "Wit is not merely an acute perception of analogies; it is a lively awareness of the fact that the obvious attitude toward a given situation is not the only possible attitude."

> There was in Donne's poetry an ambiguity which went far deeper than the mere use of obscure and difficult references. There was — as there is in the case of tragedy — an ambiguity as to the poet's ultimate attitude (p. 209).

Though we might choose a somewhat different phrasing, description in terms of attitude is, according to our analysis, substantiated by the poems. It will be recalled that most of the poems we examined were found to contain a complexity of attitudes. This complexity may, then, be considered a distinguishing feature of Donne's poetry — and of metaphysical poetry, in so far as Donne's poetry is granted to be the criterion of metaphysical poetry. Although the poems may differ among themselves in varying respects, they do, with few exceptions, have in common the feature of complexity of attitudes.

We have noted how such complexity is specifically constituted. In some poems it consists of references to two standards of value or two standards by which experiences may be interpreted. These standards may be represented thus: the special quality and significance of love, and all other activities and conditions in the world from which love is distinguished. Or the standards may derive from the distinction of human experience and the supernatural experience that follows death. Complexity resulting from the separate attitudes of love and the world is found in *The Good Morrow, The Canonization, The Sunne Rising, A Feaver, Breake of Day, A Valediction: of the Booke, A Valediction: Forbidding*

Mourning, and other poems. The complexity that derives from human life and the life after death is in *A Nocturnall upon Saint Lucies Day, The Anniversarie,* and *The Relique.* These latter poems, it may be noted, contain both kinds of complexity.

There is, as we observed in our analysis of *Aire and Angels,* another means by which complexity may exist in a poem. Such complexity results from a conception of the individual as divided into several aspects, thus allowing for differing attitudes toward separate aspects, or even toward the individual and an aspect of the individual — a conception, we remarked, comparable to that of faculty psychology. In *Aire and Angels,* for example, there is a distinction between a woman and the woman's love, with a separate attitude toward each. In *Loves Diet* love and discretion coexist independently, and they are also detached from the individual. The heart is given a status separate from the individual in *The Broken Heart, The Blossoms, The Legacie,* and *The Message.* The age-old dualism distinguishing between body and soul is found in *The Undertaking, The Extasie,* and other poems.

A third kind of complexity derives from the conventional psychology of love. Paradoxical or contradictory elements in the experience of love have traditionally been acknowledged. We find, for example, that the lover in *Twicknam Garden* would escape from certain aspects of his condition, but at the same time he would not "leave loving." He laments the falsity of women, and yet he claims to suffer from the "truth" of one woman. In *The Prohibition* the lover would be both loved and hated. At the end of *A Valediction: of My Name, in the Window* the lover says that he has been expressing hope because his case is hopeless.

Having decided that Donne's poetry is generally characterized by complexity of attitudes, we may inquire what is the nature of this complexity. It will be recalled that in every case the attitudes are in relation to specific kinds of human experience, usually the experience of love, sometimes the consideration of death. It appears, then, that a particular subject matter in the poems of Donne makes possible the complexity of attitudes, that the complexity is, indeed, inherent in the subject matter. This subject matter, it will be noticed, is of a kind to which complexity is conventionally attributed. To illustrate this we may simply repeat the different kinds of complexity that were listed: love and the world; human life and the hereafter; love and the other interests or "faculties" of the individual; the paradoxes and contradictions which are the effect of love. This is not to say that the subject of love or death necessarily introduces a complexity of attitudes, or that such complexity is possible only with respect to love and death. Our observation is simply that in the *Songs and Sonets* these subjects, especially love, are exploited for the complexity of attitudes which they imply according to convention. We have seen how in several poems a conventional dualism is treated in various ways, and we may here cite as example a poem not previously discussed. *Breake of Day* is addressed by a woman to her lover after a night together in bed. In the last stanza of the poem the opposition between love and the world of other activities is made by an analogous reference to matrimonial convention:

> Must businesse thee from hence remove?
> Oh, that's the worst disease of love,
> The poore, the foule, the false, love can
> Admit, but not the busied man.
> He which hath businesse, and makes love, doth doe
> Such wrong, as when a maryed man doth wooe.

Though it will take us beyond the frame of the individual poem, it is not irrelevant to our subject to attempt an account of poems not containing a complexity of attitudes. We may notice that these are, after all, in a relationship to the characteristic common to most of the poems. *Goe, and catche a falling starre, Confined Love,* and *Communitie* will serve as examples. Readers of these poems might feel that they are witty or that they incline toward wittiness. The poems, I believe, have the potentiality of wit because they express attitudes that may be regarded as extreme. In each of them an opinion is developed, and no allowance is made for exception to the opinion. In *Goe, and catche a falling starre* it is insisted that there are absolutely no fair women who are also true. The argument of *Confined Love* is that women ought to offer themselves promiscuously. *Communitie* says in effect that men may use women without moral responsibility because moral issue is not pertinent to woman. These statements are witty in so far as they are found surprising, in so far as they violate conventional attitudes. No wit, or surprise, would result from an argument that there are exceptions to the idealistic and romantic convention, that the convention in reality does not always operate — for the convention does not exist on such a basis. But in these poems the convention is wholly denied and is usurped by a stringent opposite. They may, therefore, achieve wittiness by oversimplification, by insisting upon a single attitude toward a question about which a complexity of attitudes is more generally admitted.

In the analyses of the poems it was noted that there are differences from poem to poem in the way that complexity of attitudes develops or is constituted. An account of these differences is, therefore, suggested.

It may be observed that in some poems, where two separate attitudes are indicated, one attitude is expressed favorably and the other is dismissed, but there is no conflict between the two. We find such relationship of attitudes in *The Good Morrow* and *The Sunne Rising*. The world of love is affirmed and maintained and the other world is distinguished from it. This is also to be found in *The Anniversarie*, though that poem has an additional complexity arising from the problem of death. In other poems, however, the possibility of conflict, or competition, between the two attitudes is suggested. It will be remembered that the speaker of *The Canonization* insists that one attitude must not impinge upon the other. The speaker of *Breake of Day* finds herself the victim of such competition, having to comply with the claims of the unfavored attitude.

In these poems the speaker is committed to one of two attitudes; he does not hold one, and then another. There are poems, however, in which movement from one attitude to another is indicated. For example, the speaker of *The Primrose* considers having for his love one who is either more or less than a woman, and then he decides that it would be best to have a natural woman. The speaker of

Loves Alchymie observes that in the course of experience one attitude is supplanted by another:

> So, lovers dreame a rich and long delight,
> But get a winter-seeming summers night.

A similar observation is made by the speaker of *A Lecture upon the Shadow*. He declares that when love diminishes at all, it has completely ended. In these three poems the attitude to which the speaker may be committed is not so much stressed as it is in poems like *The Good Morrow* and *The Canonization*. The speaker of *The Canonization*, for example, is involved in a conflict of attitudes; he is a partisan for one of the attitudes. Whereas in *The Primrose, Loves Alchymie,* and *A Lecture upon the Shadow* the speaker delivers a discourse upon attitudes, distinguishing between them, perhaps making a comparative evaluation. He pronounces upon the attitudes in general; but his statement is not initially conditioned by a particular attitude.

There are still other poems in which there is movement from one attitude to another, but in these the movement is not explained in the manner of discourse. The stress is put, rather, upon the speaker's experience of the attitudes as he holds them in a particular situation. Complexity of attitudes is thus developed in *Aire and Angels*. Here, we recall, the speaker tells a woman that she fulfills his ideal of love's object; he finds, however, that his love is inadequate for her. But he adjusts his love to the love she offers, for, he says, woman's love is less than man's. Thus he turns from the woman, who is above his love, to her love, which is beneath his. Particularized movement from one attitude to another is illustrated also by *The Prohibition*. The speaker cautions a woman about loving him, then about hating him, and finally requests that she love and hate him at the same time. In *A Valediction: of My Name, in the Window* the speaker expresses hope at some length, and then declares that he does this because there is no hope for him. It may be noticed that in these poems there is development *toward* complexity of attitudes; complexity comes as a conclusion. The speaker is, finally, not committed to one attitude alone; nor is he discoursing upon attitudes with any degree of detachment.

Donne's Poetry and Modern Criticism

Though he may at first express — or hold, or seem to hold — a single attitude, it appears in conclusion that he is committed to rival attitudes. Such poems, therefore, arrive at a tension — or at an irony, in that opposite attitudes are held simultaneously by the same individual.

A further distinction that may be noted in the relationship between the speaker and the complexity of attitudes is illustrated in *Twicknam Garden* and the *Nocturnall.* In these poems the complexity does not issue from a kind of reversal, as it does in *A Valediction: of My Name, in the Window,* where surprise may result because the complexity is not admitted until the end of the poem. Instead of development toward a tension or irony, we find that the speaker is from the very first committed to rival attitudes. This was observed in our analyses of *Twicknam Garden* and the *Nocturnall.* We indicated their dramatic nature and observed that the emotion of the speaker is in each case the subject of the poem. We referred to this in several ways: a speaker comments upon the specific situation in which he finds himself; the poem is a dramatic statement that is *private* with respect to the speaker; as the poem develops, the speaker's emotion is characterized by references to its context and to its elements; an effect of the poem is this suggestion of the nature of the speaker's emotion. The rival attitudes are, indeed, the specific occasion of the speaker's exclamation. He begins already committed to both attitudes, and as the poem develops we learn of the experience that brought on this rivalry. Hence, it becomes evident that the speaker is in a particular circumstance, a dramatic moment of his experience, much of which is, of course, "inner" experience.

The speaker of *Twicknam Garden* calls himself "selfe traytor." He would escape from what he is experiencing, and yet he would not "leave loving." He deplores the falsity of women, but finds himself distressed by the truth of one of them. Throughout the *Nocturnall* the speaker dwells upon his "nothingness," which is even more profound than the "nothingness" from which it proceeded. He is "nothing" in that he is not committed to anything — or to any one thing. A conflict of attitudes leaves him suspended, each attitude preventing him from being attached to the other. He is "nothing" at the beginning and end of the poem. The death of the woman he loved has brought him to this condition, yet he says that the word *death* "wrongs her." He would exchange his lot for that of "any beast," yet he anticipates joining his love in heaven. At the particular moment in which he speaks, he inclines in opposite directions but is committed to nothing. In each of these poems, then, the speaker does not discourse upon or expand one attitude and then another, but refers rather to the conflict — the emotion — that he entertains. It appears, therefore, that the conflict of attitudes within the mind of an individual, the individual's emotion, and the dramatic nature of the poem containing these, are the concomitant effects of each other. Such conflict implies an individual's emotion; and it is a dramatic event when an individual expounds the emotion he experiences, especially when the emotion is described in terms of past action and the attitudes toward a present situation.

In reviewing such poems as *The Good Morrow, The Canonization, A Lecture upon the Shadow, Aire and Angels* and *Twicknam Garden,* we have observed the different ways in which complexity of attitudes develops, the ways in which attitudes may be related to each other, how the development and relationship of attitudes are connected with the speaker, and finally, how all of these may contribute to the nature of a poem. Though the poems of Donne's *Songs and Sonets* generally have in common a speaker and complexity of attitudes, an obvious conclusion is that there are several patterns by which these details may exist in combination. The patterns that have been indicated should not, however, be regarded as exhaustive. Nor should the distinctions made between patterns be considered as constituting a system of classes into which the poems may be neatly divided. There are poems, no doubt, which fulfill no single pattern, but which show elements of several patterns. Our distinctions were a convenience for indicating the range of configurations in which the common characteristics of the poems may and do exist.

Since differences among the poems have been defined, questions may arise with regard to the significance of these differences. For instance, one might ask whether any particular poem is, more than another kind, characteristic of the poetry in general. This question might be settled in a way by determining which kind of poem constitutes an emphatic plurality, or perhaps a majority. But such an answer would hardly satisfy what is likely the basic motivation of the question. For one would want to know whether there is a kind of poem, frequent or not, which most essentially displays the common characteristics of the poetry.

To pursue this interest we may examine the characteristics. Do these have an *essential* nature that implies a particular kind of poetic treatment? The poems generally have a speaker and show a complexity of attitudes. One might decide, then, that the poem is most characteristic which displays these most prominently. So the argument would run. Emphasis is put upon the speaker's individuality when he is most clearly the center of a dramatic situation or predicament. And it might be said that complexity of attitudes is most pronounced when the attitudes conflict within the consciousness of a single individual. The notion of complexity does, after all, arise from a mode of consciousness, the single individual's distinction between one attitude and another. Therefore, rivalry of attitudes within the speaker's mind displays most essentially the characteristic of complexity, for the complexity is thus emphasized at its very source. Moreover, such complexity centrally involves the individuality of the speaker. It follows, then, that the speaker's individuality and the rivalry of attitudes may be two aspects of the same pattern of elements, that they converge to produce a poem of dramatic nature. That *Twicknam Garden* and the *Nocturnall* fit this description is undoubtedly apparent. In our treatment of the differences among the poems, it will be recalled, we said of these that "the conflict of attitudes within the mind of an individual, the individual's emotion, and the dramatic nature of the poem containing these, are the concomitant effects of each other." According to such reasoning, it could be maintained that *Twicknam Garden* and the *Nocturnall* represent most fully the prevailing characteristics of Donne's *Songs and Sonets*, that they supply and comply with the essential definition of metaphysical poetry.

But we will soon observe that the special status given to poems of this kind is not really tenable. A similar argument might be made for other kinds of poems. We may, in illustration, consider the kind represented by *Aire and Angels, The Prohibition,* and *A Valediction: of My Name, in the Window,* which we discussed as a group. In these, rivalry of attitudes within the mind of the speaker is not apparent until the end of a poem. Each poem shows, in fact, the process by which the speaker arrives at a consciousness of rival attitudes. It might be argued, therefore, that these poems represent the common characteristics more essentially than *Twicknam Garden* and the *Nocturnall*; for, instead of being already possessed of rival attitudes, the speaker reveals in his statement the inceptive stages of the rivalry. While one poem is a statement that issues from a condition of rival attitudes, the other is a statement that is itself the process by which the rivalry develops. This second kind of poem portrays the order of development from the primitive stages to full complexity of attitudes. Such a poem might, then, be regarded as essentially representative of the characteristics; and it has its own claims for dramatic nature.

But as we observed that a special status for *Twicknam Garden* is untenable, so we may now observe that such status is equally untenable for *The Prohibition.* Since both kinds show rival attitudes in the mind of the speaker, they might be advanced as sharing the position of being most representative. This implies that conflict of attitudes within the speaker's mind is the most essential instance of complexity; we have just followed arguments in support of this view. There is also an argument for poems in which the speaker does not hold rival attitudes, but is the partisan of a single attitude. Such partisanship distinguishes the individuality of the speaker as much as a conflict of attitudes within his mind, for he thus holds a position in contrast to the one from which he differs. Though he does not maintain a conflict, his statement is an argument for one of two competing attitudes and is thereby dramatic. Complexity is no less essentially represented by an attitude

that is held and one that is not held than by any other relationship
of attitudes. In either case there is emphasis upon the individuality of the speaker and the complexity of attitudes, and these contribute to a poem of dramatic nature. Poems of this kind are *The
Canonization, A Valediction: Forbidding Mourning, The Undertaking,* and several others. In each of these the speaker maintains
the value and spirituality of love against the naturalistic standards
of the world.

We may conclude, as a result of these considerations, that no
single treatment is most essentially representative of the common
characteristics of Donne's poems. It is noticeable, however, that
all the poems we have considered are dramatic statements made
by the speaker. This still leaves the question of the difference between such poems and those that are discourses. It will be seen
that special claims for dramatic treatment of the speaker are not
admissible. A poem that is a discourse may attain to dramatic
quality by the references that are made, by the obvious particular-
ities to which the general thesis applies. For instance, the speaker
of *Loves Alchymie* is in no specified situation at the moment of his
statement; in other words, it is not a dramatic statement, but it
concerns experiences that are dramatic:

> So, lovers dreame a rich and long delight,
> But get a winter-seeming summers night.
> . . . .
> Hope not for minde in women; at their best
> Sweetnesse and wit, they'are but *Mummy,* possest.

Similarly, the general statement of *A Lecture upon the Shadow*
has implications of the particular experience:

> Love is a growing, or full constant light;
> And his first minute, after noone, is night.

The Apparition is dramatic not so much by the present situation
of the speaker as by the scene he describes and the emotions he
predicts. We see, thus, that dramatic quality is not wholly dependent upon the speaker's relationship to the complexity of attitudes,
though it may derive from this. In some poems, as a matter of fact,

the speaker alternates between references to his own situation and the generalizations illustrated by it, as in *The Extasie*. Dramatic quality remains, however, characteristic of the poems. Attitudes presuppose the individuals by which they are held, and by drama we mean, of course, the experience of individuals.

In this attempt to demonstrate that no single treatment of complexity of attitudes is most essential and most dramatic, we have not intended to argue that among the poems of Donne there are no differences in dramatic quality and prominence of complexity. The point of our argument has been that there is no single *formula* for treatment of complexity of attitudes which makes for a poem that is most essentially characteristic or dramatic. We chose particular poems in illustration of several formulas, but do not insist, certainly, that there are no differences among these poems in dramatic quality and the emphasis on complexity. These differences are determined not by the formula, but by the specific treatment of the formula itself. Consider, for example, *The Prohibition* and the *Nocturnall*. It is perhaps obvious that a reader would find the *Nocturnall* to be the more dramatic and emphatically complex of the two. But if this is so it is because of the means by which a formula is particularized and not because of a difference in formulas. Or we might consider *The Sunne Rising* and *Breake of Day*. Both these poems represent the same formula; and the terms by which it is particularized are, to an extent, strikingly similar, as the titles indicate. Yet *The Sunne Rising* is obviously the more dramatic and essentially complex. The difference must, therefore, result from the peculiar virtues of the individual poems.

The problem of critical evaluation arises, apparently, from this consideration of the several formulas by which an essential complexity of attitudes is possible. Since the same essential complexity and the dramatic quality it may produce are equally possible by all the formulas, differences among the poems other than that of conceptual structure are in no way related to the differences among the formulas. That is, each formula, or norm, is not significant beyond the fact of its descriptive nature; and therefore, no formula may be distinguished from the others as a standard of evaluation. Complexity may be achieved as forcibly by one formula as by another, and since the formulas refer only to the development of complexity, an evaluative function cannot be ascribed to any of them. All are normative descriptions; none is a standard of evaluation. Poems having the same formula of complexity may again be cited in illustration. *The Good Morrow, Breake of Day,* and *The Sunne Rising* all have a speaker who holds the attitude of love as opposed to that of the world. Moreover, the speakers are in identical situations. *The Sunne Rising* would probably be distinguished from the others in superlative terms, and not, obviously, because of any difference in formula. The poems differ in so far as the same formula is differently treated or exploited. And these differences would be stated in terms of the peculiar characteristics of the poems. One might indicate, for example, that *The Sunne Rising* presents most vividly and extensively the elements common to all the poems. One might compare the poems with regard to images, metaphors, diction, tone, concepts, the various interrelationships of all these, and then decide that this poem is the richest, most dramatic, most vivid, most eloquent, most impressive, or use whatever superlatives are suggested by the peculiar nature of the poem.

Since the differences do not depend upon the formula of complexity, poems of different formulas could be compared according to treatment of formulas rather than differences in formulas. If *Twicknam Garden* is a "better" poem than *The Good Morrow*, it is so by virtue of the particular details in it which are found preferable to those of *The Good Morrow*. *Twicknam Garden* and *The Canonization* might be found equally good. In so far as these poems differ from one another, no single description derived from one could be applied to the other for determining its merit. To the extent that each description is exhaustive, it can refer only to the poem described; and to the extent that it may be applied beyond the poem, it is normative and not evaluative.

It should be remembered that we have been discussing only the poems of Donne's *Songs and Sonets*. We have not referred beyond them to poems that do not have complexity of attitudes by one or another of the formulas. Our conclusions may, however, be so extended, and we may state more generally the distinction between normative description and a standard of evaluation. Several conceptual structures may be used for developing complexity of attitudes, and no one of the structures is for this purpose superior to the others. Unless one puts a special value upon complexity of attitudes — or some comparable feature — there is no conceivable structure that is superior to any other. The terms of superiority would have to derive from the feature or characteristic produced by a particular structure, and the differences in structure would, therefore, be meaningful in terms of this characteristic. And, as we have observed, this implies a special value for a peculiar characteristic. The reasons that one such characteristic should be regarded as more desirable or valuable than another involve the interests of the reader; we shall eventually consider this problem.

In our first section we discovered that the structures which have been applied as standards of evaluation were most often rhetorical — or figurative — rather than conceptual structures. That is, metaphysical poetry (and therefore Donne's) was claimed to be distinguished by a structure based upon metaphorical device. But we have demonstrated, presumably, that though metaphor is frequent in Donne's poetry, there is no special use of metaphor by which structure generally develops. We learned that the characteristic structures are conceptual and that metaphor is at times instrumental in the development of these structures. The claims for the special value of a particular metaphorical structure might, consequently, be dismissed.

We should, nevertheless, give these structural standards further consideration. What has been said about conceptual structure is equally true of figurative structure. For example, even if the definition of a metaphysical poem as coterminous with a single extended metaphor were actually borne out by the poetry, there would still be no justification for isolating such structure as absolutely more valuable than any other. It would, like other descriptions, be normative and not evaluative. That is, it would be so unless the extended metaphor were valued *per se* above all other characteristics possible to poetry. But no one, of course, has postulated the extended metaphor as a standard on such unconditional grounds. If it has value, this value must arise from some purpose for which the device is used, and not from the mere presence of the device itself. We may recall Ransom's statements to the effect that extension of metaphor makes for *meantness* and *precision*. According to his arguments, a poem made of a single extended metaphor is a superior kind of poem: "The impulse to metaphysical poetry . . . consists in committing the feelings in the case . . . to their determination within the elected figure." " 'Metaphysics, or miraculism, informs a poetry which is the most original and exciting, and intellectually perhaps the most seasoned, that we know in our literature, and very probably it has few equivalents in other literatures." The seventeenth-century poets, and especially Donne, may indeed merit extremely high praise. We have already observed, however, that extended metaphor does not necessarily produce any special excellence. It is not demonstrable that the superlative qualities which Ransom ascribes to the poetry are effected by a single extended metaphor for each poem. Except for the virtue of a conspicuous figurative structure, the excellences of a poem so constituted would derive from the other elements of the poem, not alone from the general formula of structure.

According to our analyses, it is complexity of attitudes which "informs" metaphysical poetry, and no causal relationship between this complexity and extended metaphor is discernible. We have shown that the characteristic complexity exists in poems not distinguished by such figurative device. In *Twicknam Garden* no single metaphor is considerably extended or stands out as most impressive. On the other hand, a single metaphor is extended for twenty lines of *A Feaver*. If we compared the two poems we should find this structural difference between them, but the difference would not be significant beyond the fact that it exists. It would certainly not signify a difference in value, or the degree to which the poems are characteristically metaphysical.

The other definitions by which metaphorical device determines the structure of a metaphysical poem, and any claims that such structure is applicable as a standard for general evaluation, are obviously subject to the same arguments we have brought against Ransom's statements. It should be clear that the intention of this discussion has not been to disclaim the merit of metaphor, the various poetical purposes for which it may be used, and its importance in the poetry of Donne. Our thesis has been that there is no basis for regarding structure *determined by metaphor* as an absolute standard of evaluation, that Donne's poetry is not generally characterized by such structure.

A question of the value of metaphor is suggested by W. R. Moses' interesting study *The Metaphysical Conceit in the Poems of John Donne.** Following the traditional characterization of the metaphysical conceit as it was first formulated by Dr. Johnson, Moses describes the conceit as based upon a *discordia concors*, an association of the dissimilar. His treatment of the subject is more systematic than any that has previously been made. He observes that the metaphysical conceit is distinguished for the surprise it produces, the surprise resulting, of course, from the association of dissimilar objects or ideas. To account for the notion of dissimilarity, Moses avails himself of the term *imaginative category*. In the individual consciousness there are images and ideas which, because of obvious similarity in some details, are associated with each other and therefore comprise separate groups or imaginative categories. Surprise results when terms from different categories are brought into combination. Moses makes it clear that he is aware of the subjective basis of his terminology: ". . . an assumption must be made: the assumption, simply, that men are sufficiently alike so that what produces an imaginative shock in one will produce an imaginative shock in most others likewise. This assumption must be understood to operate throughout the present study" (p. 39).

Observing that surprise may result from the degree to which a conceit is extended, as well as from its violation of imaginative categories, Moses arrives at a standard for the evaluation of conceits:

* Unpublished dissertation, Vanderbilt University, 1938.

Donne's Poetry and Modern Criticism

"First, imaginative categories may be alien to each other in varying degree, so that the coupling of terms from disparate categories represents a more or less great deviation from ordinary thought sequences. To use Williamson's expression, 'imaginative distance': if a certain quantity of imaginative distance is required to establish a trope as a conceit, there may be, beyond the minimum quantity, more or less distance between the terms of the conceit. Some conceits, accordingly, may produce a great deal of imaginative surprise; others less.

"The second cause relates to the 'meantness' of the conceit. Terms not imaginatively removed to the farthest possible degree may nevertheless be developed to such an extent that they clash sharply, with a considerable amount of imaginative surprise resulting. But if the conceit is not developed, if the poet does not stick to his imagery, the imaginative surprise produced will (still assuming terms not the farthest removed from each other) be slight. Probably the finest conceits are those characterized both by greatly removed terms and by considerable development" (pp. 101–102).

Though penetrating and cautiously phrased, Moses' statements are evidently another instance of normative description presented as a standard for general evaluation. Surprise does indeed result from the "coupling of terms from disparate categories." And surprise may, strictly as surprise, be regarded as valuable. But in poetry this is hardly, if ever, the case. There are pleasant surprises, and unpleasant surprises. Unless a reader seeks simply surprise *qua* surprise, he might expect that there be apparent some perceptual — or conceptual — justification for the coupling of disparate terms. Where such justification is not discernible, the surprise would be inconsequential, meaningless, perhaps unpleasant. And the quality of surprise resulting from degree of extension would be similarly determined.

It follows from these observations that the "finest conceit" would not be determined by remoteness of terms or degree of extension. These characteristics are merely descriptive. Where they are of unusual magnitude, we have simply a most conceited conceit, a most surprising surprise. There are, moreover, other factors which participate in the reader's evaluation of a particular conceit, even when the conceit is sufficiently justified. He might be influenced by the perceptual reference made by the terms of a conceit, finding the presence of certain terms — images — especially pleasing. The conceptual burden of the conceit and the way in which this is served by the terms would most likely be even more significant. Consider, for example, this brief conceit from *The Relique*:

> (For graves have learn'd that woman-head
> To be to more then one a Bed) . . .

The imaginative distance between graves and beds, and beds and women, is presumably slight. Yet a reader might find this an extremely fine conceit, being much impressed by the references to death and sex, and deeply moved by the nature of the comment on these subjects. Conceptual character is thus seen to be of great importance in the evaluation of a conceit.

Since we are considering conceits in isolation, we might venture a comparison between two conceits. One of these will be the well-known conceit coming at the end of *A Valediction: Forbidding Mourning*. Here lovers and compasses are brought together, a large imaginative distance being thus obviously traversed; and the conceit is extended for twelve lines. We may compare with this a conceit from *A Lecture upon the Shadow*:

> Love is a growing, or full constant light;
> And his first minute, after noone, is night.

This is of brief extent. The imaginative distances between love and the noon sun, between the absence of love and night, seem less than that between lovers and compasses. Yet, is one conceit to be regarded as better than the other? There are, indeed, possible reasons for preferring the conceit of the sun above that of the compasses. The comment upon the course of love might be judged as far more impressive than that upon the unity of lovers' souls. It might be argued, moreover, that though one conceit is more extended verbally, the other is compressed and more extended conceptually. A reader might find more intellectual complexity and conceptual implication in the idea that when love passes it does so utterly and not gradually, than in the idea that lovers' souls maintain a kind of unity even when the lovers are parted.

Donne's Poetry and Modern Criticism

We should again refer to the qualified nature of our argument. It has not been insisted that the determining factor in the value of a conceit is to be found in its paraphrase. We have been concerned simply to show the relevance of the conceptual factor to evaluation, and to repeat that a structural definition is not a standard of evaluation.

It is noteworthy that we have been treating of conceits as they are detached from the poems in which they occur. This suggests an additional means by which the conceit may be evaluated, one that Moses does not consider. An extremely important basis of evaluation would no doubt be the relationship of a conceit to other elements of a poem and to the whole poem.

It may be observed, upon looking back, that we have discussed several instances of the distinction between description and evaluation. First, we indicated that no single formula for the development of complexity of attitudes is superior to others. Then we showed that poems cannot be evaluated according to a structure that is wholly determined by metaphor. And finally, we decided that the merit of individual metaphors cannot be judged simply by the degree of their extension and the imaginative distance between the terms. In each case a single aspect of structure is selected and is stated generally as a standard of evaluations. Poems may indeed be classified according to one aspect of structure, and metaphors likewise, a common element of style being thus indicated. But, as we have observed, every poem contains many elements in addition to one aspect of structure; these other elements and their relationship to the structural aspect are equally important in determining the value of a particular poem. The value of a poem is not, so to speak, already predicted by the definition of a preconceived characteristic style. It is determinable only in so far as analysis may show a particular poem to have elements that are valuable according to the many interests of a reader.

In concluding our study we shall try to give a general account of the value of Donne's poetry, to supply the terms which might be used in explaining its appeal to the reader. Of the elements present in the poems, it is natural to consider first the *complexity of attitudes* which we discovered to be the distinguishing and characteristic feature of Donne's *Songs and Sonets.* This complexity may itself be regarded as a value. It might be so held on the basis that recognition of complexity of attitudes is *realistic,* since life is extremely complex: there are various standards of interpretation that are opposed to each other; individuals seldom share identical attitudes; there are conflicts between the individual and society, and conflicts among the various interests of the same individual. Complexity of attitudes reflects, thus, the actual differences among persons and the psychological nature of the individual. There appears, then, to be a further basis for the value of complexity. It brings into prominence the *psychology of the individual,* which is itself interesting. And the emphasis on human individuality, especially when the individual maintains or is involved in an opposition of attitudes, makes for dramatic quality, which is, like psychology, self-evident in its value. The psychological stress and dramatic quality are, moreover, in conjunction with *the particular subjects of love and death,* and the interest in these is, perhaps, most evident of all.

Though in our analyses we frequently indicated and examined stylistic elements, we did not systematically develop a full account of them. But the existence of these elements and their significance to the reader are no doubt apparent. We may, for example, consider the imagery. Each image is of a particular kind, so we shall assume that the cumulative effect of the images brings the reader to a notion of the general character of the imagery. A reader may, consequently, be interested not only in the presence of imagery, but be pleased to find that it is of a distinguishable kind. And he may, furthermore, be pleased to find it is a peculiar kind— as Donne's imagery may be valued because it is found to be urban, intellectual, realistic.

Other elements similarly participate in meeting the interests of the reader. He may, for instance, like the tone produced by imagery, diction, rhythm, rhyme, stanza; he may like each of these for its own nature and for its contributing function in the development of tone. Donne's tone would, probably, be distinguished and valued because it is conversational, argumentative, and dramatic. Metaphor and other devices may likewise be valued for themselves and because they are instrumental in producing qualities such as surprise, wit, and irony. We observe, then, that an element is not only valued in itself, but for its aptness among other elements. That is, a distinguishable and purposive interrelationship among the elements may be regarded as a value. A reader is pleased by the character of elements that are verbal, figurative, and conceptual; by their discernible integration and the purpose for which they are integrated. In other words, a discernible structure is valuable. It may be so for its character as structure, for its various aspects (i.e., the constituent elements), and for its function in producing the final effect of a whole poem. Though it was not our intention in analyzing his poetry to show its possibilities of value, it may be remembered that we frequently indicated the features we have been discussing. We observed, for example, the various means by which complexity of attitudes is developed and displayed in *The Canonization, Twicknam Garden, Aire and Angels,* the *Nocturnall,* and other poems.

The way in which various elements are involved in a structure may be an additional instance of value. A reader may be favorably impressed by the ingenuity of craft which is reflected by a poem, a craft that was presumably necessary for its creation. Deciding that the deliberate integration of a complexity of elements is no usual and easy accomplishment, he may admire the spectacle of a difficult task successfully performed. He may enjoy, also, his own experience of achieving an understanding of a poem in all its detail. The "difficulty" of a poem would, then, be regarded as a value. A poem may require of a reader some time and effort before the full significance and final coherence of all its elements become apparent. (To ascribe this value, the reader must, of course, first discover significance and coherence, or have confidence that these exist and may eventually be perceived.) A "difficult" poem is, therefore, valuable in that it allows the reader to indulge his own capacities of intelligence and sensibility. Difficulty, whether for the poet or the reader, is admittedly a relative matter. Yet if one considers the concepts underlying Donne's poetry, and the nature of its other ingredient and structural elements, one will probably grant that it is, to a degree, difficult.

These observations certainly do not exhaust the characteristics, or values, of Donne's poetry. And still more certainly, there is no basis for regarding any of these specific values, or any combination of them, as the single absolute standard by which all poetry may be evaluated. If we must have generalizations, they are going to have to be extremely general, such as the proposition that a poem "be about something interesting" and that it show in some way the obvious virtues of unity, coherence, and emphasis.

ᗒᗕ Fusion and Experience

IN THE preceding essay I was concerned with what modern critics had made of Donne's poetry and with the validity and nonvalidity of their characterizations. I dealt but briefly with the concept of the fusion of thought and feeling, and I now propose to explore that subject more fully.

I

It is T. S. Eliot who is generally regarded as having discovered in Donne's poetry, and hence in the seventeenth-century poets called Metaphysical, the fusion of thought and feeling. This is so, and in a sense properly so, even when it is allowed that Sir Herbert Grierson had preceded Eliot in noting "the peculiar blend of passion and thought, feeling and ratiocination" and "passionate thinking" in the poets concerned. It is Eliot, and not Grierson, who presented the idea in such a way as to command the attention and consent of other critics and to give the idea the status among many students of literature of a seemingly permanent (i.e., valid) insight. It will clarify my subsequent discourse to announce here that I consider the insight invalid. My purpose is to show that Eliot did not have a certain kind of insight into the nature of Donne's poetry, and to show that Donne's poetry did have a certain kind of influence on Eliot's literary criticism and hence generally on criticism and critical thought of the past several decades. It remains to spell out what is meant in each case by *certain kind*.

To consider first the question of the insight, we turn inevitably to the essay "The Metaphysical Poets" (1921), that fabric of what are now familiar quotations. It is an essay not only crowded with ideas, but one in which the ideas crowd each other — indeed, for my purpose the essay, even parts of the essay, defies summarization or the making of handy quotations, for the "quotations" are always imbedded in contexts that involve "too many" ideas. Nevertheless, I must use quotations, and they are familiar:

"In Chapman especially there is a direct sensuous apprehension of thought, or recreation of thought into feeling, which is exactly what we find in Donne."

"The difference is not a simple difference of degree between poets. It is something which had happened to the mind of England between the time of Donne or Lord Herbert of Cherbury and the time of Tennyson and Browning; it is the difference between the intellectual poet and the reflective poet. Tennyson and Browning are poets, and they think; but they do not feel their thought as immediately as the odour of a rose. A thought to Donne was an experience; it modified his sensibility."

"The poets of the seventeenth century, the successors of the dramatists of the sixteenth, possessed a mechanism of sensibility which could devour any kind of experience . . . In the seventeenth century a dissociation of sensibility set in, from which we have never recovered."

It is allowable, I think, to confine the discussion to Donne, for his poetry is generally considered *the type* of metaphysical. Eliot's statements seem to say, then, and have been understood to say, that Donne's poetry differs from post-metaphysical poetry not by "a simple difference of degree" but by an actual difference *in kind*. A clear and firm line of demarcation is made between the two kinds of poetry, for the difference is plotted by the presence in Donne's poetry of the combination, or fusion, of thought and feeling, and by its absence in the other poetry. This fusion is, moreover, the product of a "mechanism of sensibility" which disappeared during the latter decades of the seventeenth century. This is not all that Eliot is saying, but it is more than enough to engage us for a while. The obvious question is, Where in Donne's poetry is there a "felt thought" or a "thought feeling"?

It has been my experience and my observation that any attempt to locate these leads to the most flagrant question-begging and to the mental snarls of amateur psychologizing. For example, even before we might get well started, we are confronted with the ambiguity of the word *feeling*, as Eliot and other critics have used it, for *feeling* means both sensation (such as touch) and emotion (such as fear). One may indicate that there are technical differences between Donne's use of metaphor and that of other poets, but there still remains the problem of explaining how any metaphor, by this technical difference, becomes a felt thought or a thought feeling. The kind of snarl to which the problem leads could be illustrated at considerable length, but I believe that another strategy would be more persuasive and is finally necessary. The strategy is, to be led not into the question, but away from it — to recognize the question as an *ignis fatuus* and to understand how it achieved that condition. The *ignis fatuus* is kindled by the notion that fusions of thought and feeling are *contained* by Donne's poetry just as images, metaphors, conceits, paradoxes are contained therein and may be located for analytical examination. But the *ignis fatuus* disappears when we recognize that the statements of Eliot and other critics about the fusion of thought and feeling are figurative, and not literal — that this fusion is itself a paradoxical metaphor. In other words, Eliot and critics of poetry after him have been practicing a mixture of analytical and impressionistic criticism, and the criticism has too readily been accepted as exclusively analytical. If Eliot had originally said (in effect, but unmistakably) that there is an *apparent* fusion of thought and feeling in Donne's poetry, it is likely that such qualification would not have led the critics to apply his remarks analytically and to have given such important status to the notion of fusion. In Eliot's remarks we have not an analysis or explanation of Donne's poetry, but a response to it. The poetry made him feel *as if* thought and feeling had been fused. This is sufficiently understandable, because we can conceive of the response and we can share it. But our response, our *impression*, is evidence of the effect of a poem. It is not an explanation or a description of it. This effect is, indeed, quite obvious, and we may surmise that it is frequently intended.

It has often been observed that surprise is a characteristic effect of Donne — and the apparent fusion is one of the variety of surprises to be found in his poetry. Thought and feeling are heterogeneous ideas that Donne yoked together, perhaps violently, but also wittily. We can see this most clearly in certain poems and passages where the fusion is not only an effect but is actually stated or suggested. "A naked thinking heart" in *The Blossome* is such a phrase. Another example is the entire poem *The Extasie*, which argues that for "pure lovers" spiritual union and physical union are indistinguishable:

> So must pure lovers soules descend
> T'affections, and to faculties,
> Which sense may reach and apprehend.

Still another example is the oft-quoted passage from "Of the Progresse of the Soule: The Second Anniversarie":

> her pure, and eloquent blood
> Spoke in her cheekes, and so distinctly wrought
> That one might almost say, her body thought.

This passage clearly shows that Donne considered "felt thought" a daring and surprising notion — at least, it is so considered in the passage. There could hardly be a stronger qualification, a more cautious and self-conscious approach to a metaphor, than the words "might almost say." Many other passages achieve the same kind of surprising effect by assuming that an abstraction, generalization or attitude is a physical object. We have an example of this in the opening lines of *Loves Diet*:

> To what a cumbersome unwieldinesse
> And burdenous corpulence my love had growne,
>   But that I did, to make it less,
>   And keep it in proportion,
> Give it a diet, made it feed upon
> That which love worst endures, *discretion*.

Of course, Donne achieved many witty and surprising effects by other means. But this kind — the identification of physical and nonphysical, the "fusion" of thought and feeling — has been peculiarly impressive and has had a notable influence on modern critical thought.

II

It turns out that our examination of the kind of "insight" Eliot had into Donne's poetry has also yielded some understanding of the kind of influence Donne's poetry has had on modern criticism. In order to pursue the matter of Donne's influence beyond Eliot, it is necessary to retread some of the ground covered in my earlier essay, and I hope that this repetition will be justified by new and relevant observations. In that essay I noted that George Williamson's book *The Donne Tradition* (1930) is an application and elaboration of Eliot's critical thoughts and expressions, especially those about the fusion of thought and feeling and the unified sensibility of the seventeenth-century poets — but I now think that Williamson did more than merely illustrate at length and in detail what Eliot had already suggested. Indeed, it seems to me that Williamson's book had an impact on subsequent criticism that has not been adequately acknowledged — and I mean by this that he added some confusions to those which Eliot had already offered. For example, Eliot *did not* give a disproportionate emphasis to the importance of the metaphysical conceit, and he *did* give some emphasis to the importance of other characteristic features, such as: "development by rapid association of thought," "brief words and sudden contrasts," and "telescoping of images and multiplied associations." Moreover, Eliot defined the conceit as "the mere explication of the content of a comparison," and also as "the elaboration (contrasted with the condensation) of a figure of speech to the farthest stage to which ingenuity can carry it." But for Williamson the conceit looms above all other features. Again and again he announces that the conceit is either the cause or the instrument of other characteristic features of metaphysical poetry and especially of Donne's. Furthermore, possibly misunderstanding Eliot's meaning, he goes on to classify practically any metaphor in this poetry as a conceit, for he distinguishes two kinds, the expanded and the condensed: "The expanded conceit is successful when the idea and the figure become one, and the condensed conceit when the image is the very body of the thought." But the most important aspect of this statement is the claim, often reiterated by Williamson, that the metaphysical conceit is the device by which the metaphysical poets fused thought and feeling. This notion, to my knowledge first formulated by Williamson, has been extensively disseminated and continues to affect some critical thinking about metaphysical poetry and even poetry in general.

It is Williamson's notion, not Eliot's, but if we look in Eliot's essay we can find what was probably its provocation for Williamson.

"Johnson, who employed the term 'metaphysical poets,' apparently having Donne, Cleveland, and Cowley chiefly in mind, remarks of them that 'the most heterogeneous ideas are yoked by violence together.' . . . But a degree of heterogeneity of material compelled into unity by the operation of the poet's mind is omnipresent in poetry. . . . we may find it in some of the best lines of Johnson himself . . . where the effect is due to a contrast of ideas, different in degree but the same in principle, as that which Johnson mildly reprehended. And in one of the finest poems of the age (a poem which could not have been written in any other age), the *Exequy* of Bishop King, the extended comparison is used with perfect success: the idea and the simile become one, in the passage in which the Bishop illustrates his impatience to see his dead wife, under the figure of a journey."

It is only a few paragraphs later that Eliot argues that the "direct sensuous apprehension of thought" is not "a simple difference of degree between poets." Hence, if King's poem is peculiar to his age, and if the extended comparison is the means by which the idea and the simile succeed in becoming one, may not Williamson have inferred that it is the conceit which fuses thought and feeling? But if this is Eliot's meaning, then he has contradicted himself not only in the essay at large, but in the close confines of a single paragraph. For if he had the fusion, the sensuous apprehension, in mind here, he surely would not have said that heterogeneous materials are "compelled into unity," that such compelled unity is "omnipresent in poetry," that this omnipresent unity of contrasting ideas is, as illustrated by Johnson's verses, "different in degree but the same in principle," and that King's "extended comparison . . . illustrates . . . under the figure of a journey." It is in this passage of the essay that Eliot comes closest to suggesting that the conceit produces the fusion, but it must also be allowed that the passage maintains a considerable distance from the notion formulated by Williamson. In this part of the essay Eliot has not yet introduced the matter of thought and feeling. By the unity of "the idea and the simile" he means the unity of effect, the adequacy with which King's terminology of journeying suggests the quality of his impatience to see his dead wife in the hereafter. Indeed, Eliot observes that some of King's lines attain an "effect of terror." It is relevant, I think, to observe that in the verses of King quoted by Eliot there are two kinds of journeys, a sea-voyage and a military march, so that it could be said that the idea and the simile become one at least twice. As for thought and feeling, is impatience an idea or a feeling? Is a journey an idea or a feeling? Impatience is an emotional experience, and a journey is a physical experience, but in so far as they are brought together in an analogy, which is a mental experience, they are heterogeneous ideas.

III

That John Crowe Ransom has believed that the metaphysical conceit is the means by which thought and feeling are fused is not so readily discernible, but this is what I hope to show. He acquired this belief either from Williamson's or from his own interpretation of Eliot. It may be recalled that for Ransom — in the essays of *The World's Body* (1938) — metaphysical poetry was the best poetry, "the most original and exciting, and intellectually perhaps the most seasoned, that we know in our literature, and very probably it has few equivalents in other literatures." And the distinguishing characteristic of metaphysical poetry was the conceit, "a single extended metaphor to bear the whole weight of the conceptual structure." A question that emerges here is, Why does metaphor so employed produce the best kind of poetry? This is the question that Ransom pursued in several of the essays of *The World's Body*, and the answer, variously stated, is essentially that such metaphor fuses thought and feeling.

Toward the end of the essay "Poets without Laurels," he describes a kind of premodern poetry as "a mechanical mixture like lemonade" in which moral and aesthetic elements are mixed, and a kind of modern poetry as one from which the moral element has been excluded. Some poetry he describes as being not even a mixture, since "lumps of morality and image lie side by side, and are tasted in succession." The "best" kind of poetry he describes by an analogy with salt (sodium chloride), in which an atom of sodium and an atom of chlorine have been combined (fused) to form "a true chemical compound." Although in this essay there is no reference to metaphysical poetry, there can be no doubt that Ransom means that this poetry is the salt that does not lose its savor. But there is, after all, a kind of reference to metaphysical poetry, and it is one that reminds us directly that Ransom's thought here is close to that of Eliot's essay. "Lumps of morality and image lie side by side, and are tasted in succession. T. S. Eliot thinks that this has been the character of a great deal of English poetry since the age of Dryden." The reference is, of course, to the "dissociation of sensibility" — before which, the poets fused thought and feeling, and after which, "they thought and felt by fits, unbalanced."

The essential theme of Ransom's criticism at this time is more directly presented in another essay, "Poetry: A Note on Ontology" — which is a kind of critic's "Goldilocks and the Three Bears." Ransom distinguishes three kinds of poetry. There is Physical Poetry, the poetry of things, but it starves the intellect. There is Platonic Poetry, the poetry of ideas, but it starves the sensibility. And finally, of course, there is Metaphysical Poetry, and this is just right. But peculiarly enough, in discussing this third kind of poetry, Ransom does not make the seemingly inevitable statement that in metaphysical poetry there is a fusion of feeling and thought, or of things and ideas. He does, however, approach this notion toward the end of the essay. Here again, his mode of discourse is dialectical. First he considers that *metaphysical*, in its medieval and seventeenth-century usage, meant "supernatural" and "miraculous." Then he identifies metaphysical poetry with the conceit. And finally, he declares that the conceit produces the miraculous. "Specifically, the miraculism arises when the poet discovers by analogy an identity between objects which is partial, though it should be considerable, and proceeds to an identification which is complete." "Platonic Poetry is too idealistic, but Physical Poetry is too realistic, and realism is tedious and does not maintain interest. The poets therefore introduce the psychological device of the miracle." Ransom's assumption is that metaphor extended to a certain degree achieves the complete identification of the terms of the metaphor. And it is implied that the terms of the metaphor are the conceptual and the sensory, thought and feeling.

Ransom's discursive and terminological strategy suggests that there is an element in his argument that has been giving him trouble. If the fusion of thought and feeling were a notion that is negotiable in the conventional terms of rational argument, it would not be necessary to invoke a miracle in its behalf. That Ransom does invoke a miracle implies that the fusion has given him considerably greater pause than it did Eliot, Williamson, and other critics. It must have appeared to Ransom that thought and feeling, unlike sodium and chlorine, do not have an affinity for each other after all — indeed, so little affinity that their complete identification is not really explicable, except by a miracle. "The psychological device of the miracle" is a curious and precarious conclusion. The mouse of metaphor has been made to bring forth a mountain. And since when is a miracle psychological — rather than superpsychological, i.e., supernatural? Furthermore, if the miracle, the fusion, is the device, where in this pattern of thought is the conceit to be fitted? At this point Ransom can no longer tell the device from the devised. Like other critics, he has stumbled into the pitfall toward which Eliot had worn the path, confusing the rhetorical and stylistic elements of poetry with the effects of poetry.

That Ransom has all along had incipient misgivings about this subject of thought and feeling is suggested by the variety and tenacity of his approaches to it. In "Shakespeare at Sonnets," one of the later essays of *The World's Body*, these misgivings emerge.

"Metaphysical poetry has received in our time a new analytical attention, and for example from Professor Grierson. (Less formally if not less influentially from Mr. T. S. Eliot.) The revival of interest in this poetry evidently suits the taste of our post-romantic generation. And Professor Grierson says in many places that what Donne does is to combine intellect and passion. But no poet would find that a practicable formula; and we may well shiver with apprehension lest theory, or the aesthetic of poetry, waver and relax and perish under such a definition. The primary business of theorists is to direct their analyses of poetry to what is objective in it, or cognitive, and they will always be safe in assuming if they like that behind any external body of knowledge there will have been feeling enough, possibly amounting to passion, to have attended the subject through his whole exercise."

It is my impression that Eliot has been not only more influential than Grierson in the matter of thought and feeling, but has also treated it with more apparent formality and more frequently. Be that as it may, it is clear that for Ransom the fusion of thought and feeling was no longer an attractive or even a tenable notion, not a "practicable formula" for either the poet or the critic — and I assume that the issue was the same, whether feeling meant passion or sensation. But it is obvious in the essay that Ransom still held that the conceit is the staple of metaphysical poetry and the cause of its superiority, for it is the conceit which accounts for the superiority of Donne's lyrics over Shakespeare's sonnets — and also for superiority among the sonnets. But if the conceit is no longer the means of fusing thought and feeling, what is its unique virtue? At one point, Ransom says, "A metaphysical poem is an intellectual labor, and all the intellect may be active in it, but it is under the presidency of the imagination." In most of the essay, however, this president is like the president of France, and it is the intellect which is like the premier, exercising all the power and getting all the attention.

To Donne's credit and at Shakespeare's expense, much is made of the logical rigor, structural discipline and systematic presentation which are produced by the conceit. Yet such qualities do not give a very full picture of poetry and are not its exclusive properties. So in the part of the essay in which this problem is confronted, Ransom considers again the matter of feeling.

". . . These poets at their best perform complete actions, very likely by means of metaphysical poems. So, on the one hand, there is an associationist poetry, a half-way action providing many charming places for the feelings to agitate themselves; and, on the other hand, there is a metaphysical poetry which elects its line of action and goes straight through to the completion of the cycle and extinction of the feelings.

"This gives us associationist poetry *versus*, I think, behavioristic. For our discussion seems to have turned psychological. If romantic poets are not fully aware of what they are doing, metaphysical poets are self-conscious and deliberate, and in fact they are very like technical psychologists. They start with feelings, they objectify these imaginatively into external actions. They think that poetry, just as behavioristic psychologists think that psychology, can make nothing out of feelings as they stand."

This is to assume a great deal about what the poets thought (and incidentally, it is also to assume that the poetry is autobiographical — which would make it romantic by some standards). And to extinguish the feelings is, indeed, to "make nothing" out of them. The feelings, so troublesome for the theorist, have been got rid of by the poets, and they have done this with their conceits, which are, of course, the "complete actions." This alleged function of the conceit seemed for Ransom to be just as valuable as its "logical rigor." Indeed, the "logical rigor" seems to be not merely, or even sufficiently, valuable in itself, but because it produces the "extinction of the feelings."

One might ask why the conceit (the single extended metaphor) should make the feelings any more extinct than does a series of associated metaphors, or whether the poets who start with feelings are properly analogous to the behavioristic psychologists who, I believe, restrict their considerations to the realm of behavior. But there are matters here of more basic import. Why, for example, should the poets be affected by the limitations of aesthetic theorists and of psychologists in regard to feelings? And why is the extinction of feeling superior to the lack of extinction? This question leads to another, the most fruitful question of all: is there not something very familiar about the extinction of feelings? My answer is, yes — that it is a version of the familiar doctrine that the poet relieves or purges himself of feelings by means of his poems. This doctrine, which is widely held, is perhaps best known in the form given it by romantic poets. There is Shelley's "Our sweetest songs are those that tell of saddest thought," and Heine's

> Aus meinen grossen Schmerzen
> Mach' ich die kleinen Lieder.

Donne speaks similarly in *The Triple Foole*:

> Grief brought to numbers cannot be so fierce
> For, he tames it, that fetters it in verse.
>
>   But when I have done so,
> Some man, his art and voice to show,
>   Doth Set and sing my paine,
> And by delighting many, frees againe
>   Griefe, which verse did restraine.
> To Love, and Griefe tribute of Verse belongs,
> But not of such as pleases when 'tis read,
>   Both are increased by such songs:
> For both their triumphs so are published,
> And I, which was two fooles, do so grow three;
> Who are a little wise, the best fooles bee.

In so far as Donne's lines imply anything relevant to the issue, they imply that the feelings are not made extinct, either in the poet or in the poem. That they are made extinct in the poem is Ransom's meaning, and the meaning is acceptable if it means no more than that the poet has unburdened himself of the feelings by bringing them under control within the poem, thus objectifying and externalizing them. But Ransom seems to mean that there are no traces of feeling left. Yet if, as he says, the poets "objectify these into external actions," are not the feelings transferred, translated, transformed rather than extinguished or annihilated? If they are transformed, what is their new form? Elsewhere in the essay, Ransom says that a metaphysical poem is an "intellectual construction." So, if the poet starts with feelings and concludes with an intellectual construction, it may then be said that the feelings have been transformed into an intellectual construction. In other words there has been — a fusion of thought and feeling.

In the earlier essays Ransom moved directly toward the notion of the fusion of thought and feeling, but when he was on the

verge of confronting it and naming it, he resorted to indirec-
tions, as if the naked fusion were somehow embarrassing and
intellectually indecent. In the later essay, he proposed that both
poets and critics would do well to be disembarrassed of the
fusion, since this definition is not a "practicable formula." But
the conceit still maintained its earlier supremacy, for it had become the disposer of the feelings, bringing them to extinction. We
have seen, however, that Ransom's argument is haunted by a
wily and vigorous ghost, and it is the ghost of the feelings. It
seemed to Ransom that the conceit could be better exalted as an
exterminator than as a fuser. But it was not a successful exterminator, for it only chased the feelings deeper into the thoughts, where
they lay concealed but not extinct, just as the notion of fusion by
conceit lay concealed in Ransom's thinking.

This notion did not, however, remain concealed. In his next
book, *The New Criticism* (1941), Ransom finally called the notion
by its name, faced it directly at its source in Eliot (with no mention of Grierson), and found it neither "credible" nor "intelligible." In this book there is a chapter on Eliot, and in the chapter
a section of over seventeen pages on Eliot's essay "The Metaphysical Poets." And the main preoccupation of the section is the subject of the fusion of thought and feeling. On this subject Ransom
made the following significant remarks:

"I confess that I know very little about that; and I must add that,
having worked to the best of my ability to find the thing Eliot
refers to in the 17th Century poets, and failed, I incline to think
there was nothing of the kind there. I have often tried — as what
critic has not — to find some description of poetry which would
regard it as a single unified experience, and exempt it from the
dilemma of logic; but we must not like some philosophers become
the fools of the shining but impractical ideal of 'unity' or of
'fusion.' The aspiration here is for some sort of fusion of two experiences that ordinarily repel one another: the abstracted exercise
of reason in hard fact and calculation; and the inclusive experience of literally everything at once. But we cannot have our
theory magical and intelligible at the same time. For it would
seem that from that precise moment when the race discovers
that what has seemed to be an undifferentiated unity is really a

complex of specialized functions, there can be no undifferentiated unity again; no return. We do not know quite how to feel
a thought. The best we can do is to conduct a thought without
denying all the innocent or irrelevant feelings in the process.
The dualism remains."

And in the next paragraph he remarks:

"But I think we must waive the psychological magic involved in
the act of feeling our thought in honor of something tamer and
more credible: the procedure of suspending the course of the
main thought while we explore the private character of the detail
items."

In this section and in the book at large there is considerable
concern with the feelings, but there is no longer any contention
that the feelings are brought to extinction by the metaphysical
conceit. Indeed, in this book Ransom was no longer impelled to
claim that the metaphysical conceit produced the best kind of
poetry. The exclusive standard of superiority seems to have been
integrally related to the fusion of thought and feeling, for with
the conscious and logical rejection of the one, the other was no
longer urged. It is significant that the Index to *The New Criticism* has no entry for "conceit," while it has numerous entries for
"structure" and "texture." It is in these latter terms that Ransom
pursued and has been pursuing the problems of poetic theory:
"the poem is a loose logical structure with an irrelevant local texture." This is the proposition that Ransom has been exploring.
While the function of the conceit, whether for fusion or extinction, was no longer the issue, it is appropriate to observe that the
logical structure suggests the thought and the local texture suggests the feeling.

IV

I have examined Ransom's work in detail and at length because
of his status and position as a critic, and because his criticism exhibits so clearly the effects which Eliot's responses to Donne's
poetry have had on modern criticism. For a further illustration of
these effects, I shall consider briefly one more critic, Cleanth
Brooks. It may be recalled that Eliot, in his essay "The Metaphysi-

cal Poets" had claimed that metaphysical poetry represented the original and essential tradition of English poetry, with the implication that later poetry represented an aberration or lapse from this tradition. Corollary to this claim was Eliot's statement to the effect that the two poetries differed not merely in degree but in kind. Brooks' criticism has often been an effort to apply the claim about the essential tradition, but to escape somehow from the implication and the corollary. Brooks differs here significantly from Ransom, for whereas Ransom tended to narrow the grounds of taste marked off by Eliot, Brooks tended to enlarge them.

In his first book, *Modern Poetry and the Tradition* (1939), Brooks said, "Our definition of metaphysical poetry, then, will have to treat the difference between metaphysical poetry and other poetry as a difference of degree, not of kind." And yet, in so much of Brooks' criticism, this difference of degree has tended to become a difference of kind. We can illustrate this by turning to his second book, *The Well Wrought Urn* (1947). The book opens with this sentence: "Few of us are prepared to accept the statement that the language of poetry is the language of paradox." This is a characteristically bold statement, for the thesis of the book is that the language of poetry is, indeed, the language of paradox. If Brooks had said that the language of Donne's poetry is the language of paradox, it is likely that more than a few of us would be prepared to accept the statement. The shocking suggestion contained in Brooks' actual statement is that much of the poetry written since the seventeenth century is, after all, like Donne's in a certain basic respect.

What Brooks has been attempting is to effect a compromise between the modern votaries of Donne and those who hold a more conventional or "old-fashioned" view of poetry. In order to establish Donne firmly as a major figure in the familiar (albeit miscellaneous) galaxy of Shakespeare, Milton, Herrick, Pope, Gray, Wordsworth, Keats, Tennyson, and Yeats, he has viewed these figures from a perspective according to which Donne's poetry is the most obviously and most firmly fixed. Toward the end of *The Well Wrought Urn* Brooks said that "the intervening poems were

to be read as one has learned to read Donne and the moderns."
For all the admirable openness of this statement, there is ground
for suspicion that something has been slipped in the back door,
and there is even some confusion as to what is the back door and
what is the front door. While Brooks' readings of the various poets
are without exception skillful and rewarding, I propose that there
is a limited value to the idea that the language of Milton or Pope
or Wordsworth is basically the language of paradox. The idea is
limited to the primacy which it gives to the poetry of Donne, for
as Brooks insists, it is Donne's poetry which gives unity to his book.
It is this primacy of Donne's poetry which makes the difference of
degree very much like a difference of kind, for it is hard to conceive of the book being reorganized with Milton or Pope or Wordsworth as the fixed point of reference.

To put the case extremely, it could be said that while Brooks
would appear to be ushering all the other poets in the front door
of a tradition of poetry, he is actually slipping Donne in the back
door. By this I would mean not that Donne is a back-door poet,
but that the idea of the tradition has been a convenient fiction for
a certain mode of criticism. And by saying fiction I do not mean
that theories and readings of Brooks and other critics have been
fallacious, but rather that the fixed Donnean perspective has produced disproportionate emphases. Brooks' essay "Milton and the
New Criticism" (*The Sewanee Review*, Winter, 1951) is an example of such emphasis. I quote from this essay.

"Our age rejoices in having recovered Donne; but in doing so we
have recovered not just Donne's poetry, but poetry. This is so generally true that for many of us the quality of poetry — as distinguished from that of the more empty rhetorics — is bound up with
functional metaphor, with dramatic tension, and with the fusion
of thought and emotion — qualities which we associate with the
poetry of Donne. Small wonder then if we try to find these qualities, or comparable qualities, in the work of anyone to whom we
give the name of poet."

This statement is admirable for the clarity with which it indicates
Brooks' position. And the position is one in which a disproportionate emphasis is given to Donne's poetry, for Brooks implies that

Donne's is the very archetype of poetry. I am confident that Brooks does not really believe that Donne's is the *ne plus ultra* of poetry, and yet his critical practice makes exactly this implication. In the essay, there are astute analyses of Milton's poetry, and to my view there is nothing "wrong" with any of his conclusions. But the general effect of the essay is wrong. Instead of throwing light on Milton where Milton *is* (wherever that may be), Brooks has attempted to lodge Milton with Donne, and to do this not through the door, but — so to speak — through the keyhole. As a result, much of Milton remains outside the door. This is admitted by Brooks in one way and another. As his title indicates, his concern was with the defense of a critical position as well as with the examination of Milton. However frankly admitted, it is finally a disturbing concern. We are left feeling that Milton has been submitted to certain critical principles rather than allowed to yield them — that the honor which the critic has bestowed on Milton was borrowed from Donne and will have to be returned, to Donne and to the critical position. As for the position itself, some of its sources are the claims Eliot had made for the metaphysical poets: their unified sensibility and their centrality in the literary tradition. In the passage quoted from Brooks, we will have noted the phrase "the fusion of thought and emotion." The phrase is appropriate enough to its immediate context, but in the larger context of modern criticism, it is redolent of confusion.

V

In Eliot's essay and in the critical thought which it has fostered there is a logical relationship between the notion of thought and feeling fused in the poetry, and the claim that the poets possessed a unified sensibility. Now it is a truism of history that the Middle Ages, an era in which religious faith was pervasive, gave way to the Renaissance and the modern era of secularism, of rational and empirical inquiry. The philosophers, Bacon, Hobbes, and Locke, particularly mark this development in the course of English culture. Loosely speaking, Eliot's phrase "a dissociation of sensibility" may be allowed to signify the changes that have occurred in the intellectual climate and cultural conditions of Western society. But this phrase and related phrases and concepts have not been used loosely, but rigidly and with an intimation of precision, especially with regard to poetry and poetic theory, so that difficulties have arisen. Where explanations and clarifications were intended, puzzles and obfuscations have been produced.

One of these puzzles, that of the fusion, we have already examined at length. But the question of the sensibility is no less puzzling than the fusions which it is presumed to have achieved. Some of the difficulty has stemmed, I believe, from Eliot's phrase "mechanism of sensibility." This is a peculiar metaphor which seems to invite logical pressure but which cannot sustain the pressure when it is applied. A mechanism suggests an organ or instrument which is either in repair or in disrepair. And Eliot's remarks, his distinction between kinds and degrees, suggest something approaching a biological mutation of species; whereas all he can reasonably mean with his terminology about sensibility — unified, mechanism, dissociation, etc. — is, to speak more loosely, that there is a habit of utterance, reflecting a habit of mind, which can be practiced in more or less degree. Eliot's own habit of utterance is relevant here, for he is often given to analogies which have a sharpness and strength of emphasis but which, after the first shocking impact, diminish in cogency under a calmer scrutiny. By a lucky accident, I have hit on this example in his essay "Philip Massinger" (1920), only after I had already written the presently obvious sentence above: "But every vital development in language is a development of feeling as well. The verse of Shakespeare and the major Shakespearean dramatists is an innovation of this kind, a true mutation of species." Eliot's use of the word *true* here suggests, as Ransom might say, that Eliot had the courage of his metaphors. But in criticism such courage, while it is momentarily appealing, is not enough — or is too much. By "species" Eliot could mean poets or poetry or both. That there is actually such confusion is proved by a statement which I notice a few paragraphs later in the essay: "Had Massinger had a nervous system as refined as that of Middleton, Tourneur, Webster, or Ford, his style would be a triumph." This statement should be considered shocking in a way that Eliot never intended. The implication is that Massinger did not share in the mutation represented by Shakespeare, or that with the appearance of Massinger the race suffered still another mutation — of the nervous system!

But to return to the metaphysical poets and their unified sensibility. There is this difficulty. Donne and certainly Marvell — the two poets most frequently cited with respect to the issues — came when the Renaissance, the dawn of the modern era, was already well under way. Donne was contemporary with Bacon, and Marvell with Hobbes. Would not, then, a unified sensibility in these poets be an anachronism? Unfortunately, I cannot give the actual sources, but I have a clear impression that Eliot and other critics have anticipated this question and have answered: Yes, it is an anachronism; sensibility had begun to disintegrate, but in poets like Donne and Marvell we have the last lingering instances of a unity that had once been general and pervasive. Such, of course, would be the case, if Donne and Marvell actually had that special kind of sensibility. But we might agree with Ransom's final view of the matter: "I incline to think there was nothing of the kind there." There was no unique fusion in the poetry, and there was no utter unity in the poets. The unity, like the fusion, has been an effect of seventeenth-century poetry on modern readers, and not a condition of the seventeenth-century poets. I suggest that the poetry of Donne and Marvell reflects not a pre-existing unity in the poets, but rather an urgent search for unity by the poets. Such a search is, I think, more familiar and conceivable than the sensory-mental unity proposed by Eliot. That this search for unity is peculiarly appropriate to the times of Donne and Marvell could be explored at length by relating it to the course of English philosophy as instigated by Bacon, to the efforts of the Cambridge Platonists, to the development of styles and themes in the work of Shakespeare and Milton, and to other matters as well. But having merely suggested these relations, I shall turn to the poetry of Donne and Marvell for evidence of the search for unity.

It may be recalled that Donne's love poetry is concerned, often wittily, with the traditional dualism of body and soul, or of body and mind. Some poems, such as *Loves Alchymie*, scorn "the loving wretch that sweares, / 'Tis not the bodies marry, but the mindes." Other poems, such as *The Undertaking*, urge the contrary:

> But he who lovelinesse within
> Hath found, all outward loathes,
> For he who colour loves, and skinne,
> Loves but their oldest clothes.

Still other poems claim for the lovers, but not for mankind in general, a transcending unity of body and soul. The effort to escape from, or to qualify, the dualism of Christian and Platonic doctrine is most clearly illustrated by *The Extasie*, a poem often cited as an example of the fusion of thought and feeling and of the unified sensibility. But actually, does not the speaker of the poem struggle through an arduous pseudo-logical dialectic in order to arrive at the lover's mystique of a unified sensibility? The poem ends,

> Loves mysteries in soules do grow,
> But yet the body is his booke.
> And if some lover, such as wee,
> Have heard this dialogue of one,
> Let him still marke us, he shall see
> Small change, when we'are to bodies gone.

The unity of soul and soul, and then of body and body, and finally of body and soul, is offered as something fittingly remarkable for the climactic conclusion of the poem.

There is surely no need to argue that the conclusion of the poem was meant to be remarkable, and yet it is relevant to note that Pierre Legouis considered the poem merely a literary and witty seduction — perhaps like *The Flea*, only more subtle and complex — with the lover speaking earnestly of souls to the lady while he leads her nearer and nearer the bed or persuades her to recline among the violets. I propose that Legouis vastly oversimplified rather than wholly misread the poem, for I believe that Legouis' view is partially justified by the subtly poised complexity in the tone of the poem. After all, Donne did not make the conclusion of the poem *too* remarkable. Where he said "Small change," he could quite as well have said "No change," and the difference here between "small" and "no" may be neither greater nor less than the distance between the tongue and the cheek. In any event, the unified sensibility is the goal toward which the poem drives rather than the post from which it started.

A comparable unity is indicated by *The Blossome*, which is otherwise a very different kind of poem from *The Extasie*. In *The Blossome* the speaker lectures his "naked thinking heart" on the fruitlessness of its commitment to an unsympathetic lady, and on the folly of the heart's continued attendance on the lady while the speaker has himself proceeded to London. The poem ends,

> I would give you
> There, to another friend, whom we shall finde
> As glad to have my body, as my minde.

Although *The Blossome* is a simpler poem than *The Extasie* in some respects, it is more complicated in others. For example, *The Blossome* shows not only the body-mind problem in the relations of the sexes, but also the heart-mind (i.e., feelings-mind) disunity within the speaker. Hence, the speaker of *The Blossome* is seeking not only a totality of personal relations with a woman, but also a unification of sensibility within himself. I would call attention to the fact that both poems are, among other things, arguments in behalf of the body — not opposing the body to the mind or the soul, but acknowledging rather the validity of its claims and the propriety of the body in the total human experience. And I would propose that such argument, by its larger implications, reveals that Donne shared to an extent that mode of thought and that complex of values which have been called Renaissance Humanism, and which was itself a search for unity. Other poems of Donne — such as *The Good Morrow, The Canonization, Twicknam Garden, The Relique* — would have yielded these observations, ultimately if not so conveniently. One of my conclusions in the preceding essay is that complexity of attitudes characterizes all of Donne's love poems, and this complexity of attitudes might otherwise be stated as a preoccupation with the unity-disunity problem.

These observations on Donne apply even more readily to Marvell, for he has treated the subjects of dualism and of unity more directly. Some of Marvell's poems are wholly traditional with respect to the dualism of body and soul. In *A Dialogue between the Resolved Soul and Created Pleasure*, the soul rejects, and hence triumphs over, the pleasurable temptations of the material world. *On a Drop of Dew* presents the dew-drop, in its precarious and tangential relation to the flower, as emblematic of the soul's relation to the body; both dew-drop and soul reflect the purity of their Christian-Platonic pre-existent state, and they desire to return "Into the Glories of th'Almighty Sun." Other poems depart from the traditional dualism which gives priority to the soul. While the familiar opposition between body and soul is maintained in *A Dialogue between the Soul and Body*, the body is permitted to make a sympathetic argument for its own claims by way of rebuttal against the complaints of the soul. In this poem Marvell has wittily, and significantly, given the last word in the debate to the body, and the poem ends,

> What but a Soul could have the wit
> To build me up for Sin so fit?
> So Architects do square and hew
> Green Trees that in the Forest grew.

Although the poem is directly based on the traditional dualism of the body-soul conflict, the search for unity along humanistic lines is implied by Marvell's distortion of the familiar argument in order to give a favorable emphasis to the claims of the body — thus introducing, if not yet a unity, at least a balance where previously imbalance had been the rule. There is, moreover, a kind of unity, or desire for unity, expressed in the last lines spoken by the body. These imply an acceptable and desirable oneness of mankind with the world of created nature.

This idea of man's unity with nature is the theme that runs through Marvell's poems about the Mower, but it is the famous *Garden* which shows most clearly and most fully the quest for the unified sensibility. It must be noted that the body-soul dualism is present in this poem, for eventually the soul casts "the Bodies Vest aside" in order to enter the boughs of a tree, where "like a Bird

it sits, and sings." But in order to do this the soul was first conveyed
by the body into the context of nature, as represented by the
garden. The entrance into the garden and the oneness with nature
are developed in the first five stanzas without any body-soul reference. Then in the sixth stanza there is the withdrawal of the mind
into itself, and thus the unity with nature has operated as a preparation for the unity within the self. Is not this intricate unity part
of the meaning of the famous lines with which the stanza ends?

> Annihilating all that's made
> To a green Thought in a green Shade.

The world of created nature, "all that's made," has been annihilated by the mind in the respect that it has been transformed
into a "green Thought." The earlier absorption into the state of
nature is followed by the absorption of nature into a state of mind.
And this development is not that of progression from one point to
another in a straight line, but that of a circle forever circling. The
greenness of the thought signifies, among other things, that nature
has been absorbed into the mind, but "in a green Shade" signifies
that the mind is still absorbed into nature. All this may be loosely
stated in familiar language without any essential distortion of
meaning: a man is at one with himself when he is at one with
nature.

It is in the seventh stanza that the soul leaves the body in order
to sit, like a bird, among the boughs of a tree. Here again I would
suggest that we do not get a "linear progression" in the development of the poem. By this I mean that the soul in the boughs has
already been anticipated by the Thought in the Shade and that
both conceptions equally signify the absorption into nature. It is
true that the stanza ends by stating in effect that the soul is preparing for "longer flight" into Platonic realms of pure Being, but
I would suggest that the soul's position among the boughs, its
absorption into nature, is precisely this preparation. According
to this interpretation, the "various Light" waved in the plumes
of the soul refers to the gradations of light and shade that filter
through the boughs. The Light is, of course, the light of (Platonic)
Truth, and the shade that I have inferred would be, again, the

"green Shade" of nature, which is also a variety of light, and hence of truth. It is my impression that Marvell's use of the Platonic reference is on the order of a "device" and that the essential subject of the poem is that of unity with and within nature. I find my impression enforced by the eighth stanza, where the poem turns from Platonic to biblical references, from Platonic Light to the earthly paradise.

> Such was that happy Garden-state,
> While Man there walk'd without a Mate:
>
> . . . .
>
> Two Paradises 'twere in one
> To live in Paradise alone.

Marvell is saying here, with obvious wittiness, that the state of nature is the ideal state of innocence, and that such innocence is at once self-sufficient and exclusively all possessing — a unity of being that is indeed Paradise enough. The wittiness which attends this meaning implies the comment that our long-lost innocence is an ideal which man may conceive but not a condition that he can experience at so late a date as the seventeenth century. The "green Thought" has been the most memorable expression in the poem. It is evidence neither of the fusion of thought and feeling nor of the unified sensibility, but rather of the fact that such notions were as startling, as attractive and as effective in the seventeenth century as they have been in ours.

VI

This extended discussion of fusion and unity would be less justified if these were matters that had been restricted to a certain stage of Eliot's literary criticism alone. Actually, they have figured less frequently, less persistently and less systematically in Eliot's criticism than in that of others, and they have reverberated widely long after they were quieted at their source.* This fact gives rise

* Eliot's statement, in *A Garland for John Donne* (1931), that there was already a "deep fissure" in Donne's sensibility is confusing. On the one hand it is an effort to maintain Eliot's theory of the unified sensibility; on the other it brings it into question, since it retracts some of the evidence on which the theory was originally based. In any event, the statement shows that Eliot developed misgivings about his earlier position on the metaphysical poets.

to two questions: (1) Why did the notion of unity appeal so strongly to Eliot at a certain stage of his critical career? (2) Why has the notion appealed so widely and so persistently to other critics? To both of these questions there is an obvious, and therefore not very impressive, answer — which is merely that unity is, by its very nature, as the ultimate reduction and clarification, intellectually appealing. Without attempting anything approaching a full account, I shall make some observations which are, I trust, of a less obvious nature. I shall begin with the first question, and I shall consider this question in regard to the fusion that is assumed in the poetry rather than the unity that is assumed in the poets.

Eliot is notoriously and, I believe, admittedly, lacking in the extended systematic organization of ideas. My proposition is that the various expressions in Eliot's criticism, and especially in "The Metaphysical Poets," which signify the fusion of thought and feeling represented a discrete (or relatively incidental) preoccupation of Eliot's thought rather than a genuinely systemic inclination of his thought. The preoccupation was this: language which successfully (for Eliot) renders the very quality of experience (especially of such experience as Eliot approved or liked). In any of Eliot's expressions of the fusion — for example, "there is a direct sensuous apprehension of thought, or a recreation of thought into feeling" — the virtue lies not so much in bringing the thought to the feeling as it does in bringing the feeling to the thought. It would, I think, be generally allowed that feeling is more readily equatable with experience than is thought, and herein lies the virtue of feeling and of the fusion of thought and feeling.

This preoccupation, that the poet's purpose is to convey by means of language what it feels like to have a thought or any other experience, is intimated at many points in the essay.

"The possible interests of a poet are unlimited; the more intelligent he is the better; the more intelligent he is the more likely that he will have interests; our only condition is that he turn them into poetry, and not merely meditate on them poetically. A philosophical theory which has entered into poetry is established, for its truth or falsity in one sense ceases to matter, and its truth in another sense is proved. The poets in question have, like other poets, various faults. But they were, at best, engaged in the task of trying to find the verbal equivalent for states of mind and feeling."

"Our civilization comprehends great variety and complexity, and this variety and complexity, playing upon a refined sensibility, must produce various and complex results. The poet must become more and more comprehensive, more allusive, more indirect, in order to force, to dislocate, if necessary, language into his meaning."

I shall restate and extend some of these remarks in such a way as to indicate their bearing on my proposition. In the first passage, the philosophical theory is established and proved true not in the usual sense, not as a theory. It is established and proved true as an experience by having "entered into poetry." The poet turns his interests or theories into poetry not when he "merely meditates on them poetically" but when he successfully renders the quality of an experience, what it feels like to have the interests or the theories. The final statement of the passage has the same import. The metaphysical poets who were "engaged in the task of trying to find" something hardly sound like the same people who had "a direct sensuous apprehension of thought," although they may have achieved something like the "recreation of thought into feeling." What they sought was "the verbal equivalent for states of mind and feeling." By states of mind here Eliot scarcely meant thoughts or theories, for these are inconceivable apart from "verbal equivalents." "State of mind" is an idiomatic expression commonly signifying a mood, an emotional condition, a temper of consciousness. It is interesting to note that Eliot used the same phrase a bit later in the essay, stating that certain "poets . . . have the same essential quality of transmuting ideas into sensations, of transforming an observation into a state of mind." The second product here is, significantly, not "ideas," but the idiomatic and ambiguous "state of mind." In the second passage, the modern poets who have to force and dislocate language do not seem to "feel their thought as immediately as the odour of a rose" any more than Tennyson and Browning did. If the "meaning" exists before the verbal equivalent has been discovered, it is because the

meaning is not a detachable or translatable idea, but an experience, a feeling, and what the poet wants is "the verbal equivalent," language which is appropriately evocative of the quality of
an experience.

Comparable instances of expression are to be found in other
early essays of Eliot. I shall consider a few of these, beginning with
one from "Philip Massinger." "And, indeed, with the end of
Chapman, Middleton, Webster, Tourneur, Donne we end a period
when the intellect was immediately at the tips of the senses. Sensation became word and word was sensation." At this point I hope
it is permissible to forego analysis of Eliot's terms and to declare
that this version of the fusion of thought and feeling implies again
the "verbal equivalent for states of mind." Discussing the publication of *Miscellaneous Poems* by Marvell in 1923, Eliot compared
with a conceit of Marvell these lines from Shakespeare's *Antony
and Cleopatra*:

> She looks like sleep,
> As she would catch another Antony
> In her strong toil of grace.

Eliot said of this passage: ". . . it is not a conceit. For instead of
contrast we have fusion: a restoration of language to contact with
things." In the Massinger essay he had said of this same passage
that it illustrates "a gift for combining, for fusing into a single
phrase, two or more diverse impressions. . . . the metaphor identifies itself with what suggests it." It is incidentally interesting to
note that Eliot attributed fusion to a passage which he did not regard as a conceit — although the distinction between contrast and
fusion in one statement is not clearly consistent with the "fusing
. . . diverse impressions" in the other. More immediately relevant
is the implication made by both statements that fusion characterizes the kind of language which renders the object of experience.
This Shakespearean touchstone is quoted yet again in another essay, "Dante" (1929), and in a context where Eliot's concern is the
poet's "attempt to make us see what he saw."

The famous "objective correlative" in "Hamlet and His Problems" (1919) contains the same meaning as the other statements

considered here. "The only way of expressing emotion in the form of art is by finding an 'objective correlative'; in other words, a set of objects, a situation, a chain of events which shall be the formula of that *particular* emotion; such that when the external facts, which must terminate in sensory experience, are given, the emotion is immediately evoked." There is already a "body of criticism" on this statement. I would only note that it says, among other things, that the art of the poet consists in the evocation of experience — and language must obviously be the medium, the ultimate "formula," of such evocation. As a final and relatively simple example of Eliot's preoccupation, I offer this sentence from his essay "Swinburne as Poet" (1920): "Language in a healthy state presents the object, is so close to the object that the two are identified." However blurred may be the distinctions and relations among thought, feeling, sensation, emotion, language, conceit, metaphor, object, experience, etc., when Eliot's numerous statements on these matters are assembled and compared, there is one meaning that runs through all the statements and that emerges clearly: the poet's language renders the quality of the experience. Eliot's several variations on this theme have produced difficulties and controversies in modern criticism, and I believe that these troubles may be partially accounted for by taking note of certain stylistic habits in Eliot's own criticism.

Although frequently analytical in some respects, Eliot's prose, like the poetry he admires, tends itself to evoke experience, and this practice is at times not in accord with the clarification of ideas. Eliot's prose mixes, confuses, appreciation with analysis, because it attempts not only to clarify an idea about the nature of poetry but at the same time to evoke a "literary" experience. In all of the statements recently quoted Eliot said in effect that language becomes identical with emotion or sensation or an object. Such expression is a generalized but nonetheless loose and appreciative account of particular "reader" experiences, as when we might say that Shakespeare's lines present the very body of the dead Cleopatra. Eliot's comment, "the metaphor identifies itself with what suggests it," is on this order of "reader" response, only more general. It is half analysis and half exclamation — indeed, a kind of fusion of thought and feeling. Eliot has said in one way and another that the poet's language is the equivalent of experience. To have said that the poet's language is potentially capable of evoking for a reader the quality of experience would have been less misleading, to himself and others, but it would also have been less emphatic and less exciting.

Eliot has said, on more than one occasion, that a poet's criticism of other poets is often intimately related to his own poetry. This is notably true for Eliot himself. The preoccupation considered here is especially well illustrated by his own work, from *Prufrock* to *Little Gidding*. Most of Eliot's nondramatic poetry is itself dramatic and experiential not only in its subject and tone but also in the very lineaments of its form. This point may be emphasized by recalling that so formalistic a critic as Yvor Winters has charged that Eliot's work, particularly *The Waste Land*, is guilty of "the fallacy of imitative form." By this expression Winters meant that Eliot and other modern poets contrived poetic forms which were intended to simulate the arbitrariness and disorder of the experiences and situations which were the subject matter of the poems, whereas they should have, in accordance with the proper function of art, imposed order on disorder. Winters' charge may be countered simply by rejecting the validity of his word *fallacy* and by replacing it with such a word as *technique* — and also by reference to the history of poetic taste and practice in the twentieth century, as well as by the familiar maxim that nothing succeeds like success. But Winters' phrase "imitative form" is a valuable perception and expression, especially for my purposes, since it calls attention to the close relation between Eliot's poetry and his critical preoccupation with "language . . . so close to the object that the two are identified." It also points toward this observation: that some primary concerns of Eliot's early criticism, however variously stated, are essentially the adaptation of Aristotle's doctrine of *mimesis*, according to which art is an imitation of nature. This remains the fact, whether Eliot was or was not aware of it. In calling for "verbal equivalents" of thoughts, emotions, sensations, and objects, he was urging the doctrine of *mimesis* as a principle of poetic practice. When he asked that poetry fuse thought, emotion, sensation (an awareness of external particulars) into language, he was asking that poetry "imitate" the inclusive totality of human experience — that it imitate the fullness of human nature.

In Eliot's concept and terminology of the language of fusion there are combined two familiar ideas. One of these is the fullness of human nature, apprehended in his expression "unified sensibility" — a concept which I have re-located, so to speak, as the search for unity. The other is the doctrine of *mimesis*. When combined, these familiar ideas produce the principle that the poet's effort is a search for unity, an attempt to create a faithful imitation of the fullness of human experience. And this can otherwise be stated as the effort to evoke verbally the quality of human experience. The combination has been, I think, more valuable for Eliot's own poetry than for his criticism. But in the criticism the ideas, however familiar, were reinterpreted and refreshed by the combination. If Eliot's critical statements have put excessive figurative pressure upon the ideas, while failing to reveal them clearly, then this is the very practice that has given provocativeness and depth of implication to both the statements and the ideas.

VII

I would turn now to the question of why Eliot's concepts of the unified sensibility and of the language of fusion appealed so widely and so persistently to other critics. My account of the appeal to Eliot himself is presumably part of the answer to this question. Not intending to explore the full complexity of the subject, I should like to add another partial answer. This will begin with the observation that the concepts did not originate with Eliot. I refer here not to such doctrines as *mimesis* but to formulations like that of Grierson — "the peculiar blend of passion and thought, feeling and ratiocination" — in his Introduction to *Metaphysical Lyrics and Poems of the Seventeenth Century*. Although it is likely that Grierson's remarks had some influence on Eliot, it is not correct to regard them as his "source." Grierson's book first appeared and was reviewed by Eliot in 1921, but Eliot was already speaking of "intellect . . . immediately at the tips of the senses" in 1920 in his essay "Philip Massinger." If one were seeking a source of convenient date, it might be found in some remarks made by Arthur Clutton-Brock in 1918. Clutton-Brock was reviewing a book called *The Best of Both Worlds: Poems of Spirit and Sense,* which was a selection from Vaughan and Marvell made by Francis Meynell.* Clutton-Brock took for his theme the title of the book, and the idea of the fusion of sense and spirit runs through his essay:

"The very title is a light thrown on the virtues of these two poets. . . . Between them, they prove that there is a quality common to both worlds because it is common to them. It was, indeed, the virtue of their age to be aware of this common quality. Many more then thought and felt in terms of both worlds; and neither religion nor science had set up a partition between them. . . . The best amateur poetry of the seventeenth century escapes from convention and dares the utmost absurdities in its freedom; but the most absurd of them, Benlowes himself, can think with the beauty of passion and feel with the precision of thought. . . . If you have the sense of beauty, which is a sense, your spirit is aware of the spirit of beauty."

Both the unified sensibility and the fusion of thought and feeling are explicit in these remarks. That Eliot had read the essay in the *Times Literary Supplement* is altogether possible, so it is conceivable that the essay had some influence upon him. But there is no certainty of this, and no need for certainty. My point is that while the concepts did not originate with Eliot, neither was there any immediate source for them. They were, as the expression goes, "in the air." Similar concepts had been prevalent among the Romantic poets, from Blake to Keats, and it was of course Coleridge who gave them formulations which were to reverberate through the nineteenth century and into our own. In seeking to justify the role of the poet, Coleridge had celebrated that power of the imagination which "reveals itself in the balance or reconciliation

* For my awareness of Clutton-Brock's essay, and of Eliot's early essays in the *Egoist,* which I quote below, I am indebted to Leland Peterson's M.A. thesis, "A Study of Various Essays on Andrew Marvell," University of Minnesota, 1956.

of opposite or discordant qualities: of sameness, with difference; of the general, with the concrete; the idea, with the image." *

Since the concepts did not originate with Eliot, it becomes necessary to revise the question in this way: why did concepts which had been more or less prevalent for a full century appeal to modern critics in the particular formulations given them by Eliot? To this question there is a seemingly simple answer: Eliot spoke with authority. But to say this is to acknowledge, even to describe, the appeal of Eliot's criticism but not to explain it. Eliot spoke his criticism, of course, with the authority of a poet, but he also spoke it in a prose style of authoritative quality. This observation leads me, not to a full answer, but to the final answer which I intend to offer. It is that the prose style of Eliot's early criticism is marked by the quality of scientific accuracy and precision, and that this scientific quality appealed strongly to other critics because it matched their own inclinations. That Eliot's inclinations, and presumptions, were decidedly scientific is often shown by his early criticism, and especially by a series of essays in the *Egoist* in 1918, from which I shall quote some passages.

"We insist in the face of a hostile majority that reading, writing, and ciphering does not complete the education of a poet. The analogy to science is close. A poet, like a scientist, is contributing toward the organic development of culture; it is just as absurd for him not to know the work of his predecessors or of men writing in other languages as it would be for a biologist to be ignorant of Mendel or DeVries. It is exactly as wasteful for a poet to do what has been done already, as for a biologist to rediscover Mendel's discoveries."

"The work of the critic is almost wholly comprehended in the 'complementary activities' of comparison and analysis . . . If the critic has performed his laboratory work well, his understanding will be evidence of appreciation."

"Criticism, like creative art, is in various ways less developed than scientific research . . . Of course, science, as well as literature, is

* For an exposition of Coleridgean elements in modern criticism, especially as adapted and transmitted by T. E. Hulme and I. A. Richards, see Murray Krieger's formidable study of modern poetic theory, *The New Apologists for Poetry* (Minneapolis: University of Minnesota Press, 1956).

dependent upon the occasional appearance of a man of genius who discovers a new method . . . But there is much useful work done in science by men who are only clever enough and well enough educated to apply a method; and in literature there *ought* to be a place for persons of equivalent capacity. . . . There might be a recognized set of tools which the critic could be taught to use, and a variety of standard patterns which he could be trained to turn out."

These remarks impress me as showing not merely an intention to clarify and emphasize certain ideas about poetry and criticism, but also as showing an urgency to claim for poetry and criticism an intellectual respectability comparable to that of science. The "analogy to science" in these very remarks is not only "close" but too close. Eliot's phrases "just as absurd" and "exactly as wasteful" in his judgments about the poet are, by the strict standards of the science he invokes, neither just nor exact. The "evolutionary" and "progressive" view of poetry expressed here is unscientifically contradicted by the contention in "Tradition and the Individual Talent" (1917) that "art never improves." Before raising further questions of consistency, I would call attention to scientific references in the better-known essays. In the one just mentioned the poet's mind is compared to a catalytic agent, "a bit of finely filiated platinum . . . introduced into a chamber containing oxygen and sulphur dioxide." In "Philip Massinger" there is the "true mutation of species" and the poet's "nervous system." In "The Metaphysical Poets" there is the "mechanism of sensibility" and the necessity for the poet to look not merely into the heart, which "is not looking deep enough,'" but to look also "into the cerebral cortex, the nervous system, and the digestive tracts." The "analogy to science" is to be seen in this criticism not only in such specific references, but also in the seemingly precise, meticulous, and factual discriminations made in regard to questions of poetry. The confident proposition and the precise analytical charting of the "dissociation of sensibility" is a discrimination of this order. So are the various statements on the fusion of thought and feeling. As I observed earlier, Eliot had a habit, a stylistic technique, of verbalizing responses and impressions (sound and persuasive enough *as such*) in a way that gave them the quality of cogent argument and scientific conclusion. Indeed, it might be said that Eliot's critical prose evoked for other critics the quality of scientific experience.

That the scientific experience was desired is shown by the record. In Ransom's criticism, it may be recalled, there were the analogies to chemistry and psychology. Such references are, however, mere signs on the surface as compared to the basic features of Ransom's critical point of view. In his earlier criticism he seemed to have arrived at a *formula* for the best kind of poetry, and this was the metaphysical conceit. The formula was used not only as a description of certain poems written in the seventeenth century, but as a standard for the degree of success in poetry of other kinds and periods, and also as the basic and exclusive rule for how good poetry should be written. The formula had the scientific virtues of measurement and prediction. Ransom's later criticism has been less evaluative in its impulse, but no less scientific. When the formula was discarded, the nature of poetry became a riddle, a problem, that one could hope to solve. His speculations on structure and texture seek for the kind of ultimate solution which the scientist achieves when he locates a material causative agent.

The same scientific reduction to formula is found in the criticism of Brooks. Structural, or functional, metaphor, which "represents the fusion of image and idea," has been the governing formula in his criticism. The argument that "the language of poetry is the language of paradox" was an attempt to stretch the formula into greater inclusiveness, to give it universal applicability and predictability. Even in his more recent work, as in the essay on Milton mentioned above, Brooks announced that all poetry was subject to the test that had been devised from a study of Donne's achievement: "in having recovered Donne . . . we have recovered not just Donne's poetry, but poetry." The causative vitamin for poetry had been scientifically isolated, and the methodology for its isolation was established.

The criticism of Allen Tate is relevant to, but not committed to, the scientific reductionism found in Eliot, Ransom, and Brooks. Certain of his essays seem to offer this reduction, but when we look for it (as I have), we find that it cannot be clearly located and named. It is as if Tate shared the inclinations of his colleagues, indulged them to some extent, but never to a final commitment. For example, an essay called "Three Types of Poetry" (1934) opens with the statement that "there are more than three kinds of poetry." The closest that Tate has come to any scientific scheme is the essay "Tension in Poetry" (1938). Here again it is necessary to note some opening remarks of the essay:

"Many poems that we ordinarily think of as good poetry — and some besides, that we neglect — have certain common features that will allow us to invent, for their sharper apprehension, the name of a single quality. I shall call that quality tension . . . There are all kinds of poetry, as many as there are good poets, as many even as there are good poems, for poets may be expected to write more than one kind of poetry; and no single critical insight may impute an exclusive validity to any one kind."

After these qualifications, Tate went on to propose a scheme by which different kinds, but not necessarily all kinds, of good poetry, could be divided into related classifications. This scheme was a scale of which the poles were denotation and connotation, and which Tate called respectively "extension" and "intension." The metaphors of metaphysical poetry he described as based on an "extensive" relationship of terms, and those of Symbolist (and Romantic) poetry as based on an "intensive" relationship. The better achievements of each kind he saw as the result of a strategy whereby there is considerable development toward the opposite pole. It is significant to note that he said of the two kinds of poetry that "both are great, and both are incomplete." The poetry that is complete, the really best poetry, he called the "poetry of tension," a poetry that occupied the whole scale, so that there is in it a "unity of all the meanings from the furthest extremes of intension and extension." That Tate regarded certain poems historically classified either metaphysical or Symbolist as having complete tension is clear from the "touchstones" which he quoted, and hence the scale is itself not a "complete" analogy.

I have given a brief and perhaps too compressed account of Tate's scheme of tension, but I hope that it will serve my purposes. The complete tension between denotation and connotation may be readily translated into the fusion of thought and feeling — but

Tate refrained from doing this. The use of the scale in regard to poetry is an "analogy to science." A scale is a methodology, but it is a methodology of which Tate merely borrowed some features, and perhaps some prestige, in order to illustrate certain observations. The scale was not adopted as a method in his criticism, not even in this particular essay. The good poem is not located at some point on the scale, but entirely covers and thus eliminates it, for the poem is not itself a scale. The scale, which is a mere illustration, and not even a perfect one (not a structural metaphor of Tate's argument) is returned to science, from which it was borrowed. And the point illustrated is referred finally not to a method of either poetry or criticism. It is referred to the effects of particular poems and to the responsible taste of the critic. Tate says as much in the essay: "Yet our recognition of the action of this unified meaning is the gift of experience, of culture, of, if you will, our humanism. Our powers of discrimination are not deductive powers, though they may be aided by them; they wait rather upon the cultivation of our total human powers, and they represent a special application of those powers to a single medium of experience — poetry."

In the preface to his most recent collection of essays, *The Man of Letters in the Modern World* (1955), Tate spoke of the error of assuming for criticism "a method that can accomplish what the responsible intelligence is alone able to do." This was the error of Eliot's early proposal (long since abandoned) that critics could be trained to use "a recognized set of tools." For indeed a defect of Eliot's criticism, a defect of Ransom, Brooks, and others, has been that the set of tools is actually recognized and has too often made of poetry the grindstone on which the tools were sharpened — for their own sake, and for the sake of "the analogy to science." It is ironical that those critics who have deplored the *scientism* of our age as a cultural scandal should have sought to participate in the positivism and prestige of scientific method. It is ironical, but it is understandable. We cannot be of our age and out of it at the same time. It is not easy to be patient in the search for unity, for patience is itself a kind of unity, a reconciling, perhaps a fusing, of thought and feeling.

Ash Wednesday

IN HIS essay on Babbitt, T. S. Eliot has said, "Given the most highly organized and temporally powerful hierarchy, with all the powers of inquisition and punishment imaginable, still the idea of the religion is the *inner* control — the appeal not to a man's behaviour but to his soul." We may assume that a devotional poem written by Eliot will constitute a record of the poet's religious experience — the personal matter of "*inner* control." The continuity which has been often remarked as existing in Eliot's work becomes definitely apparent after a study of his longer poems. *The Waste Land* looks forward, we can see now, to such a poem as *Ash Wednesday*; especially indicative are these lines from the earlier poem:

> I sat upon the shore
> Fishing, with the arid plain behind me
> Shall I at least set my lands in order?
> London Bridge is falling down falling down falling down
> *Poi s'ascose nel foco che gli affina* . . .

Setting one's lands in order amounts to approaching the practice of inner control; Cleanth Brooks observes: "The protagonist resolves to claim his tradition and rehabilitate it." In the later poem it is evident that he has been pursuing his resolution and that *Ash Wednesday* is uttered, so to speak, from *il foco che gli affina*.

In his essay on Baudelaire Eliot has implied what he considers essential for the possession — more accurately, the pursuit — of Christianity: "the greatest, the most difficult, of the Christian virtues, the virtue of humility." Significantly enough, he uses for the title of his devotional poem the name of that day in the Catholic calendar which begins a season of humility, thus indicating the tone and theme of the poem, so that Ash Wednesday comes to stand for a state of mind, a state of the soul.

The relationship which Eliot has indicated as existing between

The Man in the Name

The Waste Land and Miss Weston's *From Ritual to Romance* is paralleled, as we shall soon observe, by that existing between *Ash Wednesday* and *The Dark Night of the Soul*, a prose work of the sixteenth-century Spanish mystic St. John of the Cross. *The Dark Night of the Soul* is a companion piece to *The Ascent of Mount Carmel*, both of which the saint wrote to expound his mystical *Stanzas of the Soul*. In each of these St. John gives counsel for the religious experience of purgation and explains that those who would attain union with God must enter a condition of the soul called the "dark night." This condition is of two stages: the dark night of sense and the dark night of spirit, in which sense and spirit respectively are purged. The *Ascent*, counsel for the active way of purgation, is intended for proficients; the *Dark Night*, counsel for the passive way, for beginners. "The passive way is that wherein the soul does nothing, and God works in the soul, and it remains, as it were, patient." It is in keeping with the theme of *Ash Wednesday*, humility, that its plan comes from the counsel for the passive way.

The statements of the speaker in section 1 of *Ash Wednesday* impart a sense of the debility, humility, and vexation which are to be endured by St. John's beginner, who, to enter the dark night for the purgation of desire, must achieve a "spiritual detachment from all things, whether sensual or spiritual, and a leaning on pure faith alone and an ascent thereby to God." *

". . . those who at this time are going on to perfection . . . progress by means of humility and are greatly edified, not only thinking naught of their own affairs, but having very little satisfaction with themselves; they consider all others as far better, and usually have a holy envy of them, and an eagerness to serve God as these do. . . . And thus He leaves them so completely in the dark that they know not whither to go with their sensible imagination and meditation; for they cannot advance a step in meditation, as they were wont to do aforetime, their inward senses being submerged in this night and left with such dryness that not only do they experience no pleasure and consolation in the spiritual things and good exercises wherein they were wont to find their de-

* The translations from St. John that follow are by E. Allison Peers.

lights and pleasures, but instead, on the contrary, they find insipid-
ity and bitterness in the said things. . . .

"When the soul enters the dark night, it brings these kinds of
love under control. It strengthens and purifies the one, namely
that which is according to God; and the other it removes and
brings to an end; and in the beginning it causes both to be lost
sight of. . . ."

St. John's description of genuine purgation is recognizably expressed by Eliot in *Burnt Norton*:

> Descend lower, descend only
> Into the world of perpetual solitude,
> World not world, but that which is not world,
> Internal darkness, deprivation
> And destitution of all property,
> Desiccation of the world of sense,
> Evacuation of the world of fancy,
> Inoperancy of the world of spirit;
> This is the one way, and the other
> Is the same, not in movement
> But abstention from movement, while the world
>   moves
> In appetency, on its metalled ways
> Of time past and time future.

I

The first section of *Ash Wednesday* — indeed, the whole poem —
not only reflects superficially *The Dark Night of the Soul*, but also
contains allusions which, by their contextual significance, are in
accord with St. John's purgational system. A structural similarity
between *Ash Wednesday* and *The Waste Land* is thus suggested,
for the allusions have their place in the devotional poem by sympathetic association with the idea of the *Dark Night*. A preoccupation with the purging of desire, with the condition of "Internal
darkness, deprivation" etc., would bring a sharpened sensitivity to
whatever might suggest the condition, would impose something of
itself upon all experience and come to include within itself what
has been incidentally reminiscent of the personal problem.

The opening line is a literal translation of the first line of a *ballata* by Guido Cavalcanti: *Perch'io non spero di tornar giammai.* Rossetti's translation of it begins:

> Because I think not ever to return
> Ballad, to Tuscany, —
> Go therefore thou for me
> Straight to my lady's face,
> Who, of her noble grace,
> Shall show thee courtesy.

The statements of waning vital powers, the torment to heart and soul, the condition of the "body being now so nearly dead" and of the "dead mind" make evident a correspondence between the afflictions expressed by this contemporary of Dante and the condition of St. John's beginner, whose sensitivity, both physical and spiritual, has almost ceased to function, while the soul is in a state of despair:

"For indeed, when this purgative contemplation is most severe, the soul feels very keenly the shadow of death and the lamentations of death and the pains of hell, which consists in its feeling itself to be without God, and chastised and cast out, and unworthy of Him; . . . it believes that it is so with it forever."

Cavalcanti's line, as it is used in *Ash Wednesday*, performs much of its original function, for, as we shall note in dealing with later sections, the ideas of devotion to a woman and the religious experience of approaching union with God are held by Eliot in a single conceptual pattern.

In addition to the implications of devotion and distress which arise from the source of the line "Because I do not hope to turn again," there is yet another and perhaps more immediate meaning. To turn would be to depart from the state of purgation and humility and enter the state of existence of the hollow men who "go round the prickly pear." Eliot has used this turning elsewhere (at the beginning of his choruses from *The Rock* and in section v of *Ash Wednesday*) as a symbol of sterile activity and empty existence, applying it particularly to the modern world. But turning also symbolizes something else, something opposed to the sterile secular motion. The souls in Dante's *Purgatorio* are turning as they move up the winding mount which leads to heaven, the state of blessedness and divine love. In section III of *Ash Wednesday* the turning stair represents this conception of the motion. Eliot uses these symbolic turnings in *Burnt Norton*, where he also reminds us of the *Dark Night*:

> Here is a place of disaffection
> Time before and time after
> In a dim light: neither daylight
> Investing form with lucid stillness
> *Turning shadow into transient beauty*
> *With slow rotation suggesting permanence*
> Nor darkness to purify the soul
> Emptying the sensual with deprivation
> Cleansing affection from the temporal.
> Neither plentitude nor vacancy. Only a flicker
> Over the strained time-ridden faces
> Distracted from distraction by distraction
> Filled with fancies and empty of meaning
> Tumid apathy with no concentration
> *Men and bits of paper, whirled by the cold wind*
> That blows before and after time . . .
>
> [italics mine]

The dual meaning of this turning suggests the condition of the *Dark Night*, for, by having no hope to turn, the protagonist has no hope of responding either to the worldly or the spiritual; the faculties for doing so are become incapacitated. The portions of the line which are repeated state the different shades of meaning contained in the line: the lack of hope; and the condition of being devoid of two kinds of sensibility.

A striking illustration of the sympathetic association by which allusions are present is the line "Desiring this man's gift and that man's scope," quoted with the change of one word from Shakespeare's twenty-ninth sonnet:

> When, in disgrace with fortune and men's eyes,
> I all alone beweep my outcast state,
> And trouble deaf heaven with my bootless cries,
> And look upon myself and curse my fate,
> Wishing me like to one more rich in hope,

145]

The Man in the Name

> Featured like him, like him with friends possess'd,
> Desiring this man's art and that man's scope,
> With what I most enjoy contented least;
> Yet in these thoughts myself almost despising,
> Haply I think on thee, and then my state,
> Like to the lark at break of day arising
> From sullen earth, sings hymns at heaven's gate;
> >   For thy sweet love remember'd such wealth brings
> >   That then I scorn to change my state with kings.

It may be observed that the condition expressed here is in all its details consonant with the accompaniments and signs of purgation set forth by St. John of the Cross.

Although probably not a functional allusion, the "aged eagle" may have reference to the *Dark Night*. The term *old man* is often used for the unpurged condition of the soul:

". . . God makes it to die to all that is not naturally God, so that, once it is stripped and denuded of its former skin, He may begin to clothe it anew. And thus its youth is renewed like the eagle's and it is clothed with the new man, which, as the Apostle says, is according to God."

"Why should I mourn / The vanished power of the usual reign?" implies the futility of attempting to do anything about the condition of despair and affliction. To return to the "vanished power of the usual reign" would be a regression, a return to the state that existed before purgation began. By this implication the question becomes a statement of definite religious experience, for to suffer these afflictions is, according to St. John, to be on the way toward union with God. There is no hope of knowing the "infirm glory of the positive hour" or the "one veritable transitory power," which are respectively the modes of worldly and spiritual relief. The place "where trees flower, and springs flow" is a symbol of dual meaning, representing the consolations of sense and of spirit which are attenuated by the dark night. The protagonist, oppressed by the mere self-identity and ephemeral actuality of time and place, further expresses his wretchedness by dwelling upon the static semblance of his condition:

> time is always time
> And place is always and only place
> And what is actual is actual only for one time
> And only for one place . . .

The rejoicing which proceeds from this realization is a gesture of utter resignation, an acceptance of what seems to be irrevocable misery. So absolute is the hopelessness of his condition that it leads him to renounce the "blessed face" and the "voice" which symbolize hope and guidance. (The *face* and *voice* obviously refer to the "Lady" of section II, as well as Cavalcanti's lady, who, reflected by the spiritual guide of *Ash Wednesday*, is also an object of spiritual devotion in her original context.) This renunciation has a parallel in the *Dark Night*. St. John says of the soul that "since it believes . . . that its evil will never end . . . it suffers great pain and grief, since there is added to all this (because of the solitude and abandonment caused in it by this dark night), the fact that it finds no consolation or support in any instruction nor in any spiritual master." Of itself, the situation can yield no joy. One positive gesture is, however, possible: because there is nothing else he can do, the protagonist resigns himself to the situation and accepts it completely. In doing so by his own will, he dismisses the desire to strive and thus gains the satisfaction of consummating a volition. The passage ends with an emphatic restatement of the experience:

> Because I cannot hope to turn again
> Consequently I rejoice, having to construct something
> Upon which to rejoice.

Such rejoicing is constructed upon the resignation to inescapable misery: the positive experience comes into being only by means of the negative experience. This is ironical — and therefore humiliating.

Then come prayer and repentance, and the expressed desire for the passive and unreflective condition counseled by St. John: beginners are "to devote themselves not at all to reasoning and meditation . . . they will be doing quite sufficient if they persevere in prayer . . . troubling not themselves, in that state, about what they shall think or meditate . . . being without anxiety . . ." This aspect of the religious experience appears with more complexity in the paradoxical words

> Teach us to care and not to care
> Teach us to sit still.

Considering the precepts of St. John, it is natural that the protagonist wishes "not to care," to be "without anxiety." On the other hand, the ultimate motive of the desire rests in an actual concern with progressing in the religious experience, for one would want to follow the precept because one really did care. The paradoxical and earnest plea comes as an achievement; it is attained by the resignation contained in the earlier passage. The protagonist would not have it to do over again and hopes that "these words answer / For what is done, not to be done again." He would now be taught "to care and not to care" because he has made some progress along the way of purgation,

> Because these wings are no longer wings to fly
> But merely vans to beat the air
> The air which is now thoroughly small and dry
> Smaller and dryer than the will . . .

"Smaller and dryer than the will" is another echo from St. John's *Dark Night*: "To this end God is pleased to strip them of this old man . . . leaving the understanding dark, the will dry, the memory empty. . . ." The prayer and the section end with a quotation from the *Ave Maria* of Catholic ritual, words which are for the penitent who has faith.

II

The purgation continues in section ii, and a state (or station) of the purifying function is expressed by symbolic images, a device which Eliot commends and admires in Dante. In his essay on that poet he says, ". . . Hell is not a place but a *state* . . . Hell, though a state, is a state that can only be thought of, and perhaps only experienced, by the projection of sensory images." He also says:

"What we should consider is not so much the meaning of the images, but the reverse process, that which led a man having an idea to express it in images. We have to consider the type of mind which by nature and *practice* tended to express itself in allegory: and for a competent poet, allegory means *clear visual images*. And clear visual images are given much more intensity by having a meaning — we do not need to know what that meaning is, but in our awareness of the image we must be aware that the meaning is there too."

We may profitably follow Eliot's counsel to consider "not so much the meaning of the images, but the reverse process, that which led a man having an idea to express it in images." The idea is known to be that of purgation. We may know that the images are associated with each other and we may know that they are associated with a particular idea, but we do not know enough until we have learned upon what ground all the associations occur. When this has been learned the images will become meaningful.

We have already noted the connection between the "Lady" of section II and the lady of Cavalcanti's poem. Mario Praz remarks that the term Lady — Donna — "had quite a special connotation in Dante's circle." The *ballata* gives us an instance of the lady's function in the poetry of that circle. Worshiped with religious adoration, she is a type of the Virgin Mary, one who may bring the grace of salvation to her suitor, from whom she receives a personal devotion involving the natural and the supernatural. The sequence of the sections in *Ash Wednesday* is in part founded upon this. The Platonic lover of Cavalcanti's poem bids his soul to "worship her / Still in her purity." Such love has a religious quality and is ironically distinct from the sexual formula which describes the performance of the typist and the "young man carbuncular" in *The Waste Land*. The most eminent instance of the love which amounts to religious worship is Dante's devotion to Beatrice. Eliot has stated the idea in his essay on Dante, speaking of the experience * in the *Vita Nuova*: "It is not, I believe, meant as a descrip-

---

* "At that moment, I say most truly that the spirit of life, which hath its dwelling in the secretest chamber of the heart, began to tremble so violently that the least pulses of my body shook therewith; and in trembling it said these words: *Ecce deus fortior me, qui veniens dominabitur mihi* ("Here is a deity stronger than I; who, coming, shall rule over me"). At that moment the animate spirit, which dwelleth in the lofty chamber whither all the senses

149]

tion of what he *consciously* felt on his meeting with Beatrice, but rather as a description of what that meant on mature reflection upon it . . . the love of man and woman (or for that matter of man and man) is only explained and made reasonable by the higher love, or else is simply the coupling of animals." It is probably quite valid to associate the Lady with Beatrice, for their function is similar, although it is not necessary for the reader of *Ash Wednesday* to recall any particular appearance of Beatrice from the *Divine Comedy*. Since Eliot's poem deals with purgation, we may take note of his remark: ". . . it is in these last cantos of the *Purgatorio*, rather than in the *Paradiso*, that Beatrice appears most clearly."

Associations of the Lady also involve the "juniper tree." *The Juniper Tree*, one of Jakob Grimm's tales, is an account of a husband and wife who, having no children, but desiring one, finally acquire a boy by supernatural aid. When the wife dies in childbirth the man marries a woman who, having a daughter of her own, Marlinchen, hates the boy. She kills him, makes puddings of his flesh which she gives to her husband for food, and lies about the boy's absence. Marlinchen carries the boy's bones to a juniper tree. Then there are mist and flames, and a bird appears, singing —

> My mother she killed me,
> My father he ate me,
> My sister little Marlinchen,
> Gathered together all my bones,
> Tied them in a silken handkerchief
> Laid them beneath the juniper tree,
> Kywitt, kywitt, what a beautiful bird am I!

The bird finally causes the death of the stepmother and becomes a boy again.

The Lady, by her benevolence, corresponds to the sister Marlin-

carry their perceptions, was filled with wonder, and speaking more especially unto the spirits of the eyes, said these words: *Apparuit jam beatitudo vestra* ("Your beatitude hath now been made manifest unto you"). At that moment the natural spirit, which dwelleth there where our nourishment is administered, began to weep, and in weeping said these words: *Heu miser! quia frequenter impeditus ero deinceps* ("Alas! how often shall I be disturbed from this time forth!")." *La Vita Nuova* (Rossetti's translation).

chen. The juniper and the bones are additional links. Moreover, the story reminds us of Christian resurrection and the eating of the boy's body parallels the Communion. Eliot's use of this story agrees with his interest in the Christian elements of anthropology manifested by *The Waste Land*. The boy has passed through death and come to life again. Eliot has used devices before to express the idea that life comes through death (*v. The Waste Land, Journey of the Magi*, and *A Song for Simeon*). Another source of "under a juniper tree" strikes the same note. When Elijah was threatened by Jezebel for having slain the prophets of Baal, he went into the wilderness "and came and sat down under a juniper tree: and he requested for himself that he might die." It is possible that the proffering of "my love / To . . . the fruit of the gourd" derives from another biblical passage of the same nature. When Jonah was afflicted by the sun's heat because the gourd under which he sat had withered, "he fainted, and wished in himself to die."

The bird of Grimm's story has been carried over into the poem. It is not simply for grotesque effect that the bones happen to chirp and sing. In section IV of *Ash Wednesday* the bird sings, "Redeem the time, redeem the dream." Elsewhere in Eliot's poetry the bird and the tree occur together (cf. *The Waste Land* 1.356; *Burnt Norton* I; *Marina*). The bones in the poem reflect the tale, as well as St. John's *Dark Night*: ". . . the yearnings for God become so great in the soul that the very bones seem to be dried up by this thirst, and the natural powers to be fading away."

The book of Ezekiel is another source of the bones symbolism. It may be observed that there are in section II several allusions to chapter 37 of Ezekiel. After the Lord has passed damning judgment upon many iniquitous peoples, he promises rehabilitation and reanimation to the Israelites. He shows to the prophet a vision symbolic of renewed vitality:

"The hand of the Lord was upon me . . . and set me down in the midst of the valley which was full of bones . . . they were very dry. And he said unto me, Son of man, can these bones live? . . . So I prophesied . . . and the bones came together . . . and the flesh came up upon them . . . but there was no breath in them.

Then said he unto me, Prophesy unto the wind, prophesy, Son of man. . . . So I prophesied . . . and they lived . . . an exceeding great army.

"Then said he unto me, Son of man, these bones are the whole house of Israel: behold, they say, Our bones are dried, and our hope is lost. . . . Therefore prophesy and say unto them, Thus saith the Lord God . . . ye shall live, and I shall place you in your own land."

The chapter continues with a prophecy of the unity and blessings which God will bestow upon his people. Ezekiel ends with instructions for the dividing of the land and the negotiation of inheritance: "This is the land which ye shall divide by lot unto the tribes of Israel for inheritance, and these are their portions, saith the Lord God" (48:29).

It is significant that Eliot's first note to *The Waste Land* (l. 20, "Son of man") refers to Ezekiel. (The biblical context of this specific reference has not much importance unless we consider the entire book of Ezekiel as relative to *The Waste Land*; space forbids discussion of it.) The second note to *The Waste Land* makes a reference that applies also to section II of *Ash Wednesday*: "the burden of the grasshopper" holds the same meaning (but for a different purpose) as "the cricket no relief," both deriving from Ecclesiastes: "And the doors shall be shut in the streets, when the sound of the grinding is low, and he shall rise up at the voice of the bird, and all the daughters of music shall be brought low; Also when they shall be afraid of that which is high, and fears shall be in the way, and the almond tree shall flourish, and the grasshopper shall be a burden, and desire shall fail: because man goeth to his long home, and the mourners go about the streets" (12:4, 5). It does not seem unlikely that the bird at whose voice "he shall rise up" is connected with the idea of Grimm's tale and Eliot's use of the bird in his poetry. The grasshopper allusion implies the failing of desire. This is an additional association with the purgational dark night, during which the affections are lost sight of.

The loss of legs, heart, and liver reflects Eliot's interest in those aspects of anthropology which seem to bear upon Christian ritual. According to the article on cannibalism in the *Encyclopedia of*

Religion and Ethics, a frequent incident in folklore "is that of a child being sent out by the parent to be killed, while the assassin is ordered to bring back the victim's heart, liver, etc. . . . Grimm's story of Snow White is an instance. Here we may see a reminiscence of the practice of eating heart, liver, etc., in order to acquire the strength or soul of their owner." *The Juniper Tree* is cited as another instance. This practice and the Christian Communion are mutually reminiscent; they have become associated with the strength, the salvation, anticipated by the condition of the protagonist. The "three white leopards" which have "fed to satiety" belong to the same association. In the article "Animals" of the encyclopedia the section on the leopard relates that cannibalism and ritualistic flesh-eating are practiced by African tribes in connection with the leopard. There would not necessarily be a relevance between this article and *Ash Wednesday* were it not for an identical phrase appearing in both: "In South Africa a man who has killed a leopard remains in his hut three days; he practices continence and is *fed to satiety* [italics mine]." Although there is no special meaning brought into the poem by the coincidence of phrase with this single passage, its complete context does contain matter which recalls the Communion. The phrase and the leopards are, so to speak, handles of the association; it may very well be an unconscious one for the poet.

A quotation from chapter 3 of Genesis gives the setting of section II. When the fallen Adam and Eve hid themselves for shame of their nakedness, God walked "in the garden in the cool of the day." Besides the quality the phrase has by its allusiveness, it describes an aspect of the state, the "dream-crossed twilight," which is the subject of the poem. I remarked above that to understand the section it is necessary to learn "upon what ground all the associations occur." This "ground," as we have seen, is the idea of being purified in the purgational dark night. The images in the section, its setting, and the allusions which run through it carry the religious meaning of purgation and the way of purgation.

Eliot has said of Donne that "He knew the anguish of the marrow." As a symptom of intensity words are spoken by "that which

had been contained / In the bones." The words spoken indicate
an appreciation of the benevolent guidance of the Lady, as well as
the humility of the protagonist. The spiritual guide is responsible
for the "brightness," which is faith. Throughout the section
faith is signified by the color-symbolism of whiteness. It is by
the faith which the Lady inspires that the portions rejected by the
leopards are recovered. This faith brings and makes purposeful
the "emptiness of the apprehensions" (the forgetfulness) which St.
John declares an accompaniment of purgation.

Those familiar with the Catholic litany will appreciate the associations evoked by the solemn liturgical cadences of the words
which the bones sing to the Lady of silences. The seeming contradictions which compose the passage are analogous to the paradox
("to care and not to care") upon which the religious experience
revolves. The Lady is calm and reposeful by nature. But she is also
distressed and worried in her solicitude for the protagonist. By
being the Rose of memory and of forgetfulness she is both "Torn
and most whole." (As it is convenient, I shall defer a fuller explanation of this to the treatment of section IV.) She is "Exhausted
and life-giving" in the way that Beatrice was, having passed from
physical existence to become the inspiration of spiritual life. Her
personality is symbolical of all the spiritual aims for which the
protagonist strives; sex impulses have been sublimated into religious devotion, so that "The single Rose / Is now the Garden /
Where all loves end." The torment of "love unsatisfied" is termi-
nated in that it reaches its climax, the satisfaction of its impulse, by
a biological performance, such as the typist and the young man
enact in *The Waste Land*. This performance, however, is only an
incident in the recurring cycle of desire and satisfaction. So long
as love is merely a biological urge, forever consuming and forever
desiring, there is never ultimate satisfaction. It is in this sense
that we have

> The greater torment
> Of love satisfied
> End of the endless
> Journey to no end
> Conclusion of all that

> Is inconclusible
> Speech without word and
> Word of no speech . . .

The last two lines are a comment upon the emptiness and lack of spiritual meaning which belong to the love that must be forever desiring. A distinction is made between biological desire and spiritual love in *Burnt Norton*: "Desire is itself movement / Not in itself desirable; / Love is itself unmoving, / Only the cause and end of movement, / Timeless and undesiring." The chant of the bones ends with a note of thanksgiving. In accordance with the way of purgation the soul being purified is thankful for its present state, "the blessing of sand," from which the garden is to evolve. The scattered bones, shining with faith, say, "We are glad to be scattered, we did little good to each other." Much of the irony and all of the bitterness which these words may apparently contain are supplied by the reader. If the protagonist *cares* really, then, according to the direction he has taken, he has good reason *not to care*.

III

When section III was first published individually it bore the title *Som de l'Ecscalina* (summit of the stairway), a phrase taken from the familiar *Ara vos prec* passage of the *Purgatorio* (XXVI). The image of the stair is consistent with St. John's *Dark Night*, in which the ladder "of living faith" is used as a symbol and illustration of the purgative contemplation. The soul "is ascending and descending continually," experiencing exaltation and humiliation "until it has acquired perfect habits; and this ascending and descending will cease, since the soul will have attained to God and become united with Him, which comes to pass at the summit of the ladder; for the ladder rests and leans upon Him." St. John describes the ladder as consisting of ten steps. Eliot is most probably referring to these steps with "the figure of the ten stairs" in *Burnt Norton*, and "the saint's stair" in *A Song for Simeon*.

The progress of the protagonist, now signified by turning, is objectified by the "projection of sensory images." The terms "The same shape," "I left them twisting, turning below," and "stops and steps of the mind over the third stair" suggest the changing from one state of mind to another, or rather the function of a single dynamic state of mind. The *shape* and one of *them* are in each case the protagonist. In *Burnt Norton* the poet ponders this movement which is "neither arrest nor movement. And do not call it fixity." The "fetid air" is a sign of purification, representing that which is spiritually foul and unhealthy as the issue of purgation. The cleansing process is illustrated in the *Dark Night* by the example of fire consuming wood: ". . . it brings out and drives away all the dark and unsightly accidents which are contrary to the nature of fire." The devil with "The deceitful face of hope and of despair" embodies the tempting idea of departure from the intense submission to purgation. To persist along the way of purification it is necessary "to care and not to care." This is no ordinary attitude; it is difficult to maintain when confronted by the easy but futile adjustments of mere hope and despair, which are customary and therefore dangerously attractive.

The lurid images which are suggested to the protagonist need not be symbolical, for they occur within a symbol, one that is dramatic: the difficult effort to ascend a stair. However, the picture called to mind for the protagonist by the passage along the stair — "an old man's mouth drivelling, beyond repair" — reminds us of the *old man* that is being cast off by the experience.

"At the first turning of the third stair / Was a slotted window bellied like the fig's fruit." There is nothing extraordinary about the presence of the window. One is led to conceive of a tower with a window near the landing below the third flight. Whatever other meaning there may be is to this extent objectified. But a pertinent meaning is suggested. The preceding images readily connote despair; it may therefore be expected that the "deceitful face of hope" follows. The "slotted window" is, besides being superficially consistent, a sexual image. The fig is associated with lust. By taking window in a figurative sense one may arrive at quite a literal interpretation, if not an image: that of the female genital organ. The form of the window is a symbolic frame for the symbolic scene of beautiful sensuous images on which it opens. The "broadbacked figure" suggests a pagan fertility deity who is responsible for an appealing "Distraction, music of the flute." This sensuous beauty is hostile to the purposes of the protagonist; when it fades he gains strength. *Ash Wednesday* is again consistent with the *Dark Night*: "For to some the angel of Satan presents himself — namely, the spirit of fornication — that he may buffet their senses with abominable and violent temptations, and may trouble their spirits with vile considerations and representations which are most visible to the imagination, which things at times are a greater affliction to them than death."

The protagonist has passed through disability of the affections, achieved some success in attaining the paradoxical position of caring and not caring, and now gains "strength beyond hope and despair." The part of man that is vexed by the foibles of hope and despair is being purged.

Catholic ritual supplies the final words of the section. In the Mass, just before the priest consumes the Body and drinks the Blood of Christ, he repeats three times this prayer, while he bows low over the chalice and patin and strikes his breast thrice: "Lord, I am not worthy that thou shouldst enter under my roof. But speak the word only, and my soul shall be healed." Besides the religious connotations which the words have, they bespeak humility and faith, and an earnest dependence upon the will of God. The protagonist is still "Climbing the third stair" — with fervor and humility.

IV

Ash Wednesday may be divided into two parts, the first ending with section III. In the earlier sections the protagonist has been moving farther along through the dark night, ascending the stair according to the pattern. He reaches the third stair and is still climbing it at the end of the first part of the poem. In the last three sections he is trying to realize the causality by which he is conditioned, as well as the condition itself.

The series of questions which opens section IV implies wonder as to the identity of the Lady, the spiritual guide "who moves in the time between sleep and waking." Although the several questions imply the same answer, each of them is in terms that have a special significance. Mario Praz remarks that there is correspondence between the floral setting and the vision of Matilda in *Purgatorio* xxviii: "a lady solitary, who went along singing, and culling flower after flower, wherewith all her path was painted." One feels urged to correlate the lines with passages in other portions of Eliot's work. "Between the violet and the violet" recalls from *The Waste Land* the "violet hour" and the "violet light." Brooks observes that violet, as a quality of the twilight, has symbolic connections with a moment of time and, also, with an experience. It may be that we have here in the violet the last link in a chain of symbols: an experience, a moment of time, a sensory quality of the moment; so that "between the violet and the violet" is ultimately synonymous with "the time between sleep and waking." It is only at such moments, under such conditions, that the protagonist can consciously seize upon the one who "made strong the fountains and made fresh the springs," for it was at such a moment that her influence was first experienced.

That these terms are put in the form of questions indicates that the protagonist has not completely established his hold upon her and has not the intimate realization which Dante had of Beatrice. Eliot expresses the belief that the sexual experience of childhood which Dante describes in the *Vita Nuova* "could only have been written around a personal experience. If so the details do not matter: whether the lady was the Portinari or not, I do not care; it is quite likely that she is a blind for someone else, even for a person whose name Dante has forgotten or never known. But I cannot find it incredible that what has happened to others, should have happened to Dante with much greater intensity." The protagonist is questioning because he does not specifically remember (or visualize) the one by whom he would be led to a higher love. This is why in section ii the "Lady of silences" is "Torn and most whole / Rose of memory / Rose of forgetfulness." These lines from *Marina* involve the same meaning:

> What is this face, less clear and clearer
> The pulse in the arm, less strong and stronger —

Given or lent? more distant than stars and nearer
than the eye

. . . .

I made this, I have forgotten
And remember.

The original of the Lady, like the earthly Beatrice, was an ordinary and natural person, "Talking of trivial things." She was unaware of the effect her presence and behavior had upon the protagonist, yet the details of the experience remain significant for him, so that he imputes to her a "knowledge of eternal dolour."

The preceding sections of the poem are an account of her having made the fountains and springs of spiritual life appealing and having brought the protagonist closer to them. She has made his situation less dismal, for now the dry rock has been cooled and the sand is firm, whereas in *The Waste Land* there

> is no water but only rock
> Rock and no water and the sandy road

> . . . .

> Sweat is dry and feet are in the sand.

The words of Arnaut Daniel, the poet in purgatory, are used by the protagonist as an entreaty to the spiritual guide: *Sovegna vos* — "be mindful." Thus he expresses his desire, his willingness, to proceed further in the experience of purgation.

"Here are the years that walk between . . ." *Here* is the present condition. All the years that have passed since the first sexual-religious experience are involved in it; they have brought the condition by removing distractions, "the fiddles and the flutes." And it is only through the passage of time that this momentary experience can be recaptured, that the dreamlike person "who moves in the time between sleep and waking" can be restored. As it is stated in *Burnt Norton*, "Only through time time is conquered." The experiences and conditions recorded in the Bible, in folklore, in the writings of Dante and St. John of the Cross — "the ancient rhyme" — are restored by faith and suffering, "through a bright cloud of tears." The protagonist pleads:

The Man in the Name

> Redeem
> The time. Redeem
> The unread vision in the higher dream.

We find the phrase "redeeming the time" at the end of "Thoughts after Lambeth": "The World is trying the experiment of attempting to form a civilized but non-Christian mentality. The experiment will fail; but we must be very patient in awaiting its collapse; meanwhile redeeming the time: so that the Faith may be preserved alive through the dark ages before us; to renew and rebuild civilization, and save the World from suicide." (In each case the phrase may be an echo of Ephesians 5:15 and Colossians 4:6.) "Redeem the time," then, implies a desire that such a time as was conducive to "the higher dream" be restored and the present time atoned for.

F. R. Leavis has noted that "the higher dream" is reminiscent of some remarks in Eliot's essay on Dante. Discussing the "pageantry" of the *Paradiso*, Eliot observes: "It belongs to the world of what I call the *high dream*, and the modern world seems capable only of the *low dream*." Though in the modern world the vision— which is paradise and all it stands for — is unread, this does not mean that it has been permanently lost. It belongs to a world different from the modern, one capable of the high dream, and it is this world, this time, which the protagonist wishes to be redeemed. Notice that it is not simply the dream that is requested, but the more concrete vision. The difference becomes appreciable in conjunction with Eliot's statement upon Dante's "visual imagination . . . the trick of which we have forgotten . . . a more significant, interesting, and disciplined kind of dreaming." The protagonist himself imagines a vision as an accompaniment to the redemption which he pleads: "While jewelled unicorns draw by the gilded hearse." As Leavis observes, the unicorn belongs to the world of vision, of disciplined dreaming. The image is completed with "the gilded hearse." These objects and their embellishment constitute a scene of imaginative pageantry, one that suggests, in addition to the picture, Eliot's conception of a new life attained through death. The protagonist associates the time capable of the vision in

the higher dream with the ritual of the funeral. Moreover, the
unicorns (creatures of the imagination) have an important function in the ritual of death — death being the eve of the wished-for
life.

The supplication is, of course, addressed to the Lady. That she
should be pictured "Between the yews, behind the garden god /
Whose flute is breathless" and in section v as "The veiled sister between the slender / Yew trees" indicates that there is some ritualistic significance in the precise arrangement of the elements in the
figure. The protagonist's reflection upon his condition is equated
with the contemplation of a ritualistic symbol. The Lady's position emphasizes the difficulty with which the state is achieved, for
she can be revealed thus only when the flute of the garden god has
become breathless: in section iii the "music of the flute" is distraction. In other words, she becomes actual in proportion to the
success of the protagonist in sublimating into religious devotion
the impulses symbolized by the garden god. The yew, an ever-
green, is symbolical of immortality. The Lady being placed between the trees, we may conceive her as gathering up within herself "time past and time future," in short, all reality. We find in
Burnt Norton that past and future, though equally real with the
present, are *actual* only in the present: "At the still point . . .
Where past and future are gathered . . . Except for the point,
the still point, / There would be no dance, and there is only the
dance." That is to say, we may approach reality only through actuality, and the Lady is here the concentrated symbol of the great
past and future realities which can in no other way be perceived.
The protagonist's perception of her is imperfect, however. A complete intimacy would predicate complete revelation, and she merely "bent her head and signed but spoke no word." Although she
adds nothing of revelation, still she gives an encouraging sign. The
fountain springs up, making secure his spiritual awareness; the
bird reaffirms his petition. So long as there is no complete revelation the protagonist is right in seeking to redeem the dream, for
it is a symbol of what is as yet unrevealed, the "token of the word
unheard, unspoken." He must continue in purgation until he

reaches that state at which the immortal and spiritual essence is entirely realized, "Till the wind shake a thousand whispers from the yew." Such is also the implication in "And after this our exile," a liturgical echo from one of the "Prayers after Low Mass": "Turn then, most gracious advocate, thine eyes of mercy towards us. And after this our exile, show unto us the blessed fruit of thy womb, Jesus."

v

In section v the protagonist is pondering upon the *word*, the revelation which the world is resolutely incapable of receiving. Nonetheless, he says, the word exists. It is lost, spent, unheard, and unspoken only because unattained. And it is *the Word*, the very Word that the apostle John speaks of. "The centre of the silent Word" about which "the unstilled world still whirled" is equivalent to "the still point of the turning world . . . Where past and future are gathered" of *Burnt Norton*. A source of the idea is probably the point "where every *where* and every *when* is focused" of *Paradiso* xxix. We have previously noted the whirling movement as symbolical of the world's non-Christian attitude and activity. The modern world has violated its actual relationship to the unchanging and divine essence. But the Word is not destroyed. It is still "within / The world and for the world."

Notice that the line "O my people, what have I done unto thee" is punctuated by a period rather than a question mark. The line is from Micah 6:3: "O my people, what have I done unto thee? and wherein have I wearied thee? testify against me." These words occur also in "The Adoration of the Cross" for Good Friday, a penitential ritual. We may infer, then, that the protagonist recalls the words and exclaims them because of his religious humility and his wonder at the condition of the world. Having faith in God and the divine love, it is puzzling to him that the world should have moved "Against the Word."

He asks where the *word* shall be found, and answers himself exhaustively and emphatically, recognizing that the condition of the modern world is prohibitive of the experience which he desires. St. John's dark night is naturally suggested by the words "those who walk in darkness." The modern world does not afford the realities ("The right time and the right place") which are necessary for those who have only begun to be purged and would continue in purgation. Here in the world that is real at present there is neither "a place of grace" nor a "time to rejoice" for the partially purged, and it is inevitable that they "avoid the face" and "deny the voice." Ability to do otherwise depends not upon desire but upon condition. And the condition of the protagonist, and others like him, is that of participating in the temporal and sensual. They are of the modern world and must inescapably "walk among noise." This opinion, because one of disillusionment, is both realistic and religious. In his essay on Bradley, Eliot declares that "wisdom consists largely of scepticism and uncynical disillusion. . . . And scepticism and disillusion are a useful equipment for religious understanding." An inference of the protagonist's understanding and achievement naturally follows.

Having contemplated the circumstances, he asks whether the spiritual guide, the "veiled sister," will pray for those in the state of purgation, "those who wait / In darkness." In enduring the contradictions which make up their paradoxical condition they are "torn on the horn," for, although they desire the divinely spiritual life, they remain unpurged of worldly inclinations. They are attracted by two opposing directions, and so are torn between the seasons, times, hours, words, and powers of the worldly and the divine: at the gate of a more spiritual life, they "will not go away and cannot pray." The protagonist pleads that the "veiled sister" intercede for them.

As in the preceding section, the Lady is pictured between yew trees. From the protagonist's humble point of view, she is offended, for the insufficiently purged would enlist her solicitude. These are terrified by the world which is hostile to their interests, and by their own apparently inalterable condition. The divinely spiritual is, of course, their highest desire, and this they "affirm before the world." But when they return to their own reality, "between the rocks," and face the chosen direction, they do not *will* to advance: their denial is implicit in their condition.

The quality of the rocks (which are red and dry in *The Waste Land*) signifies that those who have chosen the spiritual way and made some progress have gained an existence more tolerable than that from which they set out, the latter being the merely secular and sensually appetitive world. Their progress may be arrested, but they have reached the last stage at which the world is an impediment to their further advancement, "the last desert between the last blue rocks / The desert in the garden the garden in the desert / Of drouth." The difference between the desert and the garden is of qualitative degree. Each is contained in the other: as the purgation of the individual continues, the desert condition is evolving toward the garden condition, which is the state of spiritual salvation. Drouth, representing spiritual want, also represents the function by which all that is foreign to the spiritual is purged away. This purgation is symbolized in "spitting from the mouth the withered apple-seed," evidently an allusion to the forbidden fruit eaten by Adam and Eve. The apple-seed, withered and being spit out, symbolizes the attentuated mundane desires which are being cast off by purgation.

VI

The first lines of the poem are repeated, except for the change of one word, as the opening lines of the final section, thus imparting formality and the quality of an expressive pattern which are characteristic of ceremonial incantation. Furthermore, this difference of one word emphasizes, by comparison with the protagonist's initial condition, the condition ultimately achieved in *Ash Wednesday*. At the first he despaired of ever being sensible to physical and spiritual attractions. But the condition has altered. He has passed through temptations and has arrived at the token, at least, of divine actuality. Now, according to his spiritual limitations and the choice he has made, his inclinations should be at a standstill. But they are not so. The purgation which has diminished the faculty for finding pleasure in the world has brought, since it was not complete, a nostalgic attraction to the pleasures that have to a great extent receded. The choice has been made and there is no question of considering the consequences in terms of reward, of "Wavering between the profit and the loss." However, though he has no desire to wish for the pleasures of the world, he inclines toward them. A confession of this follows the phrase " (Bless me father)." Among Catholics the usual form for beginning a confession is: "Bless me father; I confess to almighty God and to you, father, that I have sinned."

Attraction is exerted by the natural earth itself and its many delightful manifestations. Hence the "wide window." The nostalgic quality of the appeal is reflected by the terms of the experience:

> And the *lost* heart stiffens and rejoices
> In the *lost* lilac and the *lost* sea voices
> And the *weak* spirit quickens to *rebel*
> For the *bent* golden-rod and the *lost* sea smell
> Quickens to *recover*
> The cry of quail and the whirling plover
> And the blind eye creates
> The empty forms between the ivory gates
> And smell *renews* the salt savour of the sandy earth.

The protagonist is aware that his actual need can in no way be satisfied by the phenomena of the earth, although he is, against his wish, attracted by them. This is again implied by the "*blind* eye" which creates the "*empty* forms between the ivory gates." That is, the weakened faculties of mundane conception are indulged to experience the false promises of worldly pleasures. "Ivory gates" is an allusion to the passage in the *Aeneid* where Aeneas and the Sibyl, journeying through Hades, are informed by Anchises: "Two gates of Sleep there are, whereof the one is said to be of horn, and thereby an easy outlet is given to true shades; the other gleaming with the sheen of polished ivory, but false are the dreams sent by the spirits to the world above."

The condition of the protagonist is a "brief transit" and a "time of tension" because it is not one of repose, but a straining in two opposing directions, the worldly and the spiritual. The end of the one and the beginning of the other are a twilight, a transition from one state to another. It is in this sense a condition between the death of the worldly and the birth of the spiritual, "between dying and birth." The same purgation that would utterly remove the mundane attachment would concurrently introduce one entirely spiritual. "The place of solitude where three dreams cross" is, of course, "the time of tension." Past, present, and future are the three dreams. We have previously noted that the coexistence of these is stressed in *Burnt Norton*. These times (dreams, perhaps) meet each other at one point, the transitional condition. Other terms may be substituted for these with an addition of meaning. The three times may be respectively called the conditions unpurged, partially purged, and completely purged.

The "place of solitude" is, as in the preceding section, "Between blue rocks." In the discussion of section IV it was observed that the protagonist will maintain his position until a divine revelation comes, "Till the wind shake a thousand whispers from the yew." It was also noted that the two yews between which the Lady is placed are representative of past and future times. The protagonist now pleads,

> But when the voices shaken from the yew-tree drift away
> Let the other yew be shaken and reply.

That is, "when worldly experiences and the memory of them have passed, I hope for a revelation from the divine."

Ash Wednesday ends with a plea to the feminine principle of spiritual guidance. The first request is clear enough; the falsehoods with which spiritual pilgrims might mock themselves are, among others, complacency, the deceits of hope and despair, the "empty forms." Recurrence of the lines

> Teach us to care and not to care
> Teach us to sit still

has the same ritualistic effect as the opening lines. In connection with the earlier instance of the plea it was observed that caring and not caring constitute the patience and humility counseled by St. John of the Cross, as well as the motivating devotion. This paradox which introduces and punctuates the poem is a motif of the purgation. We have seen how it operates in section II: the images and statements which reflect a condition of defeat are symptomatic of hope and progress. The consonance which the condition has with *The Dark Night of the Soul* saves it from ironic emphasis. "Strength beyond hope and despair" of section III is at once an attainment and a resolution of the paradox. The necessity for caring and not caring persists from one stage of purgation to another. In the final stage of *Ash Wednesday* the protagonist wishes to learn "to sit still / Even among these rocks." Out of humility and devotion he seeks to maintain patience and gratefulness for the degree of progress he has been granted. Peace may be found even in an incomplete detachment from the world, in partial purgation, by realizing that the condition is in accord with the will of God. It is with hesitation that I remark at all upon the line "Our peace in His will," which is an adaptation of Dante's well-known line *"la sua voluntade è nostra pace."* T. S. Eliot's own comment upon it inspires my hesitation: "And the statement of Dante seems to me *literally true*. And I confess that it has more beauty for me now, when my experience has deepened its meaning, than it did when I first read it. So I can only conclude that I cannot, in practice, wholly separate my poetic appreciation from my personal beliefs."

"Spirit of the river, spirit of the sea" suggests Aphrodite, goddess of fertility. In this symbolism the idea of fertility has been spiritualized; the protagonist seeks a spiritual birth, the divine revelation, through the solicitous intercession of the Lady. The concluding words, which are a plea for continuation of the spiritual contact, are quotations from Catholic ritual. "Suffer me not to be separated from Thee" occurs in "Devotions of the Forty Hours," Visit IV. "And let my cry come unto Thee" is the response to the versicle "O Lord, hear my prayer." The last two lines are, as they occur in the poem, dramatically emphatic of the situation. Because of all that has gone before, they issue effectually as the protagonist's utterance, their full significance including, besides their intrinsic suitability to their place in the poem, the ritualistic force and religious meaning for which they serve in a specific ceremonial performance. The individual experience of the protagonist brings him to traditional worship.

T. S. Eliot's Rose-Garden

THE PURPOSE of this essay is to focus attention upon a specific aspect of continuity in the poetry of T. S. Eliot. I shall attempt to follow what I believe to be an important strand, a basic and persistent theme in Eliot's poetry throughout the course of his career. Consideration of this theme may begin by first taking notice of its appearance in Eliot's prose. In his essay on Dante (1929) he discusses the experience of ecstasy in childhood described in the *Vita Nuova:*

". . . Now Dante, I believe, had experiences which seemed to him of some importance . . . important in themselves; and therefore they seemed to him to have some philosophical and impersonal value. I find in it an account of a particular kind of experience: that is, of something which had actual experience (the experience of the "confession" in the modern sense) *and* intellectual and imaginative experience (the experience of thought and the experience of dream) as its materials; and which became a third kind. It seems to me of importance to grasp the simple fact that the *Vita Nuova* is neither a "confession" nor an "indiscretion" in the modern sense, nor is it a piece of Pre-Raphaelite tapestry. If you have that sense of intellectual and spiritual realities that Dante had, then a form of expression like the *Vita Nouva* cannot be classed either as "truth" or "fiction."

"In the first place, the type of sexual experience which Dante describes as occurring to him at the age of nine years is by no means impossible or unique. My only doubt (in which I found myself confirmed by a distinguished psychologist) is whether it could have taken place so *late* in life as the age of nine years. The psychologist agreed with me that it is more likely to occur at about five or six years of age. It is possible that Dante developed rather late, and it is also possible that he altered the dates to employ some other significance of the number nine. But to me it appears obvious that the *Vita Nuova* could only have been written around a personal experience. If so, the details do not matter: whether the lady was the Portinari or not, I do not care; it is quite likely that she is a blind for some one else, even for a person whose name Dante may have forgotten or never known. But I cannot find it incredible that what has happened to others should have happened to Dante with much greater intensity.

"The attitude of Dante to the fundamental experience of the *Vita Nuova* can only be understood by accustoming ourselves to find meaning in the *final causes* rather than in origins. It is not, I believe, meant as a description of what he *consciously* felt on his meeting with Beatrice, but rather as a description of what that meant on mature reflection upon it. The final cause is the attraction towards God."

Several details of Eliot's comment are of particular interest to us. He ascribes an obscurity and yet peculiar reality to the experience. He regards the experience as one not uncommon among men nor restricted to any single period or kind of period in history. He acknowledges that the experience may be variously interpreted, and he himself finds it significant beyond its phenomenal and experiential details: the experience is for him derivative of a supernatural cause; it represents implicitly and symbolically meanings that are of some intellectual complexity, meanings that are philosophical and religious.

This experience and the interpretation put upon it constitute the theme which we shall observe operating by various uses throughout Eliot's writings, from his earliest poetry to his most recent. I shall try to treat the poetry, as nearly as possible, in chronological order of its appearance. According to this plan, it seems natural and profitable to begin with a consideration of the French poem *Dans le Restaurant*, which appears in *Poems* (1920). This poem is made up, until the final section, of talk made by a shabby old waiter, uncouth and repellent in manners, to a "respectable" diner, who occasionally interrupts with indignance. For my own convenience I shall translate from the French, omitting here the diner's interruptions. The words of the "garçon délabré qui n'a rien à faire":

> In my country there is rainy weather,
> Wind, much sunshine, and rain;

The Man in the Name

> There is what one calls a beggar's washday.
>
> . . . .
>
> The willows drenched, and blossoms on the hedges —
> It is there, in a shower, that one takes shelter.
> I was seven, she was even younger.
> She was completely soaked, I gave her some primroses.
>
> . . . .
>
> I tickled her, in order to make her laugh.
> I experienced a moment of power and ecstasy.

At this point the diner's interruption is —

> Come now, old lecher, at that age . . .

But the waiter continues reminiscing:

> Sir, the fact is a hard one.
> A large dog came and bothered us;
> I was frightened, I left her half-way up the path.
> What a pity.

And now the diner finally has his say:

> Come now, you have your nerve!
> Go and wipe the streaks from your face.
> Here's my fork, scratch your head with it.
> By what right do you have experiences like mine?
> Now, here are ten sous, for the bathhouse.

Conspicuous in the words of the waiter, obviously central to the poem, is the childhood experience. Its potential significance is suggested by the intensity with which the old waiter is haunted by this experience, so haunted that he must tell of it to an unsympathetic and complete stranger. That Eliot intended the experience portrayed here as of the kind discussed in his essay on Dante is, I believe, beyond any doubt. Its being ascribed to the undignified old man illustrates that its source is basic in human nature and (to follow Eliot) in a nature beyond that. This is further emphasized by the statement of the snobbish patron: "De quel droit payes-tu des expériences comme moi?"

In his fine analysis of *The Waste Land* Cleanth Brooks has explicated the English version of the passage on the drowned Phoenician, pointing out its symbols and allusions, its several levels of

[170

meaning. But we should determine its coherent status in the French poem. To observe that the passage on drowning follows a reference to the waiter's need of a bath seems to me to be more than simply amusing. Here, as elsewhere in Eliot's poetry, water is symbolic of spiritual rebirth — a prerequisite of return to the obsessive experience. The manner by which the waiter is shown to be in need of water and the shift to the drowned man thus constitute a characteristic irony. And the shift illustrates again the "commonness" of the experience, bringing the lives of the two modern men and the ancient Phoenician within a single category. The Phoenician's death is cryptically, ironically, meant as a rebirth. The undersea current (symbol of a spiritual force) carries him "aux étapes de sa vie antérieure," presumably to an ecstatic moment in childhood and its *final cause*. The return by stages suggests a progress according to purification or purgation.

In *Dans le Restaurant* there are certain elements which, we shall notice, repeatedly characterize the theme. These are the images of water, foliage, the little girl and the proffered flowers. Another recurrent element is the waiter's remorse — remembering that he left the girl half-way up the path — for having withdrawn from the situation: "C'est dommage." The more-than-scenic significance of the images is well established in poems earlier even than *Dans le Restaurant*. For example, this obtains in *La Figlia che Piange* where, in addition to the images, there is the peculiar quality of the departure, the "pained surprise" and "resentment" of the girl — conversely related to the man's remorse. The speaker of the poem is, moreover, obviously involved in the scene; his final comment on it is explicit enough:

> I should have lost a gesture and a pose.
> Sometimes these cogitations still amaze
> The troubled midnight and the noon's repose.

Other thematic elements, incidental in the earlier poems but later to be elaborated and defined, occur in *The Love Song of J. Alfred Prufrock* and *Portrait of a Lady*.

> We have lingered in the chambers of the sea
> By sea-girls wreathed with seaweed red and brown
> Till human voices wake us, and we drown.

The Man in the Name

Prufrock's last words are a generalization. We bungle our adventures in the actual world because we are out of our true element, having strayed from the sea-girls and sea-chambers, the dreamworld that is an approach to spiritual reality. A similar hint of the "experience" is found in the *Portrait*.

> I keep my countenance,
> I remain self-possessed
> Except when a street piano, mechanical and tired
> Reiterates some worn-out common song
> With the smell of hyacinths across the garden
> Recalling things that other people have desired.
> Are these ideas right or wrong?

Here the speaker is distracted from his composure on the "actual" level by a reminder of the experience that is lost and neglected. These observations on *Prufrock* and *Portrait* are perhaps an over-reading of the poems taken singly. But I believe that they are justified in the light of later poems, and that the early passages become increasingly significant of the theme as one finds it more centrally and extensively treated in later compositions. Indeed, even the later poems will, in a sense, be over-read. Our emphasis is upon the theme, and it is often dominant in the work, but never the exclusive import — neither in *Dans le Restaurant* nor in *The Waste Land*. But on the other hand, with regard to Eliot's work as a whole, the theme is always basic as a point of view, even when there is no direct suggestion of the childhood experience.

In *Gerontion* the dramatic and imagistic details of the experience or any explicit references to it are not to be found. To the extent that this poem is allied with the theme, it is so allied generally and conceptually. If one recognizes the theme in the poems where its elements are more openly displayed, one will also see it as underlying *Gerontion*, and consequently find that poem additionally meaningful. The title and the senility portrayed throughout — the old man — represent a sense of remoteness from the experience of sexual-religious ecstasy and its significance. A similar representation (the aged eagle) is later to be observed in the first section of *Ash Wednesday*. *Gerontion* opens with the scene of old

age. Next is the statement of the coming in spring of "Christ the
tiger." This, I believe, is equivalent to the *experience*. There is
then the picture of Mr. Silvero, Hakagawa, etc., and their adjustment (or maladjustment) to it; and the old man again. The
passage that follows is of special significance, "key" for our purposes:

> After such knowledge, what forgiveness? Think now
> History has many cunning passages, contrived corridors
> And issues, deceives with whispering ambitions,
> Guides us by vanities. Think now
> She gives when our attention is distracted
> And what she gives, gives with such supple confusions
> That the giving famishes the craving. Gives too late
> What's not believed in, or if still believed,
> In memory only, reconsidered passion. Gives too soon
> Into weak hands, what's thought can be dispensed with
> Till the refusal propagates a fear.

As I read the passage, it is a statement of the difficulty of recap-
turing the experience, and yet of the need to return to it; of the
distractions which lead away from it. There is from this point of
view a criticism of man's world, a picture of the individual's predicament. What History gives is the experience. And we find here,
as elsewhere, the expression of inadequate response to it, of inability for a serious and effective attempt to reconstruct it. Further
along in the poem I find the idea of removal, of the *lost experience*,
even more particularized. It seems to me that this passage is an
apostrophe to the girl, the Lady, the partner in the experience:

> I that was near your heart was removed therefrom
> To lose beauty in terror, terror in inquisition.
> I have lost my passion: why should I need to keep it
> Since what is kept must be adulterated?
> I have lost my sight, smell, hearing, taste and touch:
> How should I use them for your closer contact?

We shall meet again in later poems the "terror" here mentioned,
and the loss of passion and the sensual faculties.

In discussing the theme as it is present in *The Waste Land* I
shall not review that poem in its entirety, but refer the reader to

Brooks' analysis. He will find, I believe, that the observations made here are consistent with Brooks' conclusions. The theme is evident in the first section, *The Burial of the Dead*. Following the song quoted from *Tristan and Isolde* is a passage comparable in its descriptive details to the scene in *Dans le Restaurant:*

> "You gave me hyacinths first a year ago;
> "They called me the hyacinth girl."
> — Yet when we came back, late, from the Hyacinth garden,
> Your arms full, and your hair wet, I could not
> Speak, and my eyes failed, I was neither
> Living nor dead, and I knew nothing,
> Looking into the heart of light, the silence.
> *Oed' und leer das Meer.*

The correspondence between the two garden scenes is surely obvious. And here, too, there is the tone of remorse. It may be noticed that the protagonist recalls not the experience in the garden, but his removal from it, his failure to see its meaning. The experience was both *life* and *death*, but its absence is neither.

The theme appears again at the end of the section, in the protagonist's speech to *Stetson*. In this passage the experience is attributed to all men of all times, to the man who was on King William Street and in the ships at Mylae, and attributed — with the quotation from Baudelaire — even to the reader. In addition to whatever other meanings it may have, I take the "corpse" to be a reference to the sexual-religious experience which has been neglected and repressed — or buried. (I am struck by the presence of the "Dog" here and the "gros chien" in *Dans le Restaurant*, but am not prepared to make anything of it.)

The section *Death by Water*, as it appears in Eliot's French poem, and its relation to the theme have been discussed above. The theme appears conspicuously again at the end of *The Waste Land*, in the passages respectively introduced by *Datta, Dayadhvam, Damyata*. There is first the statement of the intensity and persistent importance of the experience: "The awful daring of a moment's surrender." And then it is characterized as an unforgettable and desirable moment of freedom and communion: "I have heard the key / Turn in the door once and turn once only." And finally the experience is again referred to in terms nostalgic and remorseful: especially significant are the words *would have re-sponded:*

> The boat responded
> Gaily, to the hand expert with sail and oar
> The sea was calm, your heart would have responded
> Gaily, when invited, beating obedient
> To controlling hands.

I have already discussed *Ash Wednesday* at some length, indicating that the two ideas basic to the conceptual structure of the poem are the course of purgation prescribed by St. John of the Cross in his *Dark Night of the Soul*, and the principle of spiritual guidance symbolized by the "Lady" who appears prominently throughout the poem. In *Ash Wednesday* the theme which we discuss is more centrally and elaborately employed than in earlier poems, especially with regard to its religious aspect. I shall attend here only to salient points, those most obviously involved in the continuity of the theme.

The first section of *Ash Wednesday* expresses the senility and weakened sensual faculties which represent remoteness from the experience and despair of renewing it:

> Because I know I shall not know
> The one veritable transitory power . . .

The second section is addressed by the bones to the Lady. Among the abundant and complex elements of this section are those which refer to the nature of the experience, especially in the song of the bones to the "Lady of silences":

> Rose of memory
> Rose of forgetfulness
> . . . .
>
> The single Rose
> Is now the Garden
> Where all loves end
> Terminate torment
> Of love unsatisfied
> The greater torment
> Of love satisfied
> . . . .

The Man in the Name

> Grace to the Mother
> For the Garden
> Where all love ends.

The *memory* and *forgetfulness* recall Eliot's remark that "Dante may have forgotten or never known" the name of the person represented by Beatrice. This stated obscurity and elusiveness recurs in his subsequent writings. It appears again in the form of questions at the opening of the fourth section of *Ash Wednesday:* "Who walked between the violet and the violet . . ." A passage from this same section will illustrate the manner in which the theme is dramatically and symbolically developed throughout *Ash Wednesday*, as well as the significance put upon it:

> Here are the years that walk between, bearing
> Away the fiddles and the flutes, restoring
> One who moves in the time between sleep and waking . . .

The protagonist speaks from his condition of religious purgation. The present moment is seen as one resulting from and therefore containing the spiritual activity since the initial experience. This idea, it may be observed, is in accord with the coexistence of all times, as expressed elsewhere in *Ash Wednesday*, in *The Waste Land*, and *Four Quartets*. The experience is regarded as not being subject to temporal flux but as the timeless unchanging reality. It is, nevertheless, sought and approached by temporal means. For until the experience has been recreated one must act in the world of past, present, and future. Thus, intimations of the experience, the appearance of the Lady, come under special conditions, "in the time between sleep and waking." It may be noticed that in this poem and in others such moments are always characterized by a dreamlike, twilight atmosphere, as in the final section:

> In this brief transit where the dreams cross
> The dreamcrossed twilight between birth and dying . . .

In *Ash Wednesday*, more clearly and fully than in earlier poems, restoration of the childhood experience is identified with the goal of religious life, its meaning "on mature reflection upon it . . . the attraction towards God."

Similar to *Ash Wednesday* in its basic meaning, as well as in its lyrical quality, is the poem *Marina*, for which Eliot derived his "objective correlative" from Shakespeare's *Pericles*. The speaker of Eliot's poem is Pericles, Prince of Tyre, who, after years of believing that his daughter Marina is dead, finds to his amazement that she is still alive. The following passage is from the recognition scene (V. i) between father and daughter:

> PER.: But are you flesh and blood?
> Have you a working pulse? and are no fairy?
> Motion! Well; speak on. Where were you born?
> And wherefore call'd Marina?

The usefulness of this scene for Eliot's purposes is apparent: the unusual meeting between father and daughter is made dramatically to symbolize a restoration of the experience:

> What is this face, less clear and clearer
> The pulse in the arm, less strong and stronger —
> Given or lent? more distant than the stars and nearer
>   than the eye
>
> Whispers and small laughter between leaves and
>   hurrying feet
> Under sleep, where all the waters meet.

Obviously significant here are the dreamlike quality and the telling reference to the children among the foliage. And Eliot repeats in this poem the half-remembered character of the experience, the self-conscious effort for its recreation:

> I made this, I have forgotten
> And remember
> . . . . . .
> Made this unknowing, half conscious, unknown, my own.

Burnt Norton, even more than *Ash Wednesday* — more than any other of Eliot's poems — displays clearly on its surface the spiritual quest, the constant endeavor to interpret the experience and thus to relive it. The poem is a kind of essay, including within its range scenic description of the *garden* and philosophic discourse on the ultimate significance of the experience. In this poem Eliot repeats in effect and amplifies the passages in his essay on Dante. *Burnt*

The Man in the Name

Norton opens with a statement of the coexistence of all times, the ever-presence of past and future. An implication of this is that the lost experience of the past and the desired experience of the future are in no way repetitions, but exist identically in the timeless reality that is possibly available at any actual moment. As the first section of the poem progresses, it is granted, perhaps ironically, that the experience may not have actually occurred, may be only imagined; yet it is significantly implied that the experience is a goal to which one might *return*, as if it should have happened but did not, through a fault of human nature.

> What might have been is an abstraction
> Remaining a perpetual possibility
> Only in a world of speculation.
> What might have been and what has been
> Point to one end, which is always present.
> Footfalls echo in the memory
> Down the passage which we did not take
> Towards the door we never opened
> Into the rose-garden. My words echo
> Thus, in your mind.
>   But to what purpose
> Disturbing the dust on a bowl of rose-leaves
> I do not know.

Not having had the experience is comparable to a refusal of it; it is real for each of us, though we may not be awakened to that fact — just as God may exist despite the opinion of a world of infidels. In the next passage a bird speaks, beckoning "Into our first world," leading excitedly to the experience. But this is the "deception of the thrush," the deception of phenomenal details which seem by association to recall the experience: the scene that follows is not genuine, but mechanical and devitalized; the music is "unheard" and "hidden"; privacy is spoiled by an "unseen eyebeam" and the roses have the "look of flowers that are looked at." The details of the situation have been forcibly willed — "as our guests, accepted and accepting." For an instant the dry concrete pool is filled, the lotus rises (with sexual significance). But the pool is "water out of sunlight," a mirage, and disappears when a cloud passes over. The

effort is thus one of torment, disappointing in its partial and insufficient revelation. And yet, even in such attenuated form, an
intimation of the hidden experience is an unbearable strain on the
limited human capacity:

> Go said the bird, for the leaves were full of children,
> Hidden excitedly, containing laughter.
> Go, go, go, said the bird: human kind
> Cannot bear very much reality.

The second section begins with a discourse upon the reconciliation of extremes; all oppositions ("forgotten wars"), all that seems
disparate in life and in the universe, are finally discernible in a
harmonious pattern which has issued from a single source. And
this source is the "still point," describable only in paradoxical
terms: "Neither from nor towards . . . neither arrest nor movement." It is comparable to, perhaps derives from, the point in
Paradiso XXIX "where every *where* and every *when* is focused." In
Dante's poem the point is at the center of the nine circles representing the blessed orders, and the point itself represents the creative love of God, as it does in Eliot's poem:

> I can only say, *there* we have been: but I cannot say where.

The "experience" is, thus, allied with the point and partakes of its
quality:

> a grace of sense, a white light still and moving,
> *Erhebung* without motion, concentration
> Without elimination, both a new world
> And the old made explicit, understood
> In the completion of its partial ecstasy,
> The resolution of its partial horror.

This recalls the "terror" that follows the experience in *Gerontion*.
And here again are the hardly bearable reality and the circumstantial details of the temporal world by which it can be approached:

> Time past and time future
> Allow but a little consciousness
> To be conscious is not to be in time
> But only in time can the moment in the rose-garden,
> The moment in the arbour where the rain beat,

The Man in the Name

> The moment in the draughty church at smokefall
> Be remembered; involved with past and future.
> Only through time time is conquered.

The third section presents a picture of the barrier to the conquest of time and a means by which this barrier may be overcome. The barrier is the spiritual desolation of the world; it is to be overcome by the purgational system of St. John of the Cross — the descent into darkness and "perpetual solitude" — stated in compressed form at the end of the section.

A symbolic expression of St. John's *Dark Night* opens the fourth section: the day has been buried and the sun obscured. There follows then an eager questioning, "Will the sunflower turn to us," asking in effect whether life, rebirth, will come to one who waits in the prescribed passivity of purgation. And the section ends with an answer:

> After the kingfisher's wing
> Has answered light to light, and is silent, the light is still
> At the still point of the turning world.

The "kingfisher" I associate with the Fisher King of the waste land, which will be redeemed by a divine act. The passage thus means that there will be a rebirth when, through grace, the world is restored to contact with the "still point."

Many of the elements we have often observed so far are recapitulated in the final section of *Burnt Norton*. Spiritual aims, the timeless reality which is the beginning and end of all experience, are attainable only through discipline — "by the form, the pattern" — like the discipline of art. But the world presents a hindrance to discipline: "Shrieking voices . . . voices of temptation . . . The loud lament of the disconsolate chimera." And the poem concludes reaffirming the principle with which it began, the "one end, which is always present":

> Desire itself is movement
> Not in itself desirable;
> Love is itself unmoving,
> Only the cause and end of movement,
> Timeless, and undesiring

Except in the aspect of time
Caught in the form of limitation
Between un-being and being.
Sudden in a shaft of sunlight
Even while the dust moves
There rises the hidden laughter
Of children in the foliage
Quick now, here, now, always —
Ridiculous the waste sad time
Stretching before and after.

A distinction is made here between appetitive pursuit and the spiritual love which is the final "satisfaction" beyond temporal activity. The "waste sad time" is all mortal time. This passage embraces the systematic range of Eliot's conceptual materials, from the childhood experience of the rose-garden to a religious and philosophic ideology.

One who is already familiar with the several aspects of this theme would surely recognize them in Eliot's play *The Family Reunion*, even upon a first reading. Apart from the superficial structure of the play — the action-plot and the family relationships — are distinguishable Harry's many remarks upon time, experience, and a special kind of consciousness, remarks which all the family but Agatha consider nonsense and insanity. As the play develops it becomes more and more apparent that Harry's problem is not whether or not he murdered his wife, a moral problem, but a spiritual problem of longer standing to which the murder is only incidental. And this is what Harry finally discovers for himself. He is beset by a peculiar need, one which his family and the world do not understand. This need is the "experience," the advance toward spiritual rebirth and the peace of religious love — variously represented throughout Eliot's poetry and described in *Burnt Norton* as the "inner freedom from the practical desire."

I shall take notice of several instances in the play which clearly echo the theme in terms which we have seen to be its most specific representation. The first of these is in the long conversation between Harry and Mary. They discuss their childhood, their most intimate attitudes; and to Harry's question — "Is the spring not an evil time, that excites us with lying voices?" — Mary responds with surprising sympathy and understanding:

> Pain is the opposite of joy
> But joy is a kind of pain
> I believe the moment of birth
> Is when we have knowledge of death
> I believe the season of birth
> Is the season of sacrifice . . .

And thus for a moment the "experience" is suggested to Harry:

> You bring me news
> Of a door that opens at the end of a corridor,
> Sunlight and singing; when I had felt sure
> That every corridor only led to another,
> Or to a blank wall . . .

But Mary's brief communion with Harry soon fails, and it remains for his aunt Agatha to lead him to the door of the rose-garden.

The climactic scene of the play is the long dialogue of Harry and Agatha, in which she tells him of the loveless and bitter relationship of his father and mother, of her own love for his father whom she prevented from killing his mother, and of her emotional attachment to Harry himself. Just before giving this information Agatha introduces the motif of the "experience":

> There are hours when there seems to be no past or future,
> Only a present moment of pointed light
> When you want to burn. When you stretch out your hand
> To the flames. They only come once,
> Thank God, that kind. Perhaps there is another kind,
> I believe, across a whole Thibet of broken stones
> That lie, fang up, a lifetime's march. I have believed this.

And after Agatha's account, Harry exclaims —

> Look, I do not know why,
> I feel happy for a moment, as if I had come home.
> It is quite irrational, but now
> I feel quite happy, as if happiness
> Did not consist in getting what one wanted
> Or in getting rid of what can't be rid of
> But in a different vision. This is like an end.

T. S. Eliot's Rose-Garden

At this point I wish to refer to the penetrating study of *The Family Reunion* made by C. L. Barber, whose critical judgments I accept in large part. Mr. Barber presents an extremely interesting and persuasive criticism of the play from the psychoanalytic point of view. Yet I differ with his attitude that the play cannot be meaningfully interpreted except by this approach, which is illustrated by his comment on the verses just quoted: "Just because statements like this cannot be otherwise understood, one must employ psychoanalytic interpretation to get at their content — interpretation, that is, appropriate to non-communicative, asocial psychic products. In pursuing the meaning of the play, gaps appear which cannot be bridged except by following out unconscious symbolic associations." Mr. Barber's application of the psychoanalytic terms may be wholly accurate. But I think it is evident that passages such as the one on which he comments here *are* otherwise meaningful, and meaningful as the author consciously intended. It is true that one could hardly expect an audience or reader to grasp this meaning without a special preparation, a familiarity with its repeated occurrence throughout Eliot's work. If, however, one considers the play in the light of the already established continuity, the theme is no less understandable here than elsewhere. One so prepared would surely recognize the significance of the passage that comes toward the end of the dialogue between Harry and Agatha:

AGATHA: I only looked through the little door
        When the sun was shining on the rose-garden:
        And heard in the distance tiny voices
        And then a black raven flew over.
        And then I was only my own feet walking
        Away, down a concrete corridor
        In a dead air . . .
HARRY: In and out, in an endless drift
        Of shrieking forms in a circular desert . . .
AGATHA: Up and down, through the stone passages
        Of an immense and empty hospital . . .
HARRY: To and fro, dragging my feet
        Among inner shadows in the smoky wilderness . . .
        I was not there, you were not there, only our
           phantasms

> And what did not happen is as true as what did
>   happen,
> O my dear, and you walked through the little door
> And I ran to meet you in the rose-garden.
> AGATHA: This is the next moment. This is the beginning.
> We do not pass twice through the same door
> Or return to the door through which we did
>   not pass.
> I have seen the first stage: relief from what
>   happened
> Is also relief from that unfulfilled craving
> Flattered in sleep and deceived in waking.
>   You have a long journey.

The picture of agonized effort which is portrayed in the trancelike speeches of Harry and Agatha is that put upon one by the experience, the spiritual quest in an unsympathetic world. After the revelation by Agatha Harry is suddenly changed. Now he welcomes the presence of the Eumenides. Now it is clear to him that he "must go," that he must follow the "bright angels," which formerly he fled in horror. And thus once again Eliot invokes the paradoxical discipline of St. John's *Dark Night of the Soul*. We recall that the way to salvation begins in *Ash Wednesday* with spiritual and sensual debility, in *Burnt Norton* with the descent into darkness; and toward the end of the play it is stated in Harry's decisive words:

> Where does one go from a world of insanity?
> Somewhere on the other side of despair.
> To the worship in the desert, the thirst and deprivation,
> A stony sanctuary and a primitive altar,
> The heat of the sun and the icy vigil
> A care over lives of humble people,
> The lesson of ignorance, of incurable diseases.
> Such things are possible. It is love and terror
> Of what waits and wants me, and will not let me fall.

As I have said, I agree with Mr. Barber's critical judgments. The play has serious failings. Most important among these, it seems to me, is the degree of obscurity in which Eliot keeps his most important symbols; and also, his failure to integrate fully action and motivation with the dominant theme. Except for Harry and Agatha, none of the characters realizes what is happening. The central character's existence in a world of his own, though he admits it, prevents a true dramatic situation. The other characters do not know this world and refuse to know it. The nearest they come to it is their impersonal statement in the final Chorus: "We do not like the maze in the garden, because it too closely resembles the maze in the brain." But Eliot's experiment was a bold one.

The theme, as we have followed it so far, appears in a peculiarly personal application, not related to subjects that are public and historical in the most common sense. In the earlier work the experience is simply portrayed, referred to, or reflected fragmentarily. And then in *Ash Wednesday, Burnt Norton,* and *The Family Reunion* it is developed conceptually and dramatically. In Eliot's most recent work, the poems which with *Burnt Norton* have been brought together under the title *Four Quartets,* we find the theme no less personal in its significance, but also recognizably and directly related to the social scene, the World Wars and present chaos; that is, the meaning of the theme is extended from the individual to society.

East Coker has been discussed with illuminating information and sound comment in an article by James Johnson Sweeney. As a brief supplement to Sweeney's interpretation I shall indicate the presence of the "experience" in *East Coker.* The first two sections of the poem are a commentary on the cycle of history, the Renaissance and the world today, with the conclusion that there is "only a limited value / In the knowledge derived from experience," that the only wisdom is humility. In section III the darkness of the modern scene is equated with the spiritual darkness defined by St. John of the Cross: "let the darkness come upon you / Which shall be the darkness of God." Thus the darkness is a prefiguring of redemption: "the darkness shall be the light, and the stillness the dancing." And the redemption, the restoration to which purgation by humility and abjectness leads, is again represented by the "experience":

The Man in the Name

Whisper of running streams, and winter lightning.
The wild thyme unseen and the wild strawberry,
The laughter in the garden, echoed ecstasy
Not lost, but requiring, pointing to the agony
Of death and birth. You say I am repeating
Something I have said before. I shall say it again.
Shall I say it again? In order to arrive there,
To arrive where you are, to get from where you are not,
    You must go by a way wherein there is no ecstasy.

The fourth section represents the spiritual suffering by which
Christian salvation is to be attained. The last section of *East Coker*
is a personal statement of the effort for discipline that has been
made, of the meager and humble result, and yet of determination
to continue, despite the increasing difficulty of the times. And
now, not the "experience" alone is seen as significant of the essential reality in which *beginning* and *end* are identical, but all life,
all history:

Home is where one starts from. As we grow older
The world becomes stranger, the pattern more complicated
Of dead and living. Not the intense moment
Isolated, with no before and after,
But a lifetime burning in every moment
And not the lifetime of one man only
But of old stones that cannot be deciphered.

The discourse on history and its relation to the "experience" and
spiritual reality which was begun in *East Coker* is continued in
The Dry Salvages. As in *East Coker*, the meaning of reality is extended beyond the experience:

The moments of happiness — not the sense of well-being,
Fruition, fulfilment, security or affection,
Or even a very good dinner, but the sudden illumination —
We had the experience but missed the meaning,
And approach to the meaning restores the experience
In a different form, beyond any meaning
We can assign to happiness. I have said before
That the past experience revived in the meaning
Is not the experience of one life only
But of many generations — not forgetting
Something that is probably quite ineffable:

> The backward look behind the assurance
> Of recorded history, the backward half-look
> Over the shoulder, towards the primitive terror.

The "primitive terror" is represented in the poem by three principal symbols: the river, the ocean, and the rocks, all of which seem to be controlled by secular civilization but which continue actually as menacing and destructive. I have not space here to dwell upon the full meaning of the ocean, except to indicate that, in its immense shapelessness, it represents history as other than "sequence" and "development." It is thus already symbolical at the end of *East Coker*:

> We must be still and still moving
> . . . .
> Through the dark cold and the empty desolation,
> The wave cry, the wind cry, the vast waters.

In *The Dry Salvages* the symbolism is continued with the representation as "seamen" of those who are to live into the future, and with the exclamation to them "Not fare well, / But fare forward, voyagers." The final section of the poem repeats that the spiritual reality is approachable not alone in the ecstatic moment, but by a way of life:

> Men's curiosity searches past and future
> And clings to that dimension. But to apprehend
> The point of intersection of the timeless
> With time, is an occupation for the saint —
> No occupation either, but something given
> And taken, in a lifetime's death in love,
> Ardour and selflessness and self-surrender.
> For most of us, there is only the unattended
> Moment, the moment in and out of time,
> The distraction fit, lost in a shaft of sunlight,
> The wild thyme unseen, or the winter lightning
> Or the waterfall, or music heard so deeply
> That it is not heard at all, but you are the music
> While the music lasts.

And the poem ends affirming that life, even though it is short of saintliness and lacks the given ecstatic moment, may be meaningful and purposeful:

> And right action is freedom
> From past and future also.
> For most of us this is the aim
> Never here to be realised;
> Who are only undefeated
> Because we have gone on trying;
> We, content at the last
> If our temporal reversion nourish
> (Not too far from the yew-tree)
> The life of significant soil.

The three poems which follow *Burnt Norton* all make reference to World War II. Whereas the theme in *Burnt Norton* is developed on an abstract level and with no indication of an application other than personal, in the other poems the meaning of the theme is enlarged, applied to particular events in history, and thus extended beyond the personal. This tendency is more pronounced in each succeeding poem, and is most fully developed in *Little Gidding*, which is also the poem which reflects the war most fully and most immediately. In *Burnt Norton* the "waste sad time" which stretches before and after the personal experience is called ridiculous. In *The Dry Salvages* not only the personal experience but "right action is freedom / From past and future also." Thus all moments and all actions can be regarded as spiritually significant, as related to the timeless reality. In this sense, as it is stated in the final section of *Little Gidding*, ". . . history is a pattern / Of timeless moments. . . . History is now and England." And in the statement "The moment of the rose and the moment of the yew-tree / Are of equal duration," we see the rose-garden theme related to time and history — for the yew-tree, symbolic of death, is also symbolic of eternity, in which the pattern of history exists.

With the closing lines of *Little Gidding* the experience in the rose-garden is again clearly evoked:

> Through the unknown, remembered gate
> When the last of earth left to discover
> Is that which was the beginning;
> At the source of the longest river
> The voice of the hidden waterfall
> And the children in the apple-tree

Not known, because not looked for
But heard, half-heard, in the stillness
Between two waves of the sea.
Quick now, here, now, always —
A condition of complete simplicity
(Costing not less than everything) . . .

This passage is rich in symbols, themes, and ideas which are the immediate materials of *Four Quartets*, and which can be followed back through all of Eliot's poetry. In this passage, as in the whole body of the poetry, the theme of the experience in the rose-garden is of central significance. We begin to see a pattern that is both intricate and intelligible when we focus our attention on this point.

◆ Laforgue, Conrad, and T. S. Eliot

IT IS some time now since the detection of sources for the poetry of T. S. Eliot has settled into a routine. It will soon be obvious that this remark is a kind of left-handed apology for what is undertaken here. I want only, by way of introduction, to announce that I shall be making some routine detections which are, I hope, of more than routine significance. I should also announce that there are several lines of interest which will meet each other at variously distributed intersections and which at times return upon themselves.

It will help make a point to set down not only the result of a detection but also part of my experience in making it, for there is a somewhat peculiar issue here. There was a stage in the experience that was like the discovery of a sure answer, but attended by considerable unsureness as to what the question should be. I was reading an English translation of a prose work of Laforgue, the *Hamlet* of his *Moralités Légendaires,* and came upon a passage that reminded me, forcibly, of Eliot's poetry. When I turned to Laforgue's French, the impression was the same. The peculiar thing was that while Laforgue's prose seemed strikingly Eliotic, it was not immediately apparent what parts of Eliot's poetry were Laforguean in this way. The passage is from Laforgue's version of the "poor Yorick" scene, where Hamlet expounds upon the corruption of the body. Here is the French, where I italicize the key passage, and also the translation of the key passage, which I have arranged, for the purpose of emphasis, in an imitation of Eliot's verse:

"Horrible, horrible, horrible! — J'ai peut-être encore vingt ans, trente ans à vivre, et j'y passerai comme les autres. Comme les autres? — Oh Tout! quelle misère, ne plus y être! — Ah! Je veux dès demain partir, m'enquérir par le monde des procédés d'embaumement les plus adamantins. — *Elles furent aussi, les petites gens de l'Histoire, apprenant à lire, se faisant les ongles, allumant chaque soir la sale lampe, amoureux, gourmands, vaniteux, fous de compliments, de poignées de mains et de baisers, vivant de cancans de clochers, disant: 'Quel temps fera-t-il demain? Voici l'hiver qui vient . . . Nous n'avons pas eu de prunes cette année.'* — Ah! tout est bien qui n'a pas de fin. Et toi, Silence, pardonne à la Terre; la petite folle ne sait trop ce qu'elle fait; au jour de la grande addition de la Conscience devant l'Idéal, elle sera étiquettée d'un piteux *idem* dans la colonne des évolutions miniatures de l'Evolution Unique, dans la colonne des quantités négligeables. — Et puis, des mots, des mots, des mots! Ce sera là ma devise tant qu'on ne m'aura pas démontré que nos langues riment bien à une réalité transcendante."

> They also existed, the little people of History,
> Learning to read, doing their finger nails,
> Lighting their dirty lamps every evening,
> Amorous, greedy, vain, mad about compliments
> And pressures of the hand and kisses, living lives
> That were can-cans dangling in a belfry, saying
> "What will the weather be tomorrow? . . .
> Now winter will be beginning . . .
> We have had no plums this year." *

It is, of course, well known that Laforgue was an important influence on the early stages of Eliot's poetic career. But when I looked in Eliot's work up through *The Waste Land* and *The Hollow Men* I could find only general qualities, what we call an assimilated and pervasive influence, nothing that could be referred specifically to this passage of Laforgue's prose. The answer to the question, or vice versa, came only when I looked in still later work, and found it in *Animula*:

> 'Issues from the hand of God, the simple soul'
> To a flat world of changing lights and noise,
> To light, dark, dry or damp, chilly or warm;
> Moving between the legs of tables and of chairs,
> Rising or falling, grasping at kisses and toys,
> Advancing boldly, sudden to take alarm,

* The versification is mine, but the English translation of Laforgue, here and elsewhere in this essay, is that of Frances Newman, *Six Moral Tales of Jules Laforgue*, New York: Horace Liveright, 1928.

Retreating to the corner of arm and knee,
Eager to be reassured, taking pleasure
In the fragrant brilliance of the Christmas tree,
Pleasure in the wind, the sunlight and the sea;
. . . .
Issues from the hand of time the simple soul
Irresolute and selfish, misshapen, lame,
Unable to fare forward or retreat,
Fearing the warm reality, the offered good,
Denying the importunity of the blood,
Shadow of its own shadows, spectre in its own gloom,
Leaving disordered papers in a dusty room;
Living first in the silence after the viaticum.

Between the passages from Laforgue and Eliot there is correspondence of subject and imagery, rhythm and tone. For me, it was the similarity of rhythm and tone that was first felt. In each passage there is a rhythm produced by a series of grammatically parallel phrases. Alternation and variation of rhythm result from the change in length of phrase from one series to another and also from the use of single words in series. For example, in Laforgue there are the participial phrases that begin with *apprenant, se faisant, allumant, vivant, disant,* and in Eliot *moving, using, grasping, advancing, retreating,* and others. Laforgue's series of words, *amoureux, gourmands, vaniteux,* seems to find an echo in Eliot's "Irresolute and selfish, misshapen, lame."

It is, finally, the similarity of tone that gives significance to the mechanical parallelism of rhythmical elements, for as Eliot has said of the music of poetry, the music does not exist without the meaning. Eliot's poem begins with a picture of childhood and ends with a picture of death, and Laforgue's passage also suggests the span of human life, from *apprenant à lire* to *au jour de la grande addition de la Conscience devant l'Idéal.* Common elements are the references to people in relation to furniture and to weather and seasons. The word *silence* is used with special and similar meaning in both passages. Eliot's "after the viaticum" corresponds to Laforgue's *réalité transcendante.* Common also is the view of the pathetic eagerness of human need and of man's life as petty, sordid, and vain. Laforgue's Hamlet expresses here an ambivalent attitude toward the generality of mankind, implying senses both of separateness and of identification. This ambivalence is pervasive throughout much of Eliot's work, and in the final lines of *Animula* this sense of the otherness of others is suggested by the naming of Guiterriez, Boudin, and Floret, and by "this one who made a great fortune / And that one who went his own way" — yet there is also the sense of identification in the "Pray for *us*" of the last line — quoted, of course, with the change of *death* to *birth*, from the *Ave Maria*.

Eliot's title, *Animula* (derived from Hadrian's lines on death *), means "little soul" and it is possible that the word was associated by Eliot with *les petites gens*. The plausibility of this speculation is enhanced by other details. Some pages earlier in Laforgue's *Hamlet* there is a passage of poetry containing the line *O petite âme brave*, practically the French equivalent for Hadrian's Latin. Shortly after this passage is another containing the line *Simple et sans foi comme un bonjours*, adapted by Eliot in *La Figlia che Piange* as "Simple and faithless as a smile or shake of the hand." In this poem there are the lines

> As the soul leaves the body torn and bruised,
> As the mind deserts the body it has used.

Hadrian is again suggested here, for he, too, speaks of the soul departing from the body. Laforgue's *Hamlet* and Hadrian's lines both appear to be part of an established and continuing association for Eliot. One may note, incidentally, a kind of blending or linkage of associations, for with the *Hamlet* connection, Ophelia is suggested as a type of *la figlia che piange*, and thus with the Hyacinth girl and the whole intricate and pervasive pattern of the rose-garden theme in Eliot's work.

Laforgue's passage is specifically echoed again in a still later work, *Murder in the Cathedral*, where the Women of Canterbury

---

*O Animula vagula, blandula,
  Hospes comesque, corporis,
  Que nunc abibis in loca?
  Pallidula, lurida, timidula,
  Nec, ut soles, dabis joca.

represent *les petites gens de l'Histoire*. In the second Chorus of
the play they describe themselves as "the small folk drawn into the
pattern of fate, the small folk who live among small things."
In the same Chorus they speak these lines:

> Sometimes the corn has failed us,
> Sometimes the harvest is good,
> One year is a year of rain
> Another a year of dryness,
> One year the apples are abundant,
> Another year the plums are lacking.
> Yet we have gone on living,
> Living and partly living.

Like Laforgue's *petites gens,* Eliot's small folk are concerned with
weather, seasons, and crops. Both speak in a rhythm that is produced by a series of short and simple statements. It is, I think,
something of a curiosity that Eliot follows Laforgue in ending the
series of statements with the mention of the plums. The plums
and the small folk are the kind of detail, bolstered by the context,
on which one can pin one's arguments, and if it were not for the
detail, one might have doubts, or at least some timidity about
setting down one's impressions. This instance is a formidable les-
son in how elusive the question of influence may be. For example,
there may be Laforguean echoes in *Four Quartets* and Eliot's
other plays, as I shall eventually suggest, but without the benefit
of any "plums." *

At the end of his essay "Swinburne as Poet" (1920) Eliot remarks that "the language which is more important to us is that
which is struggling to digest and express new objects, new groups
of objects, new feelings, new aspects, as, for instance, the prose of
Mr. James Joyce or the earlier Conrad." It is the reference to
Conrad with which I am concerned. As far as I know, neither
Eliot himself nor anyone else has elaborated on the meaning of
this statement. We have long known, of course, from the epigraph

---

* The general impression that Laforgue's influence ceased early in Eliot's
career and that it is not shown by the plays is reflected by E. J. H. Greene's
book *T. S. Eliot et la France,* (Paris: Boivin et Cie., 1951). "Les œuvres drama-
tiques d'Eliot, *The Rock* (1934), *Murder in the Cathedral* (1935) et *The
Family Reunion* (1939), ne portent pas de traces d'influence française" (p. 136).

to *The Hollow Men* ("Mistah Kurtz — he dead") that *Heart of Darkness* has a general relevance to this poem. There is also the exchange of letters between Eliot and Ezra Pound at the time Pound had made his now famous criticism of Eliot's manuscript of *The Waste Land*.* We learn from these letters that Eliot had originally intended to use the quotation from Conrad as the epigraph to that poem. Pound had written Eliot, "I doubt if Conrad is weighty enough to stand the citation." Eliot replied, "Do you mean not use the Conrad quote or simply not put Conrad's name to it? It is much the most appropriate I can find, and somewhat elucidative." To this, Pound answered that Eliot should do as he liked. Although Eliot yielded the point, it is obvious from his remarks that Conrad was far weightier for him than he was for Pound.

What, then, is the relevance of *Heart of Darkness* to *The Waste Land*? There is in the first section of the poem the line "Looking into the heart of light, the silence," which contains a phrase suggestive of the title of Conrad's story. It has been noted† that the first song of the Thames-daughters,

> The barges drift
> With the turning tide
> Red sails
> Wide
> To leeward . . .

derives images from Conrad's description of the Thames at the opening of the story: "In the offing the sea and the sky were welded together without a joint, and in the luminous space the tanned sails of the barges drifting up with the tide seemed to stand still in red clusters of canvas sharply peaked, with gleams of vanished spirits." Eliot's use of these images is, however, not enough to explain why the reference to Conrad's story is "much the most appropriate I can find, and somewhat elucidative." In this respect, it is

---

* Eliot's letter, as well as Pound's, is printed in *The Letters of Ezra Pound 1907–1941*, edited by D. D. Paige (New York: Harcourt, Brace, 1950), pp. 169–171.

† By Elizabeth Drew, in *T. S. Eliot: The Design of His Poetry* (New York · Charles Scribner's Sons, 1949), pp. 91–2.

not the images but, in the same sentence, the phrase "with gleams of vanished spirits" that is most significant.

In the early paragraphs of the story Conrad develops this theme of the "vanished spirits":

"The old river in its broad reach rested unruffled at the decline of day, after ages of good service done to the race that peopled its banks. . . . We looked at the venerable stream not in the vivid flush of a short day that comes and departs forever, but in the august light of abiding memories. And indeed nothing is easier . . . than to evoke the great spirit of the past upon the lower reaches of the Thames. The tidal current runs to and fro in its unceasing service, crowded with memories of men and ships it had borne to the rest of home or to the battles of the sea."

After this come evocative allusions to English sea-history and its role in the development of empire. Then Marlow begins his long talk to his mates with the remarks:

"And this also has been one of the dark places of the earth. . . . I was thinking of very old times, when the Romans first came here, nineteen hundred years ago — the other day. Light came out of this river since — you say knights? Yes; but it is like a running blaze on a plain, like a flash of lightning in the clouds. We live in the flicker — may it last as long as the old earth keeps rolling! But darkness was here yesterday."

Marlow goes on to imagine the experience of the Romans who encountered the savagery and mystery of ancient England, "the growing regrets, the longing to escape, the powerless disgust, the surrender, the hate." He evokes the ancient experience not only with great vividness, but gives it a quality of the contemporaneous, rendering the past in terms of the present — "their administration was merely a squeeze, and nothing more, I suspect." This part of the story is in thematic relationship with Conrad's evocation of England's glorious sea-history and also with the tale that Marlow is to tell of his journey on another river in search of Mr. Kurtz and into the heart of darkness.

One of my purposes (others will appear) in quoting and reviewing this much of the story is to indicate a facet of relationship between the story and the poem. In both there are the "gleams of vanished spirits." Eliot's intricate and complex merging of times, places, and persons may not have been suggested by Conrad's story, but the story is in this respect appropriate and elucidative. Later in the story Marlow makes a comment which states a major theme of Eliot's poetry and a frequent preoccupation of his prose: "The mind of man is capable of anything — because everything is in it, all the past as well as all the future." The water imagery of both works is involved in this theme. Conrad develops his theme of time and history with relation to the Thames and then suggests a relation between the Thames — "darkness was here yesterday" — and the African river where yesterday's darkness still exists. In *The Waste Land* times and places are merged with reference to rivers and sea-ways: "You who were with me in the ships at Mylae!" "By the waters of Leman I sat down and wept."

There are other ways in which *Heart of Darkness* can be brought to bear upon *The Waste Land*, but since I believe that the story is also related to Eliot's later development, it is a convenient and economical strategy to say so at this time. In order to treat this subject, I shall have to quote at some length. After the account of Kurtz' death, Marlow tells of his own almost fatal illness and then of his return to the European city:

"However, as you see, I did not go to join Kurtz there and then. I did not. I remained to dream the nightmare out to the end, and to show my loyalty to Kurtz once more. Destiny. My destiny! Droll thing life is — that mysterious arrangement of merciless logic for a futile purpose. The most you can hope from it is some knowledge of yourself — that comes too late — a crop of unextinguishable regrets. I have wrestled with death. It is the most unexciting contest you can imagine. It takes place in an impalpable grayness, with nothing underfoot, with nothing around, without spectators, without clamor, without glory, without the great desire of victory, without the great fear of defeat, in a sickly atmosphere of tepid skepticism, without much belief in your own right, and still less in that of your adversary. If such is the form of ultimate wisdom, then life is a greater riddle than some of us think it to be. I was within a hair's-breadth of the last opportunity for pronouncement, and I found with humiliation that probably I would have nothing to say. This is the reason why I affirm that Kurtz was a remarkable man. He had something to say. He said it. Since I had peeped over the edge myself, I understand better the meaning of his stare, that could not see the flame of the candle but was wide enough to embrace the whole universe, piercing enough to penetrate all the hearts that beat in the darkness. He had summed up — he had judged. 'The horror!' He was a remarkable man. After all, this was the expression of some sort of belief; it had candor, it had conviction, it had a vibrating note of revolt in its whisper, it had the appalling face of a glimpsed truth — the strange commingling of desire and hate. And it is not my own extremity I remember best — a vision of grayness without form filled with physical pain, and a careless contempt for the evanescence of all things — even of this pain itself. No! It is his extremity that I seemed to have lived through. True, he had made that last stride, he had stepped over the edge, while I had been permitted to draw back my hesitating foot. And perhaps in this is the whole difference; perhaps all the wisdom, and all truth, and all sincerity, are just compressed into that inappreciable moment of time in which we step over the threshold of the invisible. Perhaps! I like to think my summing up would not have been a word of careless contempt. Better his cry — much better. It was an affirmation, a moral victory paid for by innumerable defeats, by abominable terrors, by abominable satisfactions. But it was a victory! That is why I have remained loyal to Kurtz to the last, and even beyond, when a long time after I heard once more, not his own voice, but the echo of his magnificent eloquence thrown to me from a soul as translucently pure as a cliff of crystal.

"No, they did not bury me, though there is a period of time which I remember mistily, with a shuddering wonder, like a passage through some inconceivable world that had no hope in it and no desire. I found myself back in the sepulchral city resenting the sight of people hurrying through the streets to filch a little money from each other, to devour their infamous cookery, to gulp their unwholesome beer, to dream their insignificant and silly dreams. They trespassed upon my thoughts. They were intruders whose knowledge of life was to me an irritating pretense, because I felt so sure they could not possibly know the things I knew. Their bearing, which was simply the bearing of commonplace individuals going about their business in the assurance of perfect safety, was offensive to me like the outrageous flauntings of folly in the face of a danger it is unable to comprehend. I had no particular desire to enlighten them, but I had some difficulty in restraining myself from laughing in their faces, so full of stupid importance. I dare say I was not very well at that time."

The first issue I shall raise about this passage is that of the language, which Eliot found so important in the earlier Conrad. I shall find it helpful to refer again to my own experience. Long familiar with the story, at a particular rereading I found myself hearing in this passage the accents and inflections, the familiar voice, of Eliot's poetry. The situation was like the one I had encountered with Laforgue's *Hamlet* — but of course, with some differences, and these differences become difficulties here. The story is widely known and the passage is fairly often cited in comments on Eliot, where some of the attitudes and ideas expressed by Marlow are related to *The Hollow Men* and *The Waste Land*. I was aware of all this, and had for long regarded the passage as impressively Conradian. How, then, shall I ask the reader to acknowledge what I now see and hear, what I feel, in the passage?

Perhaps it is already evident, but there may nonetheless be some purpose in pursuing the question. Hoping to emphasize the Eliotic qualities of Conrad's prose, I shall arrange parts of it in an imitation of Eliot's verse.

> It takes place in an impalpable grayness,
> With nothing underfoot, with nothing around,
> Without spectators, without clamor, without glory,
> Without the great desire of victory,
> Without the great fear of defeat,
> In a sickly atmosphere of tepid skepticism,
> Without much belief in your own right,
> And still less in that of your adversary.
>
> No, they did not bury me,
> Though there is a period of time
> Which I remember mistily, with a shuddering wonder,
> Like a passage through some inconceivable world
> That had no hope in it and no desire.
> I found myself back in the sepulchral city
> Resenting the sight of people hurrying through
>   the streets
> To filch a little money from each other,
> To devour their infamous cookery,

The Man in the Name

> To gulp their unwholesome beer,
> To dream their insignificant and silly dreams.
> They trespassed upon my thoughts.

As in the case of Laforgue, we must ask, What parts of Eliot's poetry are Conradian in this way? Since *The Waste Land* and *The Hollow Men* have a documented relationship to the story, I shall look at these poems first. In both these excerpts, and especially in the first, there are the negativity, the vacuity, the lack of desire, and the "tepid skepticism" which also inform the opening lines of *The Waste Land* and the whole of *The Hollow Men*. There are other, and perhaps more specific, elements of correspondence: In *The Waste Land*, between "A crowd flowed over London Bridge, so many" and Conrad's "the sight of people hurrying through the streets"; between "I had not thought death had undone so many" and Conrad's "sepulchral city"; between "Unreal City" and Conrad's "some inconceivable world." In *The Hollow Men*, between "shade without colour," "the twilight kingdom," and Conrad's "an impalpable grayness." These correspondences of image and idea no doubt contribute to the similarity of sound between Eliot and Conrad, yet they do not wholly explain it. But before going on to this question I should like to call attention to elements in Eliot's earlier work that may echo in the reading of Conrad. I refer to *Preludes* and note these correspondences: "smell of steaks" with "infamous cookery"; "smells of beer" with "unwholesome beer"; "the sawdust-trampled street" with "hurrying through the streets"; "early coffee-stands" and "a thousand furnished rooms" (by implication) with "to filch a little money from each other"; "the night revealing / The thousand sordid images / Of which your soul was constituted" with "to dream their insignificant and silly dreams"; "eyes / Assured of certain certainties" with "the assurance of perfect safety" and "their faces, so full of stupid importance." Finally, Eliot's poem and the passage from Conrad both end with images of grotesque laughter. It is to be noted that both writers depict the cycle of activities of the ordinary day, and that the corresponding elements are in an approximately corresponding order.

LaForgue, Conrad, and T. S. Eliot

Turning now strictly to the question of sound, we can note in the versified excerpts from Conrad not only images and ideas like those of Eliot, but also rhythmical patterns like those of Eliot's verse. In fact, it so happens that Conrad's rhythmical devices are precisely those we noticed in Laforgue's prose and in the passages of Eliot that are allied to it. These devices are series of parallel and grammatically limited phrases, with alternation and variation of rhythm produced from series to series by differing lengths and constructions of phrase. The most obvious features of this kind in the excerpts from Conrad are the prepositional and infinitive phrases. But where else in Eliot do we find this rhythmical pattern? It is present throughout *The Hollow Men* and *Ash Wednesday* and it is common in *The Waste Land*, where an obvious example is the opening passage, with its participial phrases beginning with "breeding," "mixing," "stirring," "covering," "feeding." Another example may be found near the end of the poem:

> My friend, blood shaking my heart
> The awful daring of a moment's surrender
> Which an age of prudence can never retract
> By this, and this only, we have existed
> Which is not to be found in our obituaries
> Or in memories draped by the beneficent spider
> Or under seals broken by the lean solicitor
> In our empty rooms.

Indeed, I find the pattern common throughout the entire body of Eliot's poetry, but I shall illustrate, with rigorous selection, only from the later work.

> Where there is no temple there shall be no homes,
> Though you have shelters and institutions,
> Precarious lodgings while the rent is paid,
> Subsiding basements where the rat breeds
> Or sanitary dwellings with numbered doors
> Or a house a little better than your neighbors . . .
> *The Rock*

> Only a flicker
> Over the strained time-ridden faces
> Distracted from distraction by distraction

The Man in the Name

Filled with fancies and empty of meaning
Tumid apathy with no concentration
Men and bits of paper, whirled by the cold wind
That blows before and after time . . .

Burnt Norton

a time
Older than the time of chronometers, older
Than time counted by anxious worried women
Lying awake, calculating the future,
Trying to unweave, unwind, unravel
And piece together the past and the future . . .

The Dry Salvages

Emptiness, absence, separation from God;
The horror of the effortless journey to the empty land
Which is no land, only emptiness, absence, the Void,
Where those who were men can no longer turn the mind
To distraction, delusion, escape into dream, pretence
Where the soul is no longer deceived, for there are
no objects, no tones,
No colours, no forms to distract, to divert the soul
From seeing itself, foully united forever, nothing
with nothing . . .

Murder in the Cathedral

The sudden solitude in a crowded desert
In a thick smoke, many creatures moving
Without direction, for no direction
Leads anywhere but round and round in that vapour —
Without purpose, and without principle of conduct
In flickering intervals of light and darkness;
The partial anaesthesia of suffering without feeling
And partial observation of one's own automatism
While the slow stain sinks deeper through the skin
Tainting the flesh and discolouring the bone . . .

The Family Reunion

They may remember
The vision they have had, but they cease to regret it,
Maintain themselves by the common routine,
Learn to avoid excessive expectation,
Become tolerant of themselves and others,

LaForgue, Conrad, and T. S. Eliot

Giving and taking, in the usual actions
What there is to give and take. They do not repine;
Are contented with the morning that separates
And with the evening that brings together
For casual talk before the fire
Two people who know they do not understand each other.
Breeding children whom they do not understand
And who will never understand them.

The Cocktail Party

I know what you mean. Then the flowers would fade
And the music would stop. And the walls would be broken.
And you would find yourself in a devastated area —
A bomb-site . . . willow-herb . . . a dirty public square.

The Confidential Clerk

A peculiar problem that has perhaps been pressing for some time arises from Eliot's having this characteristic rhythm in common both with Laforgue and Conrad. It is, indeed, curious that these two writers are, in the passages indicated, reminiscent of Eliot in the same way, and thus reminiscent also of each other. My own experience tells me that a reader familiar with Eliot might project Eliotic qualities onto the passages of Laforgue and Conrad, but this is possible because there is actually a coincidence of elements between the two passages. In addition to the common rhythmical patterns already noted, there are also a number of similar meanings. Laforgue's Hamlet and Conrad's Marlow both express attitudes of alienation from the ordinary routines of human existence, routines which they both evoke with comparable details and qualities. Each speaker is preoccupied with death and, moreover, with the moment of death. Almost immediately after the passage quoted from Laforgue, Hamlet makes this comment:

"Mourir! C'est entendu, on meurt sans s'en apercevoir, comme chaque soir on entre en sommeil. On n'a pas conscience du passage de la dernière pensée lucide au sommeil, à la syncope, à la Mort."

("Dying! The idea is that one can die without noticing it, just as one can go to sleep every night. One isn't conscious of the last clear idea before sleep, before syncope, or before Death.")

The Man in the Name

And this corresponds, of course, to Marlow's "I was within a hair's-breadth of the last opportunity for pronouncement, and I found with humiliation that probably I would have nothing to say." All these correspondences between Laforgue and Conrad are sufficient to suggest that Eliot has been aware of them, although with what degree of consciousness I am not prepared to say. My speculation is that the stories of Laforgue and Conrad struck in Eliot an already existing chord, and that this chord has reverberated throughout his work. Eliot has made a number of remarks which support this notion. In the first he is speaking of imagery borrowed by Chapman, in his *Bussy d'Ambois*, from Seneca:

"There is first the probability that this imagery had some personal saturation value, so to speak, for Seneca; another for Chapman, and another for myself, who have borrowed it twice from Chapman. I suggest that what gives it such intensity as it has in each case is its saturation — I will not say with 'associations', for I do not want to revert to Hartley — but with feelings too obscure for the authors even to know quite what they were" (*The Use of Poetry and the Use of Criticism*).

"I know that a poem, or a passage of a poem, may tend to realize itself first as a particular rhythm before it reaches expression in words, and that this rhythm may bring to birth the idea and the image; and I do not believe that this is an experience peculiar to myself" (*The Music of Poetry*).

These remarks, taken together, indicate that certain rhythms and images have had for Eliot a profound and abiding personal value, that they have been involved with feelings and ideas, and that all have been in a poetically creative relationship. Another and more general correspondence between Laforgue and Conrad, and one that would be significant to Eliot, lies in the fact that both passages are *spoken* (by Hamlet and Marlow) and show the qualities of the idiom to which Eliot has more than once said poetry must at times return. Closely relevant also is his remark that "poetry has as much to learn from prose as from other poetry; and I think that an interaction between prose and verse, like the interaction between language and language, is a condition of vitality in literature" (*Use of Poetry*). It is also conceivable that the passages by Laforgue and Conrad impressed Eliot and became associated for him because, among other reasons, they both show that pattern of rhythm which is characteristic of the poetry of the Bible. Any familiar passage — the Twenty-third Psalm — will illustrate. A convention of ancient Hebrew poetry, arising out of the very nature of the language, is a rhythm that is logical and grammatical rather than syllabic. This rhythm survives in translation because it is basically a rhythm of thought, of statements simply made in a succession of grammatically parallel constructions — a rhythm that arises from the nature of human utterance itself. Writers of free verse, beginning with Whitman, have often turned to this mode of rhythm as an alternative to the rhythm of metered syllables. The Bible echoes and re-echoes in Eliot's poetry, and frequently it is the device of rhythm which produces the echo. At times the style is actually biblical, and at times it is a blending of biblical and contemporary idioms, as in these lines from *The Rock*:

> In this land
> There shall be one cigarette to two men,
> To two women one half pint of bitter
> Ale. In this land
> No man has hired us.
> Our life is unwelcome, our death
> Unmentioned in "The Times."

The list of quotations from Eliot's poetry given above illustrates the persistence of a rhythmical pattern, but I should like to explore further other kinds of reverberation of the chord struck by Laforgue and Conrad, and at times with attention to some of these quotations. Recalling Marlow's remark "We live in the flicker," we may note the presence of this image in the passage from *Burnt Norton* — "Only a flicker / Over the strained time-ridden faces," and from *The Family Reunion* — "In flickering intervals of light and darkness." In the passage from *The Cocktail Party* the same image of the alternation of nights and days is suggested by "the morning that separates / And the evening that brings together." This image of recurring alternation is also to be found in the earlier work, as in the sequence from evening to morning to evening in *Preludes*, and in *Sweeney Agonistes*,

> And the morning
> And the evening
> And noontime
> And night
> Morning
> Evening
> Noontime
> Night . . .

These earlier instances might more plausibly be considered facets of the already existing chord rather than of the effected reverberation.

Turning now to the passage from *Murder in the Cathedral*, we find in this picture of unredeemed death a detailed correspondence with Marlow's account of his illness and of his return to "the sepulchral city." "The effortless journey, to the empty land / Which is no land, only emptiness, absence, the Void" is indeed "like a passage through some inconceivable world that had no hope in it and no desire." The words *dream* and *pretense* occur in both passages with similar value. The condition of "no objects, no tones, / No colours, no forms to distract, to divert the soul / From seeing itself, foully united forever, nothing with nothing," is like the condition of "an impalpable grayness, with nothing underfoot, with nothing around, without spectators, without clamor, without glory" — and is also the condition of having "nothing to say" at the "last opportunity for pronouncement." We find in these lines of the Chorus the idea of the moment of death, which is common to both Laforgue and Conrad and which appears elsewhere in Eliot's work. In *The Family Reunion* Amy, Harry's mother, remarks to his aunts and uncles,

> You none of you understand how old you are
> And death will come to you as a mild surprise,
> A momentary shudder in a vacant room.

The implication in every case is that the essential quality of the moment of death is also the essential quality of the individual in all his living. This idea is stated explicitly, with a quotation from the *Baghavad Gita*, in *The Dry Salvages*:

> At the moment which is not of action or inaction
> You can receive this: 'on whatever sphere of being
> The mind of man may be intent
> At the time of death' — that is the one action
> (And the time of death is every moment)
> Which shall fructify in the lives of others.

In the light of this, we may recall Marlow's loyalty to the remarkable Kurtz, and Marlow's statement: "Perhaps all the wisdom, and all truth, and all sincerity, are just compressed into that inappreciable moment of time in which we step over the threshold of the invisible."

There is some ambiguity in Marlow's use of the word *flicker*, or perhaps I have created this ambiguity by relating it to Eliot's use of the same word. I think that Marlow's statement does suggest the sequence of nights and days, but in its own context its immediate and logical meaning is that the light of civilization is but a flicker, a flash, in the abiding darkness that has preceded and must follow. This consideration leads me back to the image and theme of the river, with which *Heart of Darkness* opens and closes. At the opening, Conrad speaks of the service performed by the river: ". . . ages of good service done to the race that peopled its banks . . . The tidal current runs to and fro in its unceasing service . . . It had known and served all the men of whom the nation is proud." Then Marlow imagines the river of Roman times: "Sandbanks, marshes, forests, savages . . . death skulking in the air, in the water, in the bush . . . Land in a swamp, march through the woods, and in some inland post feel the savagery, the utter savagery, had closed round him — all that mysterious life of the wilderness that stirs in the forest, in the jungles, in the hearts of wild men." These two accounts, taken together, indicate the ambivalence of the river, of the natural world, and of man. Later in his tale, speaking of the experience of the Europeans in their journey up the African river, and of the savages along its banks, Marlow observes this ambivalence with emphatic directness: "We are accustomed to look upon the shackled form of a conquered monster, but there — there you could look at a thing monstrous and free. It was unearthly, and the men were — . . ."

The idea that the uncivilized is concealed insecurely within civilization is stated here and there in Eliot's writings, both the prose and the poetry. It is explicit particularly in *The Rock*, but it is in *The Dry Salvages*, where river, sea, and ships are dominant images, that the idea appears as a theme that has close parallels with Conrad's story. In the opening lines of this Quartet the river is presented as a symbol of the savagery and destructiveness lurking within civilization and within man:

> I do not know much about gods; but I think that the river
> Is a strong brown god — sullen, untamed and intractable,
> Patient to some degree, at first recognised as a frontier;
> Useful, untrustworthy, as a conveyor of commerce;
> Then only a problem confronting the builder of bridges.
> The problem once solved, the brown god is almost
>   forgotten
> By dwellers in cities — ever, however, implacable,
> Keeping his seasons and rages, destroyer, reminder
> Of what men choose to forget. Unhonoured, unpropitiated
> By worshippers of the machine, but waiting, watching
>   and waiting.
> . . . .
> The river is within us, the sea is all about us.

Eliot has assumed here a primitive view of the river as a "strong brown god" in order to suggest the essentially unchanging and limited status of man in relation to the forces of nature and within himself. The mystery and terror of man's plight in time and nature may be obscured by civilization, by instruments and concepts of his own devising, but they reside beneath these as aspects of his own identity — "what men choose to forget." An argument, so to speak, of *The Dry Salvages*, is that man is incapable of seeing his relationship to the supernatural world because he refuses to see his true and unchanging relationship to the natural world. Morally and theologically this may be stated (as Eliot has in effect stated it) as man's inability to believe in the existence of the good (and hence of God) because he refuses to admit and to recognize the existence of evil. Eliot has said of *Heart of Darkness* that it is an eminent instance of the literary evocation of evil,* and we can see how it might be regarded as a representation of the concept of original sin in fresh and secular terms. This consideration is enforced by other correspondences between Eliot and Conrad. The issue is succinctly stated in the second movement of *The Dry Salvages*:

> The backward look behind the assurance
> Of recorded history, the backward half-look
> Over the shoulder, towards the primitive terror.

Exactly such a half-look is taken by Marlow as he speaks of his response to the noisy antics of the savages on the banks of the river:

"It was unearthly, and the men were — No, they were not inhuman. . . . Yes, it was ugly enough; but if you were man enough you would admit to yourself that there was in you just the faintest trace of a response to the terrible frankness of that noise, a dim suspicion of there being a meaning in it which you — you so remote from the night of first ages — could comprehend. And why not? The mind of man is capable of anything — because everything is in it, all the past as well as all the future. What was there after all? Joy, fear, sorrow, devotion, valor, rage — who can tell? — but truth — truth stripped of its cloak of time."

Marlow relates with somewhat grim humor that he did not "go ashore for a howl and a dance" because he was too busy repairing and steering the ship, but he arrives, nonetheless, at a solemn observation: "There was surface truth enough in these things to save a wiser man." Just a few paragraphs earlier he has testified that he glimpsed the deeper truth within himself while he was engaged in guiding the ship into the weird stillness of the jungle: "One's past came back to one . . . in the shape of an unrestful and noisy dream." But it was only a glimpse. "When you have to attend to things of that sort, to the mere incidents of the surface,

* Cited by F. O. Matthiessen, *The Achievement of T. S. Eliot* (New York: Oxford, 2nd ed., 1947), p. 24. Matthiessen's reference for the source is not quite clear, but he probably refers to an unpublished lecture which Eliot gave at Harvard in the spring of 1933.

the reality — the reality, I tell you — fades. The inner truth is hidden — luckily, luckily." A similar observation is contained in *The Dry Salvages* where, toward the end of the second movement, Eliot develops the idea that "the moments of agony" have a kind of permanence,

> such permanence as time has. We appreciate this better
> In the agony of others, nearly experienced,
> Involving ourselves, than in our own.
> For our own past is covered by the currents of action,
> But the torment of others remains an experience
> Unqualified, unworn by subsequent attrition.

There is here a correspondence of "the currents of action" with Marlow's "surface truth" — but I would like to suggest that this passage has a larger relevance to *Heart of Darkness*, to its structure and to its central situation.

Although Marlow as narrator was a habitual device of Conrad, his function here takes on a special significance in the light of Eliot's statement. It is the agony of Kurtz, who did "go ashore for a howl and a dance" and so much else, in which Marlow is involved, which he appreciated and nearly experienced. While it was Kurtz who had the vision of horror, it was Marlow who had the vision of Kurtz and whose fate it was to contemplate and then to spell out the meaning of the horror. Marlow says, "It was his extremity that I seemed to have lived through," and this extremity, this victorious agony, became for Marlow a permanence, to which he was loyal "to the last, and even beyond." But the moment of Kurtz' tormented vision is transmuted into permanence not only in Marlow's "appreciation" of it, but also in the achieved art of Conrad's story. The "agony of others" is relayed, so to speak, from the *heart of darkness*, from "the whole universe . . . all the hearts that beat in the darkness" — relayed to Kurtz to Marlow to Conrad to the readers. There is in all this something of deliberate paradox, for both Conrad and Eliot convey a meaning that somehow partakes of the ineffable — a meaning that has its fullness only when the quality of ineffability has been preserved. This is managed ingeniously by Conrad. The story turns upon itself without

[210

loss of plausibility when Marlow interrupts his narrative to address his mates directly:

". . . He was just a word for me. I did not see the man in the name any more than you do. Do you see him? Do you see the story? Do you see anything? It seems to me I am trying to tell you a dream — making a vain attempt, because no relation of a dream can convey the dream-sensation, that commingling of absurdity, surprise, and bewilderment in a tremor of struggling revolt, that notion of being captured by the incredible which is of the very essence of dreams. . . .

". . . No, it is impossible; it is impossible to convey the life-sensation of any given epoch of one's existence — that which makes its truth, its meaning — its subtle and penetrating essence. It is impossible. We live, as we dream — alone. . . .

"Of course in this you fellows see more than I could then. You see me, whom you know."

In this passage, and finally in the entire story, Conrad illustrates Eliot's insight that "approach to the meaning restores the experience / In a different form" (*The Dry Salvages*). Early in the story Conrad anticipates and points up the question of ineffability by describing the still untold tale as "one of Marlow's inconclusive experiences," and by stating that to Marlow "the meaning of an episode was not inside like a kernel but outside, enveloping the tale which brought it out only as a glow brings out a haze, in the likeness of one of these misty halos that sometimes are made visible by the spectral illumination of moonshine."

I have been noting that there is a correspondence between Eliot and Conrad in regard to the questions of meaning, truth, reality, and their relationship to time, and there remains something more to be said about this correspondence. I shall pursue the subject by first reviewing, briefly, the theme of ineffability in *Four Quartets* and Eliot's plays. This theme is, indeed, one of those that are explored most persistently throughout *Four Quartets*, where there is a constant return to the interrelated problems of language, experience, and reality. As the theme is stated in *Burnt Norton* — "human kind / Cannot bear very much reality" — it suggests both Conrad's story and Eliot's plays. Specifically, we may remember Marlow's recoil from reality: "The inner truth is hidden — luckily, luckily." The identical words from *Burnt Norton* are spoken by Thomas to the Women of Canterbury at that "one moment" when they have had their vision of horror, expressed in the Chorus beginning "I have smelt them, the death-bringers," and when Thomas, finally prepared for martyrdom, has had his vision of glory, "a tremor of bliss, a wink of heaven, a whisper." Later, while Thomas' vision is being fulfilled in martyrdom, while he is being murdered, the Women say

> Every horror had its definition,
> . . . .
> But this, this is out of life, this is out of time,
> An instant eternity of evil and wrong.

Thus, both Thomas and the Women have glimpsed that reality of which humankind cannot bear very much, for it is the reality that is "out of time" — for the Saint, before his actual martyrdom, it is a tremor, a wink, a whisper of glory, and for the Women it is an "instant eternity" of horror that is beyond definition. Relevant here, as well as more generally, is Eliot's memorable pronouncement: "But the essential advantage for a poet is not, to have a beautiful world with which to deal: it is to be able to see beneath both beauty and ugliness; to see the boredom, and the horror, and the glory" (*Use of Poetry*). "Beneath both beauty and ugliness" is, of course, the reality that is beneath the surfaces of time and action — or we might better say *realities*, since there are the three levels, coexisting. The boredom is the first step, the first stage, a self-conscious disengagement from the surfaces, a seeing of the surfaces as unreal. To *see* the unreal is boredom, to see the boredom is horror, and to see the horror is glory. I have merely, and hastily, noted some of the implications of Eliot's statement, for my purpose is primarily to cite the statement, since it is necessary to move on.

In *The Family Reunion* it is, of course, Harry who is obsessed with the ineffable. Early in the play he speaks, from his world of horror, to the family:

> You will understand less after I have explained it.
> All that I could hope to make you understand
> Is only events: not what has happened.

> I tell you, life would be unendurable
> If you were wide awake. You do not know
> The noxious smell untraceable in the drains.
>
> . . . .
>
> . . . As for what happens —
> Of the past, you can only see the past,
> Not what is always present. That is what matters.
>
> That is what matters, but it is unspeakable,
> Untranslatable: I talk in general terms
> Because the particular has no language.

There is here a cluster of familiar elements. The first and last excerpts refer to an ineffable meaning that lies beneath the surface of events. In the middle excerpt there are the unbearable reality; the invisible evil symbolized here and in *Murder in the Cathedral* by smell, the most intimate and obscurest of the senses; and "what is always present . . . what matters," again the ineffable meaning that is beyond time. Toward the end of the play, reconciled to his vision of horror and having chosen the "long journey," Harry says, "I do not know the words in which to explain it." And in his parting speech to the family he says,

> I would explain, but you would none of you believe it;
> If you believed it, still you would not understand.
> You can't know why I'm going. You have not seen
> What I have seen.

To maintain the relationship with Conrad, we should recall Marlow's "truth stripped of its cloak of time"; his exclamation that it is impossible to convey one's experience, "that which makes its truth, its meaning"; and his feeling that his fellow Europeans "could not possibly know the things I knew."

In *The Cocktail Party* and *The Confidential Clerk* the theme of the ineffable is neither so prominent nor so pointed as it is in the earlier plays. This is so, I believe, because the later plays not only are contemporary in their materials but are also an attempt to approach more closely the contemporary experience. I shall soon consider this subject more fully in connection with another matter, and turn now to instances of the ineffable in the plays. Through much of *The Cocktail Party* the ineffable is represented not so much by particular instances or statements as by the relations among the characters (meaning Edward and Lavinia Chamberlayne, Celia Coplestone, and Peter Quilpe), who are all isolated, while struggling to understand themselves and each other. Their alienation, unlike Harry's, is not from a world, but again, from themselves and each other. When we do get overt and immediate references to the ineffable, they are less conspicuous, more continuous with a dramatic context of "ordinary" action than in the earlier plays. There is such a reference toward the end of Act I of *The Cocktail Party*, where Edward and Lavinia are reunited but not yet reconciled with each other.

EDWARD:
>   There was a door
> And I could not open it. I could not touch
>   the handle.
> Why could I not walk out of my prison?
> What is hell? Hell is oneself,
> Hell is alone, the other figures in it
> Merely projections. There is nothing to escape from
> And nothing to escape to. One is always alone.

LAVINIA:
> Edward, what *are* you talking about?
> Talking to yourself. Could you bear, for a moment,
> To think about me?

EDWARD:
>   It was only yesterday
> That damnation took place. And now I must
>   live with it
> Day by day, hour by hour, forever and ever.

LAVINIA:
> I think you're on the edge of a nervous
>   break-down!

Another such reference comes at the end of Act II, but it is not so much an instance as a whole episode — Celia's crucial consultation with the psychiatrist Sir Henry Harcourt-Reilly. Celia, like Edward, is reacting to the collapse of their affair with each other, and she too feels isolated in a personal hell:

> I mean that what has happened has made me aware
> That I've always been alone. That one is always alone.
> . . . .
> It no longer seems worth while to *speak* to anyone!

When the doctor describes the condition of

> final desolation
> Of solitude in the phantasmal world
> Of imagination, shuffling memories and desires

Celia says, "That is the hell I have been in." It is probably obvious
that the hellish and inarticulate isolation of Edward and Celia is
like that of Harry ("one is still alone / In an over-crowded desert,
jostled by ghosts") and of the Women of Canterbury ("emptiness,
absence, the Void") and of Marlow during his illness and on his
return to the "sepulchral city."

In *The Confidential Clerk* the theme of the ineffable reality is
even less intensely suggested than in *The Cocktail Party*. But it
is nonetheless to be found. Sir Claude Mulhammer converses with
Colby Simpkins as one frustrated artist to another and he speaks
of their art, whether music or pottery, as the *other* reality:

> it is an escape into living,
> . . . .
> . . . a world where the form is the reality,
> Of which the substantial is only a shadow.
> And when you are alone at your piano, in the evening,
> I believe you will go through the private door
> Into the real world, as I do, sometimes.

In another conversation about Colby's frustrated musical career,
Lucasta Angel remarks to him:

> But it's only the outer world that you've lost:
> You've still got your inner world — a world that's
>   more real.
> That's why you're different from the rest of us:
> You have your secret garden. To which you can retire
> And lock the gate behind you.

But nowhere in *The Confidential Clerk* is there a hint of the unbearable reality beyond time.

215]

The Man in the Name

Before considering further the differences between the earlier and later plays, I should like to show once more how the theme of the timeless and unbearable reality corresponds with *Heart of Darkness*. For this I turn to the end of the story, where Marlow, more than a year after Kurtz' death, loyally brings to Kurtz' Intended "a slim packet of letters and the girl's portrait." In this episode Conrad consummates a theme that he has been developing throughout the story: that all times are somehow identical, having their identity in a reality that binds the present to the past and the civilized to the uncivilized. This final development of the theme begins with Marlow calling at the residence of the girl in "a street as still and decorous as a well-kept alley in a cemetery." As he makes his way to the girl's apartment, he has a vision of Kurtz:

"He lived then before me; he lived as much as he had ever lived . . . I rang the bell before a mahogany door on the first floor, and while I waited he seemed to stare at me out of the glassy panel — stare with that wide and immense stare embracing, condemning, loathing all the universe. I seemed to hear the whispered cry, 'The horror! The horror!' "

And then, as Marlow meets the girl and shakes hands with her there is a merging of past and present, of death and life, of horror and glory, of light and darkness in a single moment of consciousness:

"I perceived she was one of those creatures that are not the playthings of Time. For her he had died only yesterday. And, by Jove! the impression was so powerful that for me, too, he seemed to have died only yesterday — nay, this very minute. I saw her and him in the same instant of time — his death and her sorrow — I saw her sorrow in the very moment of his death. Do you understand? I saw them together — I heard them together. She had said, with a deep catch of the breath, 'I have survived' while my strained ears seemed to hear distinctly, mingled with her tone of despairing regret, the summing-up whisper of his eternal condemnation. I asked myself what I was doing there, with a sensation of panic in my heart as though I had blundered into a place of cruel and absurd mysteries not fit for a human being to behold."

This is the ineffable meaning, the hidden truth, the reality in the moment out of time, of which humankind cannot bear very much, and it is the theme that reverberates throughout Eliot's work, the end and the beginning, whether it be "the moment in the rose-garden" or the "instant eternity of evil and wrong."

I shall assume that this matter is already sufficiently illustrated, and that no further citation from Eliot's work is necessary. But I would dwell for a moment on the correspondence of Eliot with Conrad in the paradoxical fusion of opposites. For Marlow the horror of Kurtz has become fused with the glory of the girl. For it is clear that the girl is meant to represent glory, "the heart of light" (Eliot's phrase occurring in the "Hyacinth garden" passage of *The Waste Land* and also in the "rose-garden" passage of *Burnt Norton*). She is described as "a soul as translucently pure as a cliff of crystal." Marlow sees in her "the unextinguishable light of belief and love . . . that great and saving illusion that shone with an unearthly glow in the darkness, in the triumphant darkness." ("And the light shineth in darkness, and the darkness comprehended it not"!) The conjunction of glory and horror is suggested again when Marlow, intending to tell the girl a merciful lie, says that Kurtz' last word was her name — again the cruel and absurd mystery of the glory and the horror interpenetrating each other and becoming one. Both Kurtz and the girl become a permanence for Marlow:

"I shall see this eloquent phantom as long as I live, and I shall see her, too, a tragic and familiar Shade, resembling in this gesture another one, tragic also, and bedecked with powerless charms, stretching bare brown arms over the glitter of the infernal stream, the stream of darkness."

In this passage Conrad gives still another symbolic representation of the theme that the day of the present and of civilization is essentially the same as "the night of first ages." The gesture is that of putting "out her arms as if after a retreating figure, stretching them black and with clasped pale hands across the fading and narrow sheen of the window." And the other one, "tragic also," is the African woman, "wild and gorgeous," who had had Kurtz for lover, and who had appeared on the bank of the river when the dying Kurtz was already aboard the ship that was about to leave.

The Man in the Name

She too, out of the pained frustration of love and grief, had gestured, "opened her bared arms and threw them up rigid above her head, as though in an uncontrollable desire to touch the sky." The two women, the white girl and the African, merge to become a type of *la figlia che piange*. In Eliot's poem of that title (that Laforguean poem!) there are images like those of Conrad. The girl who is to weave the sunlight in her hair is like the Intended — "her hair seemed to catch all the remaining light in a glimmer of gold." And the same girl who is to turn away with a fugitive resentment in her eyes is like the African — "She turned away slowly, walked on, following the bank, and passed into the bushes to the left. Once only her eyes gleamed back at us in the dusk of the thickets before she disappeared." The last lines of Eliot's poem might be lines for the Marlow who sees all his life the gestures of the composite woman:

> And I wonder how they should have been together!
> I should have lost a gesture and a pose.
> Sometimes these cogitations still amaze
> The troubled midnight and the noon's repose.

"How they should have been together," Kurtz and the Intended, Kurtz and the African, and then all of them, everything, the horror and the glory, all incredibly, unbearably, yet irrevocably fused in Marlow's vision and his memory of the vision — this is the amazing question that emerges from Marlow's tale and Conrad's story. "Do you understand? I saw them together — I heard them together."

There is one matter of correspondence between Eliot and Conrad, and also Laforgue, which I have deferred until the last because there is also involved an apparent development and change in Eliot's attitude. The theme I refer to harks back to those key "Eliotic" passages of Laforgue and Conrad, expressed respectively in each as *les petites gens de l'Histoire* and "commonplace individuals going about their business." In each case there is a protagonist (Hamlet, Marlow) who stands apart from the generality of mankind. An attitude of isolation has commonly been noted in Eliot's work, from the poems of *Prufrock* through *The Waste Land*. In the light of this issue, Eliot may be regarded as sharing with those

[218

generations of the late nineteenth and early twentieth centuries the obsession expressed by Pater's injunction to burn with a hard gemlike flame. For Eliot the flame eventually became the flame of religious love, of the Christian and self-sacrificing saint — a figure nonetheless isolated from others. Such a figure we have, of course, in *Murder in the Cathedral*, where Thomas is a type of the saint and the Women are a type of the ordinary people, and the two types are at a polar distance from each other. This relationship is meaningful according to Christian doctrine and tradition, but it is also of the pattern of the individual isolated from society.

It was noted earlier that there is an actual echoing of Laforgue's *petites gens* in *Murder in the Cathedral*. The Women are the *"petites gens,"* the "small folk," a point re-emphasized at the very end of the play: "we acknowledge ourselves as type of the common man, / Of the men and women who shut the door and sit by the fire." In *The Family Reunion* there is no such precise echoing of Laforgue or of Conrad on this score, but the same materials are obviously present. In the earlier part of the play Harry is the individual who, with his vision of the hidden reality, is isolated from society, from the members of his family. And in the latter part, if he does not achieve, at least he approaches the type of the saint. In the climactic scene of recognition and reversal (Part II, Scene ii), his Aunt Agatha says of him

> It is possible
> You are the consciousness of your unhappy family,
> Its bird sent flying through the purgatorial flame.

And at the end of the scene Harry declares his commitment, in a kind of catalogue ,to the saintly life:

> To the worship in the desert, the thirst and
>   deprivation,
> A stony sanctuary and a primitive altar,
> The heat of the sun and the icy vigil,
> A care over lives of humble people,
> The lesson of ignorance, of incurable diseases.

Curiously enough, despite their material means and high social position, Harry's family are another kind of humble people, comparable in several respects to the Women of Canterbury — particularly the two aunts and two uncles, who constitute a Chorus in the play. Like the Women, they are but "living and partly living," engrossed in the surfaces of life, unaware of, yet fearing, the deeper and hidden reality. It is at those moments in the play when they speak together as the Chorus that they give such an account of themselves:

> Hold tight, hold tight, we must insist that the world is
> what we have always taken it to be.
>
> . . . .
>
> We understand the ordinary business of living,
>
> . . . .
>
> But the circle of our understanding
> Is a very restricted area.
> Except for a limited number
> Of strictly practical purposes
> We do not know what we are doing.

Eliot's first two plays show a clear parallelism with each other. In each there is the pattern of isolation from ordinary living found in Laforgue and Conrad. The isolation is spotlighted against the background of ordinary living, the ineffable depths against the known surfaces. The later plays differ in these respects from the earlier. If most of Eliot's work has been an expression of alienation from the world, the last two plays show that the lonely pilgrimage has eventually turned him back toward it. This change, this reconciliation, is implied by Eliot's own criticism of *The Family Reunion*, made in his lecture *Poetry and Drama* (1950):

"A more serious evidence [of the play's weaknesses] is that we are left in a divided frame of mind, not knowing whether to consider the play the tragedy of the mother or the salvation of the son. The two situations are not reconciled. I find a confirmation of this in the fact that my sympathies now have come to be all with the mother, who seems to me, except perhaps for the chauffeur, the only complete human being in the play; and my hero now strikes me as an insufferable prig."

This remark has struck me as curious, for I had never doubted Eliot's intention — I had never felt any ambiguity about who was the protagonist in *The Family Reunion*. It was definitely Harry. Eliot still calls him "my hero." Whatever its weaknesses are, the ambiguity is not in the play, but in Eliot's recently developed attitude. Within the framework of the play, Harry is the most complete human being, for he becomes increasingly conscious of the deeper reality, while the mother is only the most forceful person and most fully realized persona in the world of the aunts and uncles, the world of appearances, "what we have always taken it to be . . . the ordinary business of living." Eliot's mentioning the chauffeur is a hyperbole by which emphasis is given to his own newly developed attitude, for the chauffeur has no facet of "completeness," but is merely an ordinary person. He is a stock figure of literary convention, the lowly person and minor character who stands outside the dramatic complication while making a few simple but wise remarks from the sidelines.

The new attitude is, of course, a qualification and partial reversal of the old. Whereas Eliot had for so long divided personal experience and the world at large into the real and the unreal, there is in his latest work a steady drift away from such monism and toward a more traditional dualism. In *The Family Reunion* (in the play itself, not in Eliot's new view of it) there is only one way to reality and it is the way that Harry takes. But in *The Cocktail Party* there are two ways, and

Neither way is better.
Both ways are necessary. It is also necessary
To make a choice between them.

One way, by now familiar in Eliot's work, is the way of the saint, the extraordinary way chosen by Celia Coplestone. The other way is "the common routine . . . casual talk before the fire." (For the context of these phrases see above, in the list of quotations illustrating the Laforgue-Conrad pattern of rhythm, the passage from *The Cocktail Party*.) It is this way, chosen by Edward and Lavinia Chamberlayne, which recalls Laforgue's *petites gens* and Conrad's commonplace individuals, and it recalls also the Women of Canterbury and Harry's aunts and uncles. But not until *The Cocktail Party* (and the later Quartets) is this ordinary way given such sympathetic attention and such emphatic approval. There is a phrase occurring in *The Family Reunion* and in *The Cocktail Party* which, considered in the respective contexts, illustrates nicely the change in attitude that has taken place between the two plays. In the earlier, the aunts and uncles, speaking together as Chorus and in the rhythms recalling *les petites gens*, say

> the transparent deception
> The keeping up of appearances
> The making the best of a bad job
> All twined and tangled together, all are recorded.

In the later play, when it is clear that the Chamberlaynes will be reconciled and that neither will go to the sanitorium, there is this passage:

EDWARD:
> Lavinia, we must make the best of a bad job.
>
> . . . .

REILLY:
>   When you find, Mr. Chamberlayne,
> The best of a bad job is all any of us make of it —
> Except of course, the saints — such as those who go
> To the sanitorium — you will forget this phrase,
> And in forgetting it will alter the condition.

The recurring phrase has a somewhat different meaning in each case. In the first there is irony and distaste, in the second there is sympathy, approval, and hopefulness. In *The Cocktail Party* there is no ambiguity of the kind Eliot attributes to *The Family Reunion*, but there is a kind of dualism, of the ordinary and extraordinary ways, and it is the ordinary — making the best of a bad job — that is the embracing subject and in the foreground of the play.

The Confidential Clerk shows a still further development of the new attitude. This may be indicated by making comparisons among the plays. After the religious pageant of St. Thomas, all of them have contemporary settings. In the first of these there is the haunted hero isolated, to the technical detriment of the play, from the other characters. In the next there are the four people, Edward and Lavinia Chamberlayne, Celia Coplestone, and Peter Quilpe, whose fates are more or less manipulated by those quasi-super-

natural busybodies, Julia, Alex, and Dr. Harcourt-Reilly. But in
the last, whatever its implausibilities, there is a greater realism of
character and of character relationship. There are, so to speak, no
flat characters, none who are merely dramatic props, such as the
aunts and uncles in *The Family Reunion*, Julia and Alex in *The
Cocktail Party*. No character in *The Confidential Clerk* is merely
dramatic machinery. The characters are different people, not symbols of different categories of reality. Whereas in *The Cocktail
Party* two approaches to reality, two ways of living, are distinguished and defined, *The Confidential Clerk* shows a concern for
reconciling and integrating the two aspects of reality. In their first
long dialogue, when Sir Claude and Colby are discussing their
arts, pottery and music, which evoke for them a special reality, Sir
Claude remarks that the art in each case, like his wife's occult
investigations, is "a kind of substitute for religion." And he adds,

> I dare say truly religious people —
> I've never known any — can find some unity.
> Then there are also the men of genius.
> There are others, it seems to me, who have at
>   best to live
> In two worlds — each a kind of make-believe.
> That's you and me.

The two worlds or two realities are not opposites (*The Family
Reunion*) or alternatives (*The Cocktail Party*) but complementary. This theme is represented in *The Confidential Clerk* by a
symbolic image that is familiar and recurrent in Eliot's work. Very
early in the play, when Eggerson and Sir Claude are discussing
Colby's living quarters, Eggerson makes a suggestion:

> He's expressed such an interest in my garden
> That I think he ought to have window boxes.
> Some day he'll want a garden of his own.

Later, when Lucasta tells Colby that he has a garden where there
are music and flowers that are exclusively his own, he answers that
this garden and the ordinary world are equally real in being
equally unreal —

> that's just the trouble. They seem so unrelated.
> I turn the key and walk through the gate

And there I am . . . alone, in my 'garden.'
Alone, that's the thing. That's why it's not real.
You know, I think that Eggerson's garden
Is more real than mine. . . .

. . . .

       he retires to his garden — literally,
And also in the same sense that I retire to mine.
But he doesn't feel alone there. And when he
   comes out
He has marrows, or beetroot, or peas . . . for
   Mrs. Eggerson.

. . . .

What I mean is, my garden's no less unreal to me
Than the world outside it. If you have two lives
Which have nothing whatever to do with each other —
Well, they're both unreal. But for Eggerson
His garden is part of one single world.

. . . .

If I were religious, God would walk in my garden
And that would make the world outside it real
And acceptable, I think.

The mystical, or at least metaphysically symbolic, rose-garden has
given way to, or been merged with, the actual vegetable garden —
Eggerson's garden. At the end of the play it is Eggerson who informs Colby that he (Colby) is religious and who predicts for him
a vocation in the church. As for Eggerson himself, it turns out
that he is the Vicar's Warden and has always been a Christian,
despite Sir Claude's remark earlier that he has never known any
truly religious people, although he has known Eggerson for practically a lifetime. While the other characters — Sir Claude, Lady
Elizabeth, and Mrs. Guzzard — struggle and compete with each
other for a son — for Colby — it is Eggerson, also in need of a son,
who effortlessly wins him for his own home and as church organist
in his parish of Joshua Park. (There may be a deliberate significance in that name, for Joshua — *Yehoshua* — is the Hebrew of
which the Hellenized form is Jesus. Hence, Jesus Park: God in
the garden.) Colby is in some ways the same type of Eliotic charac-

ter as Thomas, Harry and Celia Coplestone, and yet, significantly, he is not a type of the saint. Both Colby and Eggerson are confidential clerks, but it is a mild irony of the play that it is Eggerson who is *the* confidential (trusting, believing) clerk, the humble hero of the play, for Eggerson is one of *les petites gens*, a commonplace Christian, both ordinary and extraordinary at once.

There is one more point of difference between the plays that seems worth making here. In *The Cocktail Party* the doctor's description to Celia of the "common routine," though he calls it "a good life," is somewhat depressing. He pictures man and wife as

> Two people who know they do not understand each other,
> Breeding children whom they do not understand
> And who will never understand them.

In this statement the common lot — the relation of husband and wife, of parent and child, of person and person — is viewed as one static condition which is the negation of another static condition, understanding. It is as if understanding, in this reference, were an ultimate insight, a contemplation once and for all of an abiding truth. Behind this use of the word *understand* is the idea of the essential reality which, by definition, is the object requiring such ultimate understanding, so that this use of it, with reference to human relationships, is somewhat irrelevant. The question of understanding is raised again in *The Confidential Clerk* as if to correct or to qualify the statement of the earlier play. In their long intimate dialogue, Colby tells Lucasta:

> I meant there's no end to understanding a person.
> All one can do is to understand them better,
> To keep up with them; so that as the other changes
> You can understand the change as soon as it happens,
> Though you couldn't have predicted it.

And the play ends precisely on the question of understanding between parents and children. Lady Elizabeth says, "Claude, we've got to try to understand our children." And Kaghan, speaking of himself and his future wife, Lucasta, says, "And we should like to understand *you*."

After *The Family Reunion* Eliot's plays show a waning empha-

sis on the isolated individual and the ineffable reality, and a growing interest in the common lot and the ordinary reality. It may be
noted, for whatever it is worth, that the later plays show an increasing unity of situation and of action but diminish steadily in the
intensity of poetic language.

Change of attitude is less prominent in *Four Quartets* than in
the plays, and there are probable explanations why this is so. For
one thing, the poem is a single work under a single title. *Four
Quartets* was, moreover, composed within a briefer span of time
than the plays. A listing of publication dates is significant here:
Burnt Norton, 1935; *Murder in the Cathedral*, 1935; *The Family
Reunion*, 1939; *East Coker*, 1940; *The Dry Salvages*, 1941; *Little
Gidding*, 1942; *Four Quartets*, 1943; *The Cocktail Party*, 1949;
The Confidential Clerk, 1953. It is to be noted that there is a considerable time span between *Burnt Norton* and *East Coker*, that
The Family Reunion was written before *East Coker*, and that the
last three Quartets were written in relatively quick succession.
Conceivably Eliot planned *Four Quartets* as a single work only
some time after he had written *Burnt Norton*, which was published as an individual poem in the book *Collected Poems 1909–
1935*. If this is so, it is consistent with Eliot's frequent practice
of making a new composition have a retroactive effect upon his
earlier work, and with his statements to the effect that each of a
writer's compositions has, besides its own unity, a place in the
larger unity of his entire work. *Four Quartets* has, indeed, this
kind of ambiguity, for its title is that of a single work and yet col-
lective in its meaning.

But to return to the change of attitude, it is most marked between *Burnt Norton* on the one hand and the later pieces on the
other. Compared with the other Quartets, *Burnt Norton* is in
greater degree abstract and personal, more steadily preoccupied
with the discontinuity between reality and the temporal world —
"To be conscious is not to be in time." Such references as are made
to the world, to people, are in the mood of alienation — for example, "the strained time-ridden faces" and "The loud lament of
the disconsolate chimera." But the other Quartets abound with

references, and sympathetic references, to the life of the external world. In *East Coker* there are the people of Sir Thomas Elyot's sixteenth-century England, "The association of man and woman." In *The Dry Salvages* there are the "anxious worried women." And in *Little Gidding* there is the concern with history and England. Whereas *Burnt Norton* is preoccupied with the quest for the personal experience of the moment out of time —

> Ridiculous the waste sad time
> Stretching before and after —

in *The Dry Salvages* it is stated that

> right action is freedom
> From past and future also.
> For most of us, this is the aim
> Never here to be realised;
> Who are only undefeated
> Because we have gone on trying.

All of the Quartets are personal, but a difference may be indicated by calling *Burnt Norton private* and the others *intimate*. Eliot has himself made a distinction, in *The Three Voices of Poetry* (1953), which is applicable here. "The first is the voice of the poet talking to himself — or to nobody. The second is the voice of the poet addressing an audience, whether large or small."

In the later Quartets the second voice is relatively stronger and more frequent. Change of attitude is not only generally implicit in the later Quartets but is also an immediate subject — as in *East Coker*:

> one has only learnt to get the better of words
> For the thing one no longer has to say, or the way
> in which
> One is no longer disposed to say it.

The change of attitude may be accounted for by what we call simply, and vaguely, development, and also, of course, by Eliot's continuing commitment to Christian belief. But it is to be noted that the change first appears, is first announced, in *East Coker*, the first of the later Quartets, all of which were written during World War II. An obvious inference is that the change was produced by the impact of the war. In these Quartets, there is a steady increase in reference to the war, a progressive integration of that subject with Eliot's enduring themes — an adjustment of the themes to the subject. In *Four Quartets* the second voice intends to speak not only to an audience, but for an audience, for a people in the circumstantial plight of war, and also for people in the universal plight of living, for *les petites gens de l'Histoire* and for "commonplace individuals going about their business." The change of attitude in the later Quartets and the later plays was not so much a change in principles as in mood. The position remained the same while the perspective was extended and broadened. It was not the identity but the identification that had changed.

My subject has been the relationship of Eliot's poetry to Laforgue's *Hamlet* and especially to Conrad's *Heart of Darkness*. If there is something of the miscellaneous about my discussion, I hope that this quality, besides being a limitation, is also a valid comment on the complexity of the subject. The complexity of Eliot's literary relationships exists, of course, not only with respect to one or two writers, but to many. There are places in Eliot's work, and general aspects of his work, for which I have offered Conrad as, so to speak, a source, but for which other writers could equally be claimed — Dante, St. John of the Cross, Baudelaire, for example, and perhaps still others. It is characteristic of Eliot to echo not only an individual source, but whole congeries of sources at once. We have seen that there are certain ideas and a particular pattern of rhythm which Eliot took neither from Laforgue nor Conrad, alone, but from both — or was it from the Bible?

A familiar theme of Eliot's criticism, since "Tradition and the Individual Talent," has been the use which one writer makes of others, particularly of his predecessors. In that early essay he said, with regard to the poet, that "not only the best, but the most individual parts of his work may be those in which the dead poets, his ancestors, assert their immortality most vigorously." He also said that it is not "preposterous that the past should be altered by the present as much as the present is directed by the past." Although Conrad was not strictly a poet, and although he was still alive when his earlier prose first began to affect Eliot's poetry, these remarks are true about the relationship of the two writers. There are qualities in each which are enhanced, which emerge with greater fullness and clarity in the light of the relationship. Each writer nourishes and augments the other without a loss resulting in either quarter. The remarkable thing, the thing that is not, after all, "preposterous" is that the earlier writer should be "altered" by the later. For has not Eliot's use of Conrad's story probed new depths of its meaning and shown new virtues of its thematic form? It is not that Eliot has imposed any meaning or form on Conrad, but that he has uncovered (and in that sense, altered) what was already there. If this is so, it illustrates a singuluar virtue of Eliot's work. Since Ben Jonson — indeed, since Horace — there has been conscious theorizing about the writer's use of other writers, and the principle of influence has provided seemingly endless tasks for modern scholarship. But no writer has illustrated the fact of influence so forcefully, so variously, and so dramatically as Eliot has. There is a respect in which Eliot's eminence as a critic is better documented by his poetry than by his prose. A diligent reading of Eliot's poetry becomes often a diligent reading of his sources and brings a new perspective on the sources. He said in the essay, "No poet, no artist of any art, has his complete meaning alone" — and as he takes us among other writers to complete his own meaning, he makes their meaning more complete also. Like the successful critic, he teaches us to share his ability to read. He leads us, as Virgil led Dante, not only into regions previously unknown, but also to a fuller understanding and a deeper appreciation of what was already familiar.

AFTER-NOTES *

By "the earlier Conrad" Eliot meant, I believe, other works as well as *Heart of Darkness*, but it was this story which evidently

* The titles and publication dates of Conrad's works referred to here are as follows: *An Outcast of the Islands*, 1896; *An Outpost of Progress* and *The Return*, contained in *Tales of Unrest*, 1898; *Lord Jim*, 1900; *Youth* and *Heart of Darkness*, contained in *Youth*, 1902; *Amy Foster*, contained in *Typhoon and Other Stories*, 1903; *The Shadow-Line*, 1917.

made the deepest and most influential impression upon him. Although not specified as such, it is obviously the earlier Conrad, and especially *Heart of Darkness*, that Eliot characterized when, in 1919, he gave Conrad the highest praise, while contrasting him with Kipling:

. . . some poets, like Shakespeare or Dante or Villon, and some novelists, like Mr. Conrad, have, in contrast to ideas or concepts, points of view, or "worlds" — what are incorrectly called "philosophies." Mr. Conrad is very germane to the question, because he is in many ways the antithesis of Mr. Kipling. He is, for one thing, the antithesis of Empire (as well as democracy); his characters are the denial of Empire, of Nation, of Race almost, they are fearfully alone with the Wilderness. Mr. Conrad has no ideas, but he has a point of view, a "world"; it can hardly be defined, but it pervades his work and is unmistakable." *

While it may be hard to define the "world" that pervades all of Conrad's work, the theme of man "fearfully alone with the Wilderness" is certainly most pervasive and predominant in the earlier novels and stories, and it is represented most vividly and definitively by *Heart of Darkness*.

In my deliberate reading of Conrad's earlier fiction I have found nothing comparable to *Heart of Darkness* for extensive and complex relationship with Eliot's poetry. The experience of reading did, however, clarify Eliot's reference to the earlier Conrad in general rather than to the particular story. In this earlier fiction, even when there are no precise sources, if one anticipates a relationship with, a suggestion of, Eliot, one finds it in the quality of the effect produced by Conrad's subject and meaning and style. One finds recurrently in Conrad what Eliot called, in the essay on Swinburne, "Language . . . so close to the object that the two are identified," and Conrad's "objects" are often like those rendered by Eliot's language, too. This proposition cannot be readily demonstrated, and I am not inclined to amass a copious body of excerpts from Conrad to urge so elusive and tenuous a point, although I believe that the point is actually valid. But I shall quote

* "Kipling Redivivus," *Athenaeum*, May 9, 1919, pp. 297–298. This is a review of Kipling's volume of poems *The Years Between*.

here a characteristic passage. It is a comment by Marlow, in *Lord Jim*, on Jim's predicament in the remoteness of Patusan:

"I suppose I must have fallen into a sentimental mood; I only know that I stood there long enough for the sense of utter solitude to get hold of me so completely that all I had lately seen, all I had heard, and the very human speech itself, seemed to have passed away out of existence, living only for a while longer in my memory, as though I had been the last of mankind. It was a strange and melancholy illusion, evolved half-consciously like all our illusions, which I suspect only to be visions of remote unattainable truth, seen dimly. This was, indeed, one of the lost, forgotten, unknown places of the earth; I had looked under its obscure surface, and I felt that when to-morrow I had left it forever, it would slip out of existence, to live only in my memory till I myself passed into oblivion. I have that feeling about me now; perhaps it is that feeling which had incited me to tell you the story, to try to hand over to you, as it were, its very existence, its reality — the truth disclosed in a moment of illusion."

This passage is like many others with which Conrad or Marlow or some other narrator intrudes, so to speak, upon the story in order to probe its meaning — not to give a judgment or an opinion or an explanation, but to suggest briefly, intensely, dramatically "that feeling" which is an essential part of a meaning — "its very existence, its reality" — a meaning, it appears, not otherwise translatable. Common to this passage and others is that truth which lies beneath the surface, and also the word *illusion* which, as Conrad uses it, is centrally relevant to his intellectual and emotional outlook. This subject — or "object" — so frequent in Conrad's work, is equally frequent in Eliot's. There are in Eliot's poetry many "moments" — the moment of consciousness, the moment of distraction, the moment of vision — which are comparable to Conrad's "moment of illusion." Conrad's language in such passages shows a psychological impressionism and a dramatic mode of evocation which are also to be found in Eliot's poetry.

As stated above, no single passage is a wholly adequate illustration of those recurring effects in Conrad's writing which, in their cumulative aspect, justify Eliot's praise and at the same time suggest Eliot's poetry. The passage I have quoted is but one among a variety of examples. There are other passages where the object rendered is not an inner experience but an external atmosphere or situation.

In addition to such passages of only general relevance between the two writers, I have, in my reading of Conrad, also come upon a number of actual passages echoed by Eliot's poetry. These I excluded from my essay because Eliot's relation with *Heart of Darkness* appeared sufficiently complex and has its own discrete unity. Before offering these sources and echoes I should say that I am aware of the possibility of having become oversensitized by my preoccupation, of having "found" too readily what I was quite consciously looking for.

1. *An Outpost of Progress* (1898) is a shorter and simpler story than *Heart of Darkness* (1902), but it is similar in theme and is also about the ivory trade in Africa. Here, too, Conrad is concerned with the impact of primitive savagery upon the civilized, and with that forbidding reality of human existence which lies beneath both savagery and civilization:

"Few men realize that their life, the very essence of their character, their capabilities and their audacities are only the expression of their belief in the safety of their surroundings . . . But the contact with pure unmitigated savagery, with primitive nature and primitive man, brings sudden and profound trouble into the heart. To the sentiment of being alone of one's kind, to the clear perception of the loneliness of one's thoughts, of one's sensations — to the negation of the habitual, which is safe, there is added the affirmation of the unusual, which is dangerous; a suggestion of things vague, uncontrollable, and repulsive, whose discomposing intrusion excites the imagination and tries the civilized nerves of the foolish and the wise alike."

This theme of the familiar and the usual is applied with ironical parallelism to both Europeans and Africans. In a single paragraph Conrad comments respectively on Kayerts and Carlier, the two white men at the trading outpost:

"He regretted the streets, the pavements, the cafés, his friends of many years; all the things he used to see, day after day; all the thoughts suggested by familiar things — the thoughts effortless, monotonous and soothing of a government clerk; he regretted all the gossip, the small enmities, the mild venom, and the little jokes of government offices."

"He regretted the clink of saber and spurs on a fine afternoon, the barrack-room witticisms, the girls of garrison towns."

Several paragraphs later in the story there is this comment on the black workers at the outpost, who are languishing in exile from their own tribe, which is in a remote part of Africa:

"They were not happy, regretting the festive incantations, the sorceries, the human sacrifices of their own land; where they also had parents, brothers, sisters, admired chiefs, respected magicians, loved friends, and other ties supposed generally to be human."

These passages, conspicuous for their combination of similarity and contrast and for the resulting irony, are, I believe, echoed by Eliot in his poem, *Journey of the Magi*:

> There were times we regretted
> The summer palaces on slopes, the terraces,
> And the silken girls bringing sherbet.

Eliot's poem has otherwise no significant relation to Conrad's story. But the passage quoted here is strikingly similar to those of Conrad. Both writers use the word *regret* with its meaning of "miss poignantly," and in each case the word is followed by an appropriate and comparable series of references.

Toward the end of the story, when Kayerts and Carlier are both suffering from the effects of their prolonged isolation, they squabble over a trifling matter of rations, soon become violent, and Kayerts fatally shoots Carlier. In Conrad's dramatic account of Kayert's mental response to the predicament there is this passage:

"Then he tried to imagine himself dead, and Carlier sitting in his chair watching him; and his attempt met with such unexpected success, that in a few moments he became not at all sure who was dead and who was alive. This extraordinary achievement of his fancy startled him, however, and by a clever and timely effort of mind he saved himself just in time from becoming Carlier."

I find this passage — especially the expression "who was dead and who was alive" — echoed by Eliot in the second "Fragment" of

Sweeney Agonistes. Sweeney has been telling his companions of a man who "once did a girl in."

> He didn't know if he was alive
> and the girl was dead
> He didn't know if the girl was alive
> and he was dead
> He didn't know if they both were alive
> or both were dead
> If he was alive then the milkman wasn't
> and the rent collector wasn't
> And if they were alive then he was dead.

Conrad's story, both in its comment and in its action, is concerned with the reality that lies beneath ordinary awareness, and Sweeney's account of the man who "did a girl in" implies, for all its absurd grotesqueness, the same subject. Sweeney's man, like Kayerts, is estranged by his evil deed from the ordinary world, the world of the milkman and the rent-collector. Relevant here is Eliot's Baudelairean concept that the experience of evil, even the conscious practice of evil, has a positive value, as compared to the amoral attitude, in that it affirms the existence of an absolute morality.

2. In Conrad's second novel, *An Outcast of the Islands* (1896), there is a passage which is a highly plausible source of some lines in *What the Thunder Said*, the last section of *The Waste Land.* The passage comes at that point in the novel when Willems, the outcast, is abandoned by Lingard, the benefactor whom he betrayed — abandoned as a kind of prisoner in the jungle remoteness of a Malayan island. I shall italicize some words and phrases for convenient reference.

". . . Only his eyes seemed to live, as they followed the canoe on its course that carried it away from him, steadily, unhesitatingly, finally, as if it were going not up the great river into the momentous excitement of Sambir, but straight into the past, into the *past* crowded yet *empty*, like an old cemetery full of *neglected graves,* where lie dead hopes that never return.

"From time to time he felt on his face the passing warm touch of an immense breath coming from beyond the forest, like the short panting of an oppressed world. Then the heavy air round him was pierced by a sharp *gust* of wind, *bringing* with it the fresh, *damp* feel of the falling *rain*; and all the innumerable tree-tops of the forests swayed to the left and sprang back again in a tumultuous balancing of nodding branches and shuddering leaves. A light frown ran over the river, the *clouds stirred* slowly, changing their aspect but not their place, as if they had turned ponderously over; and when the sudden movement had died out in a quickened tremor of the slenderest twigs, there was *a short period of formidable immobility* above and below, during which the *voice of the thunder* was heard, *speaking* in a sustained, emphatic and vibrating roll, with violent louder bursts of crashing sound, like a wrathful and threatening *discourse of an angry god."*

Here are Eliot's lines:

> In this decayed hole among the mountains
> In the faint moonlight, the grass is singing
> Over the tumbled graves, about the chapel
> There is the empty chapel, only the wind's home.
> It has no windows, and the door swings,
> Dry bones can harm no one.
> Only a cock stood on the rooftree
> Co co rico co co rico
> In a flash of lightning. Then a damp gust
> Bringing rain
>
> Ganga was sunken, and the limp leaves
> Waited for rain, while the black clouds
> Gathered far distant, over Himavant.
> The jungle crouched, humped in silence.
> Then spoke the thunder
> DA

The similarities are most obvious in the latter parts of the two passages where, in each case, there is description of a storm. Any two descriptions of the same kind of storm will inevitably make a number of similar references and thus probably use even the same words. But the similarities here are compelling beyond such plausible coincidence. In the context of the Conrad-Eliot relationship, Eliot's "damp gust / Bringing rain" is surely suggested by Conrad's use of precisely the same words in close proximity.

The Man in the Name

This kind of evidence is enough to provoke a search for other signs — and they are discovered. Eliot's "the black clouds / Gathered" corresponds with Conrad's clouds which "stirred slowly, changing their aspect." Having warmed to the issue, do we not feel a resonance between Eliot's next image — "The jungle crouched, humped in silence" — and Conrad's tree-tops which "swayed . . . and sprang back again," and also with the atmospheric condition preceding the thunder, "a short period of formidable immobility"? And the two passages end with an emphatic correspondence: "the voice of the thunder . . . speaking . . . discourse of an angry god" — "DA. *Datta . . . Dayadhvam . . . Damyata*." In addition to these details, which are in closely parallel sequences, it may be noted that both storms are in eastern jungles.

If we are persuaded that Eliot's verses echo, in condensed form, Conrad's description of the oncoming storm, we may allow that there are also some correspondences between the earlier parts of both passages — although here the relationships are not nearly so immediate. The most striking similarity is that of Eliot's "tumbled graves" and Conrad's "neglected graves." Eliot's "empty chapel" is surely symbolic, among other things, of the past, and is in this respect equivalent to Conrad's "past crowded yet empty . . . where lie dead hopes that never return." These correspondences might seem forced if they were not actually reinforced by the context and by the impressive sequential parallelism between the details in the entire passages of both writers.

The inherent qualities of Conrad's passage — the language so close to its object — are enough to explain Eliot's use of it, but there are also supporting reasons why Eliot should have been impressed by this scene of Conrad's novel and should have used it where he did in *The Waste Land*. Willem's plight of being isolated in a savage wilderness, cut off from civilization, readily recalls similar plights of characters in *Heart of Darkness* and *An Outpost of Progress*. The remainder of Conrad's paragraph about the storm, a bit less than a single page of the novel, is truly one of the most water-laden passages that has ever been written, and the word *water* itself occurs in it eleven times. It should be recalled in this connection that *What the Thunder Said* opens with a passage containing a reference to "thunder of spring over distant mountains." The passage following, lines 331 through 358, beginning "Here is no water but only rock," is the memorable description of the absence of water, vividly evocative of both dryness and its opposite. Curiously enough, the word *water* occurs precisely eleven times in the twenty-eight lines! The exact numerical equation is, of course, of no significance whatsoever. (My desire to convey the nature of Conrad's prose without actually quoting it led me into this counting of words.) But the collocation of all these materials in Conrad and in Eliot is significant. In writing the watery-waterless passage with its "dry sterile thunder without rain," Eliot's preoccupations could have recalled to him Conrad's thunderous storm which produced "heavy big drops . . . with sonorous and rapid beats upon the dry earth" — "Drip drop drip drop drop drop drop." Or Conrad's storm could have already been within the focus of Eliot's imagination, already assimilated into Eliot's impulses and purposes. In any event, there is a rich pattern of correspondences between the final pages of Part IV, Chapter Four, of Conrad's novel and the last section of Eliot's poem.

3. Eliot's symbolic imagery of the rose-garden is certainly traditional and archetypal, and yet it is known that some of the passages in which this imagery appears derive details and qualities from particular sources. These sources are D. H. Lawrence's story *The Shadow in the Rose Garden*, the opening pages of *Alice in Wonderland*, where Alice is at first too big to get through the little door beyond which there is a lovely garden, and Kipling's story *They*, where there is a preternatural circumstance of children's laughter in the shrubbery.* To this multiplicity of sources may also be added the opening sentences of Conrad's novel *The Shadow-Line*.

"Only the young have such moments. I don't mean the very young. No. The very young have, properly speaking, no moments.

* See L. L. Martz, "The Wheel and the Point," in my *T. S. Eliot: A Selected Critique* (New York: Rinehart, 1948), pp. 448–450; also Helen Gardner, *The Art of T. S. Eliot* (New York: Dutton, 1950), p. 160.

The Man in the Name

It is the privilege of early youth to live in advance of its days in the beautiful continuity of hope which knows no pauses and no introspection.

"One closes behind one the little gate of mere boyishness — and enters an enchanted garden. Its very shades glow with promise. Every turn of the path has its seduction. And it isn't because it is an undiscovered country. One knows well enough that all mankind had streamed that way. It is the charm of universal experience from which one expects an uncommon or personal sensation — a bit of one's own.

"One goes on recognising the landmarks of the predecessors, excited, amused, taking the hard luck and the good luck together — the kicks and the halfpence, as the saying is — the picturesque common lot that holds so many possibilities for the deserving or perhaps for the lucky. Yes. One goes on. And the time, too, goes on, till one perceives ahead a shadow-line warning one that the region of early youth, too, must be left behind.

"This is the period of life in which such moments of which I have spoken are likely to come. What moments? Why the moments of boredom, of weariness, of dissatisfaction."

All the sources, including this one of Conrad, are most clearly in evidence in the first section of *Burnt Norton* and in the climactic dialogue of Harry and Agatha in *The Family Reunion*. I should like to indicate first those elements in Eliot's poetry which have correspondences in Conrad's prose as well as in some of the other sources. The most obvious and inclusive material, the common ground, is of course, the garden itself. In Eliot there are the "passage" and the "alley" (*Burnt Norton*), like Conrad's "path"; "the door . . . / Into the rose-garden," "the first gate" (*Burnt Norton*) and "the little door" (*The Family Reunion*), like Conrad's "little gate"; "a cloud passed" (*Burnt Norton*) and "a black raven flew over" (*The Family Reunion*), like Conrad's "shadow-line."

I shall indicate next those elements of Eliot's poetry which correspond more immediately with Conrad than with any of the other sources. The most explicit correspondence in any of the sources with "Through the first gate, / Into our first world" of *Burnt Norton* is Conrad's "little gate of mere boyishness" and also his "region of early youth." It is in Conrad, as in Eliot, that the garden and allied details are used in a clearly symbolic rather than in a circumstantial or allegorical fashion. Eliot's use of first-person plural pronouns and possessives — "the passage which *we* did not take," "the door *we* never opened," "*our* first world" — accords with Conrad's "*all mankind* had streamed that way . . . the charm of *universal* experience" and "*one* perceives ahead a shadow-line warning *one*." The Conrad source underscores, and may even partially explicate, Eliot's symbolization of the universal experience of early youth and the passing of early youth. Both passages are discourses on time. Toward the end of the second section of *Burnt Norton* there is "the moment in the rose-garden," and the word *moments*, used with the same quality of meaning, occurs repeatedly in Conrad's passage. The word *moment* is, indeed, of central and singular importance in Eliot's poetic vocabulary. *The Shadow-Line* (1917) is no longer "the earlier Conrad," and after the opening paragraphs there is nothing in it that is suggestive of the Conrad-Eliot relationship.

4. This final note will treat a number of points of relationship between Eliot and Conrad. None of them is so extensive as those already given, and they vary in character among themselves. Any of them could be mere coincidence. On the other hand, there may very well be points of relationship which I have failed to recognize. But the points presented here, as an accumulation, and within the larger context of the subject, are ultimately relevant.

I had known for some time that the phrase "a handful of dust," in the first section of *The Waste Land*, appears also in John Donne's *Meditations* IV: "What's become of man's great extent and proportion when himself shrinks himself and consumes himself to a handful of dust?" I had vaguely surmised that the phrase came from the Bible. After I had found this same phrase — not once, but twice — in Conrad, I consulted Bible concordances and other appropriate dictionaries, but with negative results. The twelfth edition of *Bartlett's Familiar Quotations* (1955) contains the phrase in its Index, but the only reference is to the lines from *The Waste Land*, quoted in its section on Eliot. (But I still feel that the phrase may have some ultimate source — it is that kind of phrase.) I shall consider first the occurrence in Conrad's story *The Return*. The story opens with an account of the desperate and agonized thoughts of a successful English businessman who, on returning home in the evening, finds a note from his wife saying that she has deserted him for another man. This account contains the sentence, "He was afraid with that penetrating faltering fear that seems, in the very middle of a beat, to turn one's heart into a handful of dust." The subject, fear, in addition to the phrase, suggests that it is this statement that is being echoed in Eliot's line, "I will show you fear in a handful of dust." (*The Return*, a story concerned with the crisis of moral and spiritual awakening, is otherwise suggestive at several points of likely echoings in *The Waste Land*, as indicated by R. L. Morris, "Eliot's 'Game of Chess' and Conrad's 'The Return'," *Modern Language Notes*, LXV, 6.) And yet, recalling Eliot's practice of combining multiple sources in a single reference or echo, we should also consider this passage from Conrad's story *Youth*:

"I remember my youth and the feeling that will never come back any more — the feeling that I could last forever, outlast the sea, the earth, and all men; the deceitful feeling that lures us on to joys, to perils, to love, to vain effort — to death; the triumphant conviction of strength, the heat of life in the handful of dust, the glow in the heart that with every year grows dim, grows cold, grows small, and expires — and expires, too soon, too soon, before life itself."

There are a number of possible explanations why this phrase should occur in the three writers. There may be some common source of which I am unaware, or there may have been a multiple coincidence — or other possibilities between these extremes. The most attractive explanation for the course of this discussion is that Eliot, having come upon the phrase once in Donne and twice in Conrad, was sufficiently impressed by it to use it in his own poem. That Eliot had read Donne's *Meditations* is beyond question, and that he had read Conrad's stories is more than likely. *The Return* appeared in the volume *Tales of Unrest*, which also contains *An*

Outpost of Progress, and *Youth* is the title story of the volume containing *Heart of Darkness*.

There are further reasons why the passage from *Youth* is interesting here. The style is strikingly marked by that rhythm — produced by the repetition of words and constructions — which is pervasive in Eliot's verse and intrinsic to the Bible. An appropriate biblical example, and a favorite of Eliot's, would be the opening verses of Ecclesiastes 12, beginning "Remember now thy Creator in the days of thy youth, while the evil days come not," and ending "Then shall the dust return to the earth as it was: and the spirit shall return unto God who gave it." The passage from *Youth*, like some other points of relationship or parallelism between Eliot and Conrad, has the same import as the verses from Ecclesiastes — the vicissitudes of life and the stages of human decay that follow with the passing of time. Another such passage is the one in *The Shadow-Line*, and the two are, I think, of a kind to be readily associated. I say this by way of introducing some lines from Eliot which have, for me, also entered into the association. They are from the description of old age in *Little Gidding*.

> Let me disclose the gifts reserved for age
>   To set a crown upon your lifetime's effort.
>   First, the cold friction of expiring sense
> Without enchantment, offering no promise
>   But bitter tastelessness of shadow fruit
>   As body and soul begin to fall asunder.
> Second, the conscious impotence of rage
>   At human folly, and the laceration
>   Of laughter at what ceases to amuse.
> And last, the rending pain of re-enactment
>   Of all that you have done, and been; the shame
>   Of motives late revealed, and the awareness
> Of things ill done and done to other's harm
>   Which once you took for exercise of virtue.

In Eliot's lines there are similarities to Conrad's prose in diction as well as in meaning. Eliot's words *cold* and *expiring* have equivalents in *Youth*, and the words *enchantment*, *promise*, and *shadow* have them in *The Shadow-Line*. Eliot's verses give not only a painful picture of waning vitality but also of the vanities and delusions

which attend the period of greatest vitality, and the same ambivalence is present in *Youth*. In both passages, Conrad's and
Eliot's, there is reference to an awareness which survives the death
of other faculties and which, before the end of life, sits in exacting
judgment on the life that has been lived.

I have offered these considerations not primarily to suggest that
Eliot, in the second section of *Little Gidding*, is echoing Conrad,
but rather to indicate further the range of likeness between the
two writers — of likeness even when no specific echoing is necessarily involved. I shall end these notes with one more point relevant to this issue, a point of verbal parallelism between the first
section of *Little Gidding* and Conrad's *Amy Foster*. I refer to these
passages:

> And what the dead had no speech for, when living,
> They can tell you being dead: the communication
> Of the dead is tongued with fire beyond the language
>   of the living.

"Her face he remembered as the only comprehensible face amongst
all these faces that were as closed, as mysterious, and as mute as
the faces of the dead who are possessed of a knowledge beyond the
comprehension of the living."

There is nothing of further relevance in the immediate or larger
contexts of the passages. If we were to ask Eliot the obvious question about this and other correspondences and if he were to answer
that he could neither affirm nor deny, should we not then have
an obvious and sufficient answer? Perhaps too obvious and more
than sufficient, for it is now a matter of public record that Eliot
used for one poem a reference to Conrad that had been intended
for another, a reference which, he said, "is much the most appropriate I can find, and somewhat elucidative."

INDEX

Index

The Man in the Name

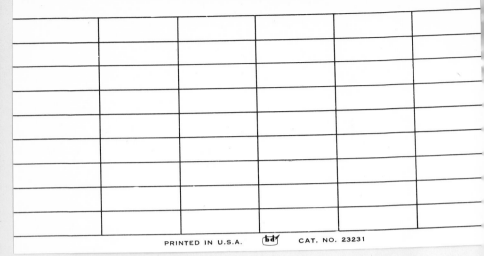